HAPPY 50th
Rod Ferr

TOP DOG!

TOP DOG!

A FIFTY YEAR HISTORY OF B.C.'S
MOST LISTENED TO RADIO STATION

BY CHUCK DAVIS
ASSOCIATE EDITOR HAL DAVIS

Canada Wide Magazines Ltd./Vancouver, Canada

Published and produced for CKNW 98 (Westcom Radio Group) by

Canada Wide Magazines Ltd.
#401 - 4180 Lougheed Hwy.
Burnaby, B.C., Canada V5C 6A7

Canadian Cataloguing in Publication Data

Davis, Chuck, 1935 –
        Top Dog: A Fifty Year History of CKNW. B.C.'s Most Listened to Radio Station

ISBN 0-9697585-0-2

1. CKNW (Radio station: New Westminster, B.C.) — History. I. Title.

PN1991.3.C3N49 1993   C93-090492-3
                384.54'53'0971133

Project Manager: Sandy Crawford
Associate Editor: Hal Davis
Designer: Cathy Mullaly
Production Manager: Corinne Smith
Typography: Debbie Craig
Photo Research: Scott Glazier, Cher Van de Sande
Photo Credits: CKNW (2, 6, 15, 25, 26, 36, 37, 38, 41, 42, 47, 50, 52, 53, 58, 63, 66, 70, 85, 86, 94, 95, 96,
                97, 99, 101, 102, 107, 111, 117, 119, 124, 127, 144)
        Jim Harrison (149)
        Robert Kenney (143,147,149,152,153, dust jacket cover)
        Brad Ledwidge (Inside front and back dust jacket)
        Courtesy of The Province (19, 109)
        Ron Sangha (140)
        Vancouver Public Library (33, 39, 54, 61, 65, 67, 68, 73, 74, 79, 90, 92, 93, 103, 104, 106)
        Courtesy of Vancouver Sun (5, 8, 18, 19, 20, 23, 24, 45, 76, 80, 81, 112, 115, 130, 133, 136, 138)
        Jeff Winnick (128)

Every effort has been made to correctly credit the photographs appearing in this book. If you know
of any errors or omissions, please write the publishers and future editions will be corrected.

Printed in Canada

To be completely frank, I wanted to write this book. I'm glad I didn't.

Because I have been so intimately associated with the growth and development of CKNW for most of its first fifty years, as a program director and a general manager, I would have found it virtually impossible to select the events and to outline the contributions of the many individuals who are the story of the station, and to put them into perspective. I think that Chuck has done a

masterful job. I regret, as he does, that the limitations of space forced him to edit out of the original manuscript hundreds of names, stories and pictures . . . enough to fill at least one more book of this size.

Although we share the same last name, Chuck and I are not even close to being "kissing cousins," but through the work we have done together on this document, I am proud to have become a "book-relation."

As the station approaches its fiftieth anniversary, we at CKNW feel that the thousands of people on the Lower Mainland of B.C., who tune to us daily for information and entertainment, might find interesting the story of how this

pip-squeak upstart of a cowboy station on the banks of the Fraser River became part of the fabric of their lives.

I hope that you enjoy this history of CKNW as much as those of us who were a part of it did in living it. To paraphrase the closing I used during the thirty-five years I presented the eight o'clock news each morning: "Have a good read now, d'ya hear!"

— Hal Davis

CONTENTS

THIS BOOK WAS ON THE VERGE OF GOING TO THE PRINTER WHEN CKNW'S LATEST RATINGS APPEARED. EVEN CKNW's staff, used to seeing the station at Number One — where it has been for more than 35 of its 50 years — was startled by the new numbers: they showed more than 650,000 people listened to NW sometime during the week. They showed morning man Brian "Frosty" Forst had more than three times the audience of his closest rival, and that every single personality on the air had better numbers: Rafe Mair, Bill Good, Rick Honey, Jack Cullen, et al. It was an astonishing testimonial to the quality of NW's talent, to the excellence of its news and sports teams, to its genius for promotion, and to its determined focus on serving the community.

That last reference is heartfelt: "CKNW," says open-liner Rafe Mair, "has never forgotten it's a community-based station." Retired executive Erm Fiorillo: "No other station ever got involved in the community the way NW did." This book will show you some of the ways.

There's something more. Former manager Ted Smith: "CKNW doesn't know how to lose. It only knows how to win. Because of that, we've put together the most incredible pool of talent in radio in Canada. Winners want to be associated with winners. I don't think there is anybody who works at NW who isn't proud to work there."

That was one reason this book was just about the most enjoyable project of my writing career. The opportunity to meet (or renew acquaintance) with so many skilled broadcasting professionals, both on the air and behind the scenes, was genuine joy from start to finish. CKNW's promotion head John Plul, who commissioned me to do the book, laughingly said "Davis is having too much fun! Why are we paying him?"

Working with associate editor Hal Davis was a privilege: Hal's nearly 50-year tenure at NW makes him an invaluable resource. He was hugely helpful, always cordial, recalled a thousand stories and told them over damn good coffee. When the book threatened to rival Gone With The Wind in length, Hal's editing was thoughtful and — almost — painless.

Did we get the station's whole story within these pages? Let Erm Fiorillo, an NW financial official for four decades, answer that: "Just mention to anyone you work at CKNW, or any station for that matter, and their first question is, 'Are you on the air?' When you tell them no, I'm in sales, or accounting, or traffic, here's what you get: 'Oh.'

"To our listeners," Erm continues, "the on-air personality is the one they really love to meet. But it's the little guys who helped to build the station. You never hear their names, never hear them on the air. I always got a kick out of telling someone who expected to hear I'm on the air that I was just the financial director . . . That's when the conversation turned to the weather."

This book, alas, must plead guilty to a similar stance. Over 50 years many hundreds of people have passed through CKNW, some staying many years, others only a few, some for mere days or weeks. Many of them made important contributions to the station's success, but the very nature of their work guaranteed them obscurity: the accountants, the personnel officers, traffic managers, continuity writers, engineers and technicians, the secretaries, receptionists, maintenance workers, record librarians, account executives, promotion staff . . . they are as essential, and as invisible, as the army of behind-the-scenes workers on a movie set.

So to Shirley Drouin, and Rod Walter, Sheila Hassell, Rose Marks, Gina Steeves, Ann Papay, Harold Clare, Joan Johnson, Anne Bolton, John Donaldson, Maureen Stoney, Wendy Cox-Walker, Hazel Lougheed, Marjorie Sanford, Phil Oakes, Mary Jane Tokar, and Dolores Avramenko, a tip of the CKNW hat. To Bill Collins, Harry Watts, Ruth Kelly, Pat Jacura, Eileen 'Sparky' Sparks, Don Macdonald, Don McLeod, Fred Whiting, Johnny Rennie, Rae Davis, Doug Champion, Earle Toppings, and Anita Bereza: many thanks! To Mary Bishop, Joan Johnston, Jules Ross, Bruce Carlson, Len Carlson and Donna Covent . . . and hundreds and hundreds more . . . to all the mighty mob, on and off the air, who contributed so much to the success of this most successful of radio stations, heartfelt gratitude.

To the more than 150 people I interviewed, my thanks . . . and apologies to those who ended up on the cutting-room floor. Sandy Crawford, the book's project manager, tried to accommodate my pleadings for more pages but, understandably, there had to be a limit. I'm delighted with the look of the book; what a super job designer Cathy Mullaly has done. And how lucky we were to have the sprightly artwork of Stan Buchanan available from the NW archives. My thanks to John and Kathy Cochlin of Kara Data Services for their valuable electronic assistance!

I have 38 years experience in broadcasting (oddly, none with CKNW, except for some research and writing on an Expo 86 series), and I can tell you that stations with NW's proportion of long service employees are extremely rare. Dick Abbott, with 40 years at Top Dog, gives one reason: "The key at CKNW is support. It's a family. There is no hierarchy. At staff parties engineers don't just sit with engineers and on-air with on-air. We mingle. Frank Griffiths will greet you with a beer. His wife Emily is there. I remember when I was in my late 20s I started having trouble with my hearing. Hal Davis sent me to a specialist, and he told me, 'It's nerves, that's all. You've got double hearing.' The station sent me to Hawaii for a rest! They paid the shot. Well, on the plane, not long after we took off, there was an announcement; 'Is Mr. Abbott on the plane?' My first thought was, God, it's the kids, something's wrong. Well, it was a bottle of champagne. Bill Hughes and Hal Davis had sent it for me."

But in the final analysis, NW got to be Top Dog — and stays there — for one good reason. Ted Smith says it well: "We're there to inform, sure, but we're also there to entertain . . . and CKNW entertains superbly."

— *Chuck Davis*

It was 1937, and a heavy fog lay over Vancouver.

A young broadcaster named Des McDermot had just finished his shift at

Radio CKMO and, at 9 p.m., was heading home. He saw a car, its lights dimmed,

creeping through the fog-shrouded streets, attempting to park. The wife

of the driver, holding a toddler, was leaning out her window and giving her husband

directions. Des went over and helped the little family park. The driver, a tall,

vigorous fellow, got out. "Say," he called out, "we're new in town, are there any

radio stations around here?" "Sure," Des said, "I've just come from one, CKMO,

right there at 812 Robson. And CJOR's right around the corner."

"That's fine," the man replied, "I'm going to drop in on them."

He stuck out a big hand. "Thanks for your help. My name's Bill Rea."

No one, Des included, knew it at the time, but radio in metropolitan

Vancouver was about to change forever.

Bill Rea (fourth from left) and CKNW staff at the New Westminster Market dock, 1946.

"Many A Day We Went Without Heat"

THE SECOND WORLD WAR WAS FOUR MONTHS OLD WHEN THE '40s began — it would come to dominate the decade here as elsewhere. The famous TUTS, Theatre Under The Stars, began in 1940. A Canadian comic book hero, Johnny Canuck, started driving Adolf Hitler crazy. "Ach!" der Führer splutters to his generals in a 1941 summer issue, "Fools! You promise arrest, but dot svine Canuck goes on destroying our var machine!" In real life, gun installations were set up along the B.C. coast, even in Stanley Park. Canada declared war against Japan within hours of the attack on Pearl Harbor, and gas masks went on sale locally. "Victory gardens" sprang up all over town, and meatless Tuesdays began.

Blackouts began on the Pacific coast, and windows were covered, when ordered, with "blackout paper." Cars drove — when they could — with hooded headlights; students learned how to use gas masks, and ration books made their appearance all across Canada. Canadian Pacific Airlines was formed under the dynamic leadership of bush pilot Grant McConachie and the Alaska Highway opened.

On the very day CKNW had its "official" sign-on, September 1, 1944 (two weeks after it actually went on the air), Canadian troops liberated Dieppe — the scene two years earlier of a bitter defeat for Canada.

Jim Cox raved about Rocket Richard scoring 50 goals in 50 games, and Bill Hughes — then on radio in Trail — was a trifle late on May 8, 1945 in informing his listeners of victory in Europe. Victory in Japan and war's end came just three months later. On June 20, 1945 the first troop train to bring men back from the war pulled into Vancouver's CPR station to be met by a huge crowd . . . and CKNW News. Several of NW's early staffers were fresh out of the services, some hired while still in uniform.

In 1946 something called a "computer" was developed at a Philadelphia university, and margarine was legalized. Thousands of women who had been employed during the war suddenly found themselves out of work. Vancouver city council withdrew an order setting aside separate swimming days at Crystal Pool for "colored" and Orientals.

The Orphans' Fund started in 1946.

An amazingly sturdy program called Roving Mike had its origins in a show called the Market Broadcast. The venue: the New Westminster Public Market, where Bill Rea interviewed passersby.

At 16 Bill Rea tried to buy a radio station. He had been interested in radio in school, and like virtually every boy his age had a crystal set by his bedside. Radio stations were popping up all around Canada and the U.S. in the early '20s, and it was exciting to try to pick them out of the air, and to compare with your friends the stations you had picked up and were able to put a name and location to. But young Bill wasn't content just to listen. The Alberta and Pacific Grain Co. owned a small radio station in Edmonton's Royal George Hotel, and put it up for sale for a few hundred dollars. Bill asked his father to lend him the money to buy it. The elder Rea declined. Bill was too young, and besides, he confidently told his young son, "radio has no future." ∎

CKNW's long history of live sports broadcasts began in the '40s, with Jim Cox's lacrosse play-by-play. Cox would soon be working himself to exhaustion with coverage of WHL hockey, once making three train trips to Saskatoon and back in two weeks to cover league playoffs.

And Canada's first phone-in talk show was launched on CKNW in 1946 with The Pastor's Study.

In 1947 NW began broadcasting 24 hours a day, the first station in B.C. to do so.

NW salesman Al Klenman would sign up Woodward's Stores in 1948, the first time that venerable merchant had opted for radio advertising. It was a tribute to NW's growing importance. And, that same year, the station's coverage of provincial politics was launched when Jim Cox did complete coverage of election returns, with background and color provided by a 28-year-old Vancouver Sun reporter named Pierre Berton. Jim went on to become the station's news director in '49, thinks the election coverage may have started NW's reputation as a strong news station. "It was good for both sides," he says. "The Sun got radio publicity everywhere, and NW got access to The Sun's province-wide reportage of election results." Joe Chesney: "Bill Rea was strong on local news. 'If a shingle blows off Mrs. Jones' roof in Burnaby, and lands in New Westminster, that's NEWS.'"

The decade ended nicely for NW, with a power boost to 1000 watts at a new spot on the dial: on January 2, 1949 it switched to 1320.

1949 had other highlights for CKNW: on December 19 it began broadcasting from new studios on the second floor of 227 Columbia Street, the Swanrite Building. Erm Fiorillo: "227 Columbia was right next door to the Columbia Funeral Home. The building was new, erected by a business acquaintance of Rea's, and this fellow squeezed his dollars. There was many a day when we went without heat because the building's owner forgot to pay his oil bill. There was a well for an elevator in the building, but no elevator was ever installed."

CKNW occupied three-quarters of the building's second floor, soon would fill that floor and a portion of the third. When live programming was eventually phased out, it left a lot of studio space unused.

In 1949 Jack Cullen brought the Owl Prowl over from CKMO; Bill Hughes moved into sales, his first step up the corporate ladder at CKNW; the station started a popular feature called Are You Listening?; and a former Disney artist named Peter Carter-Paige created for Bill Rea a new mascot/logo for the station. It was an odd-looking dog, sort of a Dalmatian Pluto, and it would be identified with the station for decades. Letters on the pooch's fur spelled out CKNW.

Frank Walden, NW's accountant and one of its directors, recalls walking into Rea's office one day and seeing the dog for the first time. Rea had had a big model of it made, and it was sitting on his desk. "What in hell is that?" Walden asked.

"That's our new mascot," Rea said proudly. "You'll be seeing it everywhere. I'm calling it Top Dog. CKNW is going to be 'Top Dog'."

Walden snorted. "That won't work."

Oh, yeah?

"Keep The Music Rolling"

Radio was thriving in Greater Vancouver in the wartime summer of 1944. On August 15 you could choose from CBR, CJOR, CKWX and CKMO. Local shows included Moments in Melody; Dinner Diversions; Twiddle, Biddle and Bop; and The Royal

Public service was Bill Rea's forte. Here he is (right) at a ceremony which dedicated a swing to children at a Vancouver school.

Canadian Navy Presents. U.S. network stations that Tuesday were bringing us Ginny Sims, Lum and Abner, George Burns and Gracie Allen, and the crime drama Big Town. Most stations featured live orchestras at night.

Curiously, one station wasn't listed. Turn to the pages of The Province or The Sun where radio listings were printed and check them for August 15, the day CKNW signed on. You won't see those call letters.

You won't see them a month later, either. Or the next month, or the next. As far as the newspapers were concerned, the arrival on the scene of CKNW was a non-event. But on the second floor at 732 Columbia Street in New Westminster, in the Hotel Windsor building, above the Fraser Cafe, there was excitement. Bill Rea, a 35-year-old radio time salesman, dance hall manager and band leader, had assembled an eager little group of people to staff his new station.

They were broadcasting before the workmen finished reshaping the place.

"Carl, the Careful Carpenter" would thoughtfully pause in his hammering when anyone turned on the mike. Ferdy Baglo, the station's first music director, was busily cataloguing its modest collection of 78s, some of which still bore the marks of a fire at CKMO, which had owned the records previously. Announcer Don Wilson, program director Bill Fox and chief announcer Bill Duncan pushed their way through the station's tiny rooms, dodging a small mob of teenagers invited to share in hosting the

For all his bluster and occasional insensitivity Bill Rea had a big heart. In the spring of 1947, soon after Hal Davis returned to CKNW from the Lorne Greene Academy in Toronto he became seriously ill. "I was in hospital for a month. They couldn't diagnose what the problem was. Well, Bill Rea paid my full salary all the time I was away. And I had just started! That sort of sealed the bargain for me. I decided to stay with NW." ∎

While at CJOR Bill Rea single-handedly organized a hugely successful drive to get his listeners to donate 10 cents to buy cigarettes for Canadian soldiers overseas. He'd been getting letters from soldier friends saying cigarettes were difficult to obtain. Rea convinced Sam Cohen of the rapidly growing Army & Navy Stores — Rea's voice was heard on their commercials on three Vancouver stations — to sponsor the promotion. Cohen went further. He promised to match dollar for dollar all the donations received. This was the first cigarette fund in Canada, and resulted in more than 10 million being shipped overseas to our men. Cohen was so pleased with the results he repeated the drive on radio stations in Edmonton and Regina. And when Rea started CKNW Cohen was an enthusiastic supporter. ∎

Ross MacIntyre, engineer until 1945.

afternoon High School Jamboree show. (One of those kids, Jim Cox, three weeks past his 16th birthday, fell in love with broadcasting and would stay with CKNW for more than 40 years.) Engineer Ross MacIntyre was "really pushing the station's 250 watts; the tubes were white hot." In the tiny sales office three "account executives" shared one desk. The continuity office, where commercials were written, was relatively big.

Smallest of all, "like a hallway," someone said, was the newsroom.

The grandest space in the station was the main studio, with room for an audience of 40 and a piano. Little Annabelle Rea played the piano on opening day to help launch her father's station. When CKNW wasn't playing records it was featuring live performers, and anybody walking by could drop in to the station to watch . . . or perform. There was an informality to NW in those days. "If anyone could string a guitar and play three chords," Jim Cox says, "we'd put 'em on the air."

The guitar was the most frequently heard instrument at CKNW, with fiddles and accordions strongly represented. What CKNW was featuring — to the snickers of sophisticates in Vancouver radio — was what was derisively called "cowboy" or "western" or even "hillbilly" music. Gene Autry, Roy Rogers, The Sons of the Pioneers, Bob Wills, Wilf Carter, Roy Acuff, Hank Snow . . . these were the recording stars at CKNW. And people like Evan Kemp, Curly Johnson, Jack Jensen and other locals were heard live.

"They laughed at Bill when he started that station," his sister Margaret recalls. "All that cowboy music, and away out in *New Westminster.*"

The station was on the banks of the Fraser River, the transmitter just feet from the dikes that held the river back at freshet time. The station's ground system actually ran through the dike into the water.

Sometime during that August 15, 1944 a young sailor stationed at Esquimalt near Victoria was hunched over his ship's radio equipment and heard CKNW on its first day. "Everyone used to listen to Seattle those days," he recalled, "but I was roaming the dial and picked up this new station at 1230 kc. I got rid of it instantly! Cowboy music! Yeukhhh!" The sailor's name was Jack Cullen.

Bill Rea was unfazed by the reaction of the uptowners whose tastes ran more to Bach or Benny Goodman. Western music had been good to him, and it got the new station off to a distinctive and down-home, friendly start. There were plenty of listeners out there who thought it was just fine.

Rea was doing something else new: playing a *lot* of music. No soap operas or cops-and-robbers dramas interrupted the flow. "I think cowboy songs are a whole lot better," he told the staff. "Such songs all tell a story — a clean, wholesome story about the outdoors." Years later, Rea told Jack Cullen CKNW was the first all-music station in Canada. He'd been inspired, he said, by a woman in New York City, a radio station owner named Bernice Judas, whose programming philosophy was: Keep The Music Rolling.

Rea's new station had another distinction right from the start: a very strong emphasis on news. CKNW may not have been in the newspaper radio listings, but they had taken out some want-ads. NW wanted people to know they were: ON THE AIR NOW! At 1230 kc On Your Radio Dial — CKNW — Bringing You NEWS EVERY HOUR On The Hour From 6 A.M. Until MIDNIGHT.

If they couldn't get into the regular listings free, they would buy announcements of their arrival. And note what was stressed in that very first CKNW advertisement: news every hour. Hourly news on radio was nowhere to be found in B.C. in those days, except on this newcomer.

And they were doing it out of a newsroom the size of a hallway. But the newsroom's size was no indication of its status.

The importance given to news by CKNW has paid dividends to the station every day of its existence. An amazing 50 years after NW signed on, it is still considered the leader in local radio news, and, to this day, all around the province in rival radio stations, and in TV stations, and in newspapers, radios are tuned to CKNW.

But news was still only a part of the success of Rea's station.

"Bill," says Margaret Rea, "started everything that's still there today! Hourly newscasts. On the air 24 hours. The Roving Mike. 'Block' programming. Community involvement. Phoning in with news tips. The Orphans' Fund. Everything!"

Bill Fox interviewing returning troops during World War II, 1945.

Who was this man, Bill Rea? He's been described as "volatile," "mercurial," "jumpy," "impetuous," "brilliant," "bombastic," and "generous." "You loved him and you hated him." A "super-salesman and a lover of people," a "human dynamo," he could fire you one day, hire you back the next. He was "brash," "eccentric," "tireless," capable of sudden flashes of rage, and just as sudden a return to sunny optimism and good cheer. He was capable sometimes of behaving like a pouting, spiteful child.

And he had a genius for radio.

"Bill had a feel," long-time NW executive Erm Fiorillo says, "for what his listeners wanted to hear in music, he had the knack of picking songs that would later become hits, and he had the knack of choosing on-air people who were to become personalities that would attract listeners to his station."

He cut a swath through radio in British Columbia no one has ever come close to equalling. "This guy," Fiorillo said, "this eccentric, outgoing, outspoken, articulate, bombastic super-salesman and lover of people had only one goal in mind, and that was to make CKNW the most listened-to station in B.C."

"Bill Rea," says Joe Chesney, an early morning man, "pushed CKNW to the top through the sheer force of his personality."

You could see it coming.

". . . as corny a program as ever came out of a loudspeaker . . ."

William Rea, Jr. was born in Edmonton December 27, 1908. His father, also William, of Scottish descent, was born in Walton, Ontario. He had been the principal of Edmonton High School, was now, at 32, an articling law student. The elder Rea was a man of wide-ranging intellectual curiosity. At 50 he taught himself Greek so he could read the classics of that literature in the original tongue.

Bill's mother, Alice Blanche (Wooster) Rea, was also a University of Toronto graduate and, although she never taught, had studied to be a teacher. Bill, a tall and athletic young man, and his two sisters (Jean was born in 1912, Margaret in 1917) would grow up in a comfortable home full of books and informed conversation.

Tragically, Bill's mother died in March, 1920. Bill was 11.

On V-J Day in August of 1945 CKNW sent Jim Cox downtown with a pack transmitter. Thousands of people jammed Granville Street, and 17-year-old Jim Cox struggled through them capturing their excitement. "This huge thing was strapped to my back, and for all its weight it had a range of one block. I went down to the New Westminster train station, too, to cover the return of the Westminster Regiment. When HMS Implacable, the British aircraft carrier, sailed into Vancouver I interviewed the fellows. They were Canadian and British, and they'd been prisoners of war in Hong Kong." Those interviews were transcribed onto acetate discs at dockside, then rushed to CKNW. ∎

Bill Rea, circa 1940's.

Joe Chesney has a funny memory of the lengths Bill Rea would go for promotional attention for NW. It happens there had been a long rainless stretch, and the drought was causing real concern in the fertile Fraser Valley. "Bill told me to go to Vancouver International Airport and charter a plane. It was an Avro Anson, and Jim Spilsbury was the pilot. I took up a bucket of dry ice to seed the clouds for rain. As I remember, the rains did come . . . and the Bartenders' Union blamed us for spoiling their picnic in Stanley Park!" ∎

Bright, endlessly energetic, he showed his mettle quickly at school. "We all started at Mackay Avenue School," Margaret recalls. "Bill skipped three grades. He graduated at 14." Too young for university, Bill looked for work. There was nothing exceptional about those early jobs: he "crated boxes around," worked at a drug store, and so on.

He enrolled at the University of Alberta in 1924 at 15 . . . almost immediately ran into trouble. "He wouldn't take direction," Margaret laughs. "They told him, 'You can't wear a hat,' so he wore a hat. They said, 'You have to wear a regulation tie,' so he wore a bow-tie. He was an individualist."

The University of Alberta didn't have what the ambitious young Bill Rea wanted, and he left in 1927 for Northwestern University in Evanston, Ill. It had an excellent reputation, especially for business-oriented courses. "Bill took commerce there," says Margaret, "specializing in advertising."

Rea came back to Edmonton in 1932 without graduating and immediately went to work selling advertising in The Edmonton Bulletin. He must have been thinking about radio still, because before long he'd moved over to CJCA, part of a chain owned by an Alberta company, Taylor and Pearson. (Later, they would become Taylor Pearson Carson.)

He was hired as a time salesman, began hitting the pavement, dropping in to local shops, talking excitedly about the potential of radio advertising.

He was a natural, succeeded immediately. It helped that radio had become established. Some cities even had more than one station now, there were regular programs, and "radio personalities" were being created, people who became celebrities just by being on the air. Bill turned Jean, his younger sister, into just such a star. She'd taken home economics at university, so he arranged for her to do a daily radio program as a dietitian, giving out recipes and home care advice. He sold commercials on the show to local and national advertisers. Besides giving Jean a chance to use her training, it also gave Rea some idea of the possibilities of radio.

And along about here he fell in love. He had gone to a University of Alberta dance hall with Jean, and not long after they arrived and were checking out the crowd, his sister nudged him and said, "There's a cute blonde over there." The cute blonde was named Marjorie Foster. Bill asked her for a dance, then another, and another, and finally took her home. He must have made an amazing impression on Marjorie: she had come to the dance with her fiancé!

Bill and Marjorie were married January 2, 1934 and would be together until Bill's death almost 50 years later. (Marjorie died in April, 1991.)

In 1937 Bill and Marjorie, now the parents of a little girl, Annabelle, moved to Trail. Taylor Pearson Carson owned CJAT there, and transferred Bill with a promotion to commercial manager. The family's time in Trail was brief. "My parents had concerns about my health because of the smelter there," Annabelle says, "so they decided to leave. We weren't there very long, a few months."

It was still 1937 when the little family moved to Vancouver. Bill, now 29, was on the verge of his remarkable career in B.C. broadcasting. He started at George Chandler's CJOR, and this seems to be where his involvement with western music began. There was a program called Ranger's Cabin on OR — whether Bill inherited that show or started it himself isn't clear. At any rate, it became a great success with a mix of live and recorded music from sagebrush and corral. And in it was the seed of CKNW.

"Ranger's Cabin," radio reviewer Dick Diespecker wrote, "as corny a program as ever came out of a loudspeaker. But corny or not, he never had the slightest difficulty in keeping it loaded with sponsors and maintaining the highest listenership for that period of the day in Vancouver."

When Rea moved as a time salesman to CKMO he brought the Ranger's Cabin with him. "It was the only program on that station that ever made any money," says Ferdy Baglo, who was at MO when Rea arrived. The Ranger's Cabin theme song, Back in the Saddle Again, by Gene Autry, became a familiar sound in thousands of Lower Mainland homes. Bill got a real kick opening and reading the mounds of listeners' letters that came every day. The popularity of "hillbilly" music was not lost on him.

While he was at CKMO Rea put in his application to establish CKNW. He was encouraged by Sam Cohen, and New Westminster MLA (later Senator) Tom Reid. "He really wanted a *Vancouver* station," early associate Frank Walden says, "but if he couldn't get in the front door he'd go around to the back."

Rea began thinking about the live entertainment business. Right under that August 15, 1944 newspaper ad announcing the new station was another, reading: "Dance Tuesday! Dance Thursday! Dance Friday! with Bill Rea's Band, at the Cool TOWN HALL, West Pender at Burrard." And right below that is yet another ad, this one reading: "Saturday Dancing at the Horticultural Hall, North Vancouver, with the All-Modern Bill Rea's Band!"

It's likely Rea's experience with Ranger's Cabin had inspired him to go for this extra source of income. Given his own upbringing, growing up in a home where it's highly unlikely cowboy songs rang out daily, one suspects he started Bill Rea's Band for coolly practical reasons, a route to success.

It was, and then some.

The band was a five-player group touring small towns in the Lower Mainland and the Fraser Valley, and showing up regularly in city dance halls like the Town Hall Ballroom in the Driard Hotel at 1027 West Pender, and the Alexandra Ballroom at 804 Hornby at Robson. Marjorie took tickets at the door. The band became a fixture, popping up everywhere, with Bill "slapping the bull fiddle" and even singing now and then. "He wasn't particularly musical," his sister Margaret recalls, "but he had a lot of enthusiasm." Bill later laughingly claimed he was the least talented member of Local 145 of the Musicians' Union.

The band thrived. Bill, in fact, eventually bought the dance halls he had formerly rented, and held on to ownership of the Town Hall years after he moved away from B.C.

And money the band had earned was part of the $30,000 Rea somehow got together in 1944 to establish CKNW.

Where did that $30,000 — a *lot* of money in 1944 — come from? Accountant Alex Reid, who had CKNW as a client when it opened, says he has "no idea" where Bill got the money. "I never asked him."

Rea was sole owner. NW began as a proprietorship, so no records were needed to indicate repayment of any loans made . . . if any were made.

Sam Cohen of Army & Navy Stores assured him he would advertise on the new station. That would have been welcome financial and moral support.

And there was another factor: "CKNW," says Jim Cox, "was the only radio station in Canada to sign on during the war. Everyone wondered, where did Bill Rea get the equipment? Rea's father told me he sat down with C.D. Howe and said, 'Mr. Howe,

Jim Cox's enthusiasm got him an interview with jazzman Count Basie. Wire recording had just come in, and NW jumped at the new technology. "We met Basie and his band at the border and got on their bus. I recorded the interview, then we got off the bus at New Westminster. While Basie was in the bus enroute to Vancouver, listening to the radio, we were playing the interview back on the air. Basie was tremendously impressed with this new technology — that I could interview him on the bus, and then just go and play it. 'I've travelled all over,' he told me, 'and I've never heard an instant playback like that.' And we got a scoop: we had the story on the air while the other stations were waiting for the Count at the Vancouver end." ∎

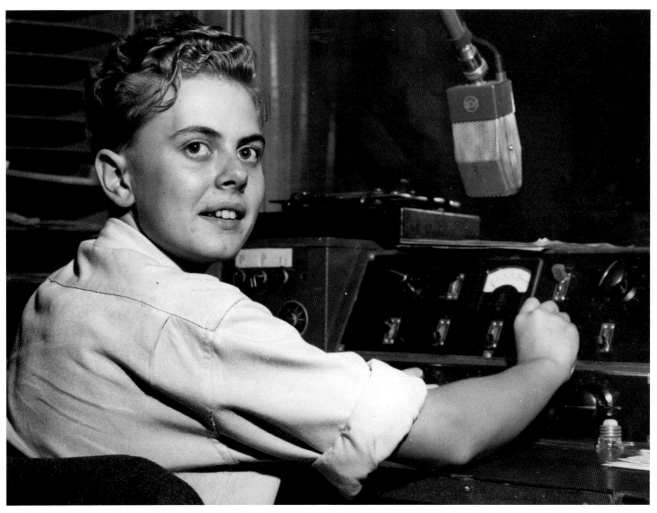

A very young Arnie Nelson (a regular performer on Ranger's Cabin) at CKNW's first console in "A" control.

Arnold Nelson turned up so faithfully to perform, it prompted Bill Rea to offer him a regular after-school spot on Ranger's Cabin. For 10-year-old Arnold, it was heaven.

"Listeners started writing in; they really liked this new boy soprano's voice. Bill Rea started calling me the mascot of the show. The other kids at school ribbed me, but I kept going. One day Bill says, 'They tell me you've been excellent; never miss a shift.

I want Sonny to have that station'." Howe, in 1943-44, was minister of munitions and supply, a formidable man famed for his tough, decisive nature. (And, yes, Bill Rea, Sr. called his son 'Sonny.' Years later, Anne Bolton remembered her boss telling her, "At my age it's nice to have your dad call you Sonny!")

A 1952 Sun story indicates MP Tom Reid "went to bat" with the CBC on Rea's behalf, so that was likely a factor in the war-time startup, too.

If the $30,000 did all come from band and dance-hall income, that must count as a remarkable achievement for the time. And it's not impossible, given the driving ambition and endless improvisational genius of the man who started the station.

Rea showed that improvisational flair right from Day One at CKNW. The station frequently reminded listeners it was running with no commercials.

On September 1, 1944, two weeks after the unofficial sign-on, the commercials started. And CKNW began doing what it has done so consistently, so professionally, so superbly ever since: attracting listeners, keeping listeners, and making money.

". . . too much of that radio station . . ."

When they hired 16-year-old Jim Cox in 1944 CKNW got a lot for its $13.85 a week. "I'd do the morning show every day, 6 a.m. to 8 a.m., then go to school. Then I did High School Jamboree from 3 to 5 in the afternoon, ended up doing that every day, too.

"It was an exciting time," Jim says. "Once NW signed on I was hooked. I'd always been a radio nut, listened from the time I was seven: Manhattan Merry-Go-Round, Amos and Andy, Jack Benny, Fred Allen . . . and I'd always collected records, especially big bands. I went back to Duke of Connaught in September, 1945 for my senior matriculation. But there was just too much of that radio station. I pulled out of school in October."

Evelyn Stensgaard, owner of the Windsor Hotel where NW had its studios, remembers Jim nearly 50 years later. "He always made so much noise clumping down the stairs after sign-off," she laughs, "it woke us up."

Following Bill Rea's instructions, Jim's evening shows leaned more toward novelty music than big bands, with a lot of up-tempo material, heavy on English music-hall, The Hoosier Hot Shots, and other lively groups. "The kind of music we play," Rea told him, "is the kind a pensioner in White Rock can clap his hands to." Rea had definite ideas on programming, and listened constantly to ensure people followed his orders.

"Never play two records together," he told Cox and the others. "The listener begins to ignore the voice, *and that's bad for commercials.* And every time you open your mouth give the listener some information."

Over the console was a sign demanding: SMILE! YOUR LISTENER WILL LIKE YOU!

One night Jim played some Dixieland. The phone rang and Hal Davis picked it up. It was Bill Rea. "Oh say Ha-al, who picked the music for the last segment?" Davis: "I guess it was Jim." "Let me speak to him." Cox: "Hello Bill — I picked it." Rea: "You're fired!!' (Hal heard it through the phone right across the room.) Cox: "Thank you, Bill, goodnight," and he hung up. Next afternoon as the afternoon shift came in, Rea materialized. "Oh say Ha-al, where's Jim?' "You fired him last night, Bill.' "Ahhhhh!' said Bill and left. Twenty minutes later, after getting the call he was waiting for, Jim was back picking approved music for the program that night.

"Bill sat sulking in the bathtub . . ."

At 17, Ferdy Baglo moved from CKMO to CKNW the day NW started. Ferdy, NW's first music director, would work there from 1944 until 1950, often perplexed by Bill Rea's "strange mixture" of generosity and volatility. "I remember one Christmas, two NW people brought Christmas trees to the station. Bill was furious. *He* was the one who brought Christmas trees in, no one else. He cancelled the Christmas bonuses, cancelled the staff party. He could be like that, like a flash fire. Everyone was angry — they'd been counting on that money. Bill went home, sat soaking in the bathtub, sulking, still angry . . . with Marjorie banging on the door, trying to get him to talk."

Yet in 1947 the generosity showed when Ferdy took a doctor-ordered break from work. Rea bought Ferdy a camera to take on a five-month trip on a Norwegian freighter. "Bill was very generous to me. He taught me everything about showmanship.

"In 1950 I went over to CKDA in Victoria for a year, then came back to CKNW in 1951 as transmitter operator. I started doing the late-night show, then went back into the record library and helped Len Hopkins revamp it. In 1952 I left CKNW for good, and went to CKOM in Saskatoon. But I continued doing a weekly taped NW show called Scandinavia, sponsored by Hagen's Travel. I did that show until 1958, when Norm Grohmann took it over."

I think I'd like to start *paying* you.' He gave me $20. In 1945 that was a LOT of money. And I think I probably got $20 a month or so from then on."

He picked up a new skill while appearing on Roundup with Jack Jensen. "I learned to sing harmony. I sang with Jack; he really liked it, he'd never had harmony before." That was important, because it played a part in the formation of the Rhythm Pals. ∎

Bill Fox (left) as 'Barometer Bill' with Bill Hughes, 1948.

Ferdy later went into the ministry and in 1972 got his STM degree. He grins. "My thesis was Communications in Mission."

Today, he lives in retirement in Chilliwack.

"I want you to be my program director . . ."

Bill Fox was a CKWX staff announcer, did a show called the Red White & Blue quiz. One day, as Fox ended his shift at WX, a little man in horn-rimmed glasses drove up and introduced himself. He was Dave Armstrong, and he was to be the sales manager at a new radio station in New Westminster, owned by a fellow named Bill Rea. "He wants to talk to you."

"We drove down to the York," says Fox, "and there's Bill Rea in the beer parlor buying beer for everyone. He says, 'How'd you like to come work at CKNW?' Well, I said I didn't know, the station wasn't even on the air yet. "How much are you making at CKWX?' I told him: $140 a month. 'I'll give you $160,' he says, 'and I want you to be my program director!' He'd just met me! Well, that sounded like a pretty good idea, so I said yes. I was 26.

"I started doing a quiz show called the Fair Sex Quiz. Ladies would come to the station, and I'd ask them all sorts of silly questions. Their prizes would be kitchen gadgets."

Bill left NW and returned a couple of times. In 1958, on his second return, he was "pretty much in news. I was the first one to go out in the Sunbeam Bread News Cruiser.

"One thing I did at CKNW was well-known at the time: I was a kind of tongue-in-cheek weather forecaster, 'Barometer Bill.' It was just a fun thing, and not meant to poke fun at the official forecasts. Bill Hughes liked it, and encouraged me to keep doing it. But we had a formal complaint from Ottawa that said we were ridiculing their forecasts! Of course, that wasn't true. We got letters of support from listeners."

In those days no one played around with weather on the air!

"In 1963 I left CKNW for good, and got the second of my *two* five-year-service watches from the station."

Roving Mike

Roving Mike, the world's longest-running radio program, began in 1944 as a morning show on Fridays and Saturdays when the New Westminster Public Market was open. As this book went to press, the 15,000th airing of the show loomed. From the beginning to 1950 the host was Bill Rea; since then it's been Bill Hughes.

Because he talked to Interurban commuters, Rea tended to have a lot of repeat guests. He would ask them a question of the day. "If they didn't know the details," Hughes smiles, "he'd be happy to explain it and share his views. Bill was a strong Liberal, and he used the show as a political soap box."

Hughes changed direction, started talking to people about themselves. When the show moved in 1952 to the bus depot, and he began interviewing Greyhound passengers, it hit its stride. "I discovered how much more interesting it was to meet people

Shortly after he started at CKNW, Warren Barker got what he later described as the biggest scare of his professional career: "Bill Rea came in, talking a mile a minute as usual, told me he had to dash off somewhere, and gave me the Ranger's Cabin show to do. It was starting in just a few minutes! I was petrified: I'd been at the station for all of three days, I'd never done a live show, never operated, didn't know what switch was the microphone, how to get the turntables going. But the CKNW

from elsewhere. People seemed to enjoy hearing about the prairie farmers and the small towns in Ontario."

Today he chats with passengers on the Gray Line Bus at Tsawwassen.

Since 1951 Roving Mike has been heard six mornings a week at 8:45. One reason for the show's interest is Bill's own wide knowledge of world locations. Often he has been to the spot from which his guests have come, and will astonish them with his knowledge of local landmarks and conditions. That tends to open people up, make them more talkative.

The number used on the Roving Mike Show is predicated on its beginning as the Market Show. Hal Davis recalls somebody saying, after the show had been on about three years, "Let's number them." Hal sat down with a sharpened pencil and a calendar, calculated the number of times the show had been on since it began, began numbering them the next day.

On June 26, 1984, when Bill hosted the 12,000th edition of Roving Mike, it made the Guinness Book of Records. He told Lori Pappajohn of the Royal City Record, "People are friendly and in a great mood on vacation. There are only three or four in a hundred who refuse to speak. With couples, one is always more talkative than the other. I've never met talkative twosomes. And older people are more interesting because they're more relaxed and don't care what they say."

George Garrett, who has been filling in regularly for Bill since 1965, once spent the whole program talking to one man — the only passenger on the bus! "I don't know what I would have done if his English had been bad!"

"We rant and rave and tear our hair . . ."

Following a suggestion from accountant Frank Walden, Bill Rea named his company the International Broadcasting Company, and used that name on air right after the CKNW call letters. It was an ambitious title — meant, no doubt, to impress listeners and potential sponsors.

A 1945 Christmas card, describing CKNW as Your Port of Good Listening, pictures 25 people, headed by Rea as Owner and Manager. The card, which includes staff photos, and tongue-in-cheek "poetry," gives a nice indication of NW's flavor in its first full year.

David Armstrong is commercial manager, and the station's one account executive is a beaming MacIntosh "Tosh" MacDonald. (Rea, Armstrong and MacDonald all sold air time.) The title "account executive," incidentally, may have been brought to B.C. radio by Bill Rea; perhaps he had heard it used in Chicago. It had a certain tone, more impressive than "time salesman."

Chief engineer was Ross MacIntyre, and two young fellows named Eric Risbey and James Dagg manned the struggling little 250-watt transmitter. "We rant and rave and tear our hair to keep the station on the air."

There was more poetry on the next page: "We supply the looks *and* keep the books!" Dulcie Bergenham was receptionist, Anne Papay handled traffic (making sure programs

Trio was there as part of the program, and they helped me over some of the technical hurdles.

"This wasn't a unique event: Rea worked on the principle of teaching a kid to swim by throwing him in the water." ∎

The CKNW Trio performed live on Ranger's Cabin.

Record companies once refused to let radio stations play their records. If people could hear songs free on the radio, they argued, they wouldn't buy them in the stores. By the time NW signed on, all the major companies but one had come to their senses, realizing radio exposure was free advertising. The one exception was Decca Canada, whose major star at the time — and he was a *giant* star — was crooner Bing Crosby. Bill Rea loved Crosby's records, and had so many he could present a half-hour of Crosby's music every evening at 7.

How did he get away with it? Jim Cox: "I'd go on and say 'The owner of this radio station has collected Bing Crosby records for years, but because no equipment is available at his home this is the only way he can hear them!'" Sometimes Rea himself explained "his phonograph was broken."

NW got away with this bizarre and illegal procedure for some time. Decca Canada eventually joined the rest of the industry in allowing its records, including those of Bing Crosby, to be aired.

and commercials got on the air at the correct time), and Rosalie Ontko was the station's accountant. "Secretary to Mr. Rea" was Sheila Hassell. The continuity department ("They write the stuff and take the guff") was headed by Dorothy Tupper, who worked with Lillian Jackson and Allan MacNab.

The announcers, all neatly coiffed, wear suits and ties. Chief announcer was Bill Duncan, whose staff included Warren Johnstone, Len Chapple, Wally Grant, Jim Cox and Charles Rogers. The news department was a one-man operation: Mike Giraud. (Giraud would eventually move to CBC Radio, later became their international assignment editor.)

Margarette Duncan handled publicity, and musical director was young Ferdy Baglo: "He's mighty important, we want you to know — if there ain't no music, there ain't no show!" Live music was a big factor, and the last page of the card shows Curly Johnson, Evan Kemp and Jack Jensen . . . each sporting a guitar and dressed as a singing cowboy. "We bring the Songs of the West to you — Monday to Sunday the Whole Year thru!"

The card reflects the eager, informal and lively flavor of the new station. It was still a bit formless, a little seat-of-the-pants, but it was learning fast.

Just For Fun

Just For Fun was 'must listening' for CKNW fans from virtually the beginning of the station until the late 1960s. It was the highest-rated, and certainly the funniest, Sunday morning show in local radio.

Al McNab fathered the program by playing novelty and comedy records. When McNab left NW in 1946 Hal Davis was asked to write Just For Fun. Host Doug Bruce dubbed the new writer "Hallucinations P. Davis." Then Hal and "Wallopin' Warren Johnstone" took over the on-air duties, too. Hal would write and perform "commercials" that satirized real spots heard on the air.

Spike Jones was often heard with his City Slickers, maiming sweet love songs like Cocktails for Two and Laura. The Hoosier Hotshots were favorites. "Who can ever forget," asks Hal Davis today, "the Hotshots' heartfelt rendition of 'Does the Spearmint Lose Its Flavor on the Bedpost Overnight?'

"Characters created on the program," Hal recalls, "and played by various NW personalities, included the brilliant young conductor Jascha Yabettcha — who led the Simpletown Symphony Orchestra in such classics as 'She Was Only a Jockey's Daughter, But All the Horsemen Knew 'er,' and announcer Elmer Slurp, who flogged Zero, 'the deodorant that doesn't kill underarm odor — It makes your armpits disappear so no one knows where the stink is coming from.'"

There were real sponsors, too. In the early years Bolivar Hatcheries promoted their Skookum Chicks which, thanks to Hal's commercials, were vested with superhuman powers. Clothier Murray Goldman contributed jokes — most of them deliberately bad. Toward the end of its run, Just For Fun was written by 'Wistful Warren' Barker and, latterly, Bob Hughes. Lyndon Grove, who worked at NW in the mid-50s, recalls he did some scripts for JFF, and got $10 each.

And Hal had a succession of on-air co-stars, including Norm Grohmann.

The party ended in the late 1960s, when manager Mel Cooper canned the show. It was the highest-rated program in its time period, but Cooper thought the show had become old hat. Sponsored programs were being phased out, anyway . . . and then the ubiquitous disc jockey took over.

"Don't call me down in front of the staff..."

Al Reusch, a Vancouver musician in the late '30s, was CKNW's first production manager. "It was April, 1945. At Bill Rea's request I started in production and, two weeks later, was chief announcer." Al was another of the legion of people who filled in on Rea's shows when he was away on holidays.

Reusch also co-hosted, with Al McNab, a 15-minute show called How Smart We Aren't. These two would walk into the studio and improvise and ad-lib gags . . . and began to develop a following. One day they ad-libbed gags on the name Custer . . . and that made people in the little town of Custer, Washington angry! Bill Rea was delighted. "An international incident!"

"I remember I got really angry at Bill; he was always changing my program schedules. I'd post a schedule for the announcers, and I'd come in the next day and see XXXs all through it. 'Well, Al,' he'd say, 'you're not used to block programming.' That's why I left. He wouldn't talk about it. I followed him one day, shouting at him, the copy staff heard. Rea got really mad: 'Don't call me down in front of the staff, you won't last long.' 'Well, Bill,' I said, 'I don't know if I *want* to last long.'"

He didn't.

No big loss for Al: he would later go on to found Aragon Records, one of the major recording studios in B.C. musical history.

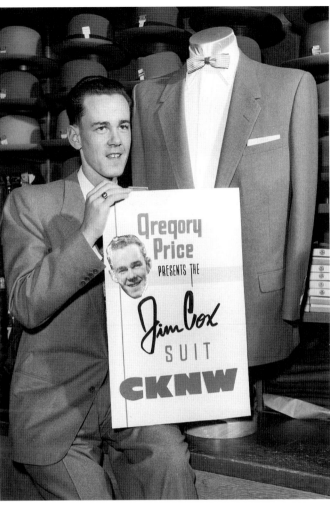

Jim Cox modelling the 'Jim Cox' suit for client Gregory Price in 1949.

The Orphans' Fund

In 1945 NW launched a phenomenon as well-known as anything the station has ever done: The CKNW Orphans' Fund.

Hal Davis, who now administers the fund, remembers its origins: "In the 1940s orphaned and unwanted children in the Fraser Valley were collected in New Westminster in the Loyal Protestant Home. It was customary for the city to recognize them at Christmas. As part of that tradition CKNW appealed to its listeners for funds for treats for the children.

"Bill Rea," says Erm Fiorillo, "insisted from the very day the Fund was born that NW would pick up all the operating expenses for the Fund — 100 per cent of every dime raised would go to benefit orphaned children. That was a policy unheard of in charity circles at that time." To this day, all administrative and other expenses of the Fund are covered by CKNW.

"That first year," Hal continues, "$1,200 was raised, and the station bought Christmas treats for the children . . . including radios which could be tuned to the new station. The project was so successful it was repeated in subsequent years, and the tradition of raising money to provide treats for children at Christmas was established. Some money was raised through direct listener contribution, but originally most came through station projects using the staff as volunteers."

Incidentally, restrictions on the number of commercials in the early days seemed somewhat looser. Jim Cox remembers packing no fewer than 12 60-second commercials into the Crosby show, a program just 30 minutes long. Part of the reason was a ruling that no spot announcements were allowed after 7:30. From that point, prime time for radio then, only fully-sponsored shows were okayed. ■

Arnold Nelson with Frankie Laine and Bruce Gifford (above) and a very young Arnie performing in the CKNW studio (below right).

Jack Cullen was tireless in his efforts to get music no one else had. He'd lug two heavy Magnacorders (40 pounds each!) up to movie house projection booths, and with two alligator clips and a screwdriver do the technical work necessary to record music off the new movies being shown. Decades later, his listeners enjoy these one-of-a-kind treasures. Cullen interviewed Duke Ellington for three hours, from 2 to 5 a.m. one morning, and Ellington came back later because he needed

If Bill Rea had done nothing else, his creation of the Orphans' Fund would have made him a major figure in B.C. history. As this book was being written, an announcement was made that total contributions since the Fund began had topped $10 million. You'll read much more about this tremendously successful initiative in later pages.

"I was beside myself with joy . . ."

"When I heard Bill Rea was starting a station in New Westminster, I was beside myself with joy." The reason for Arnie Nelson's happiness was that, at age 10, he loved Bill Rea's show, The Ranger's Cabin, on CKMO.

Young Arnold made a little cardboard CKNW mike and got his mom to take a photograph of him at the mike holding his guitar. He did more: he started showing up to perform on NW's amateur talent Children's Hour. Host was announcer Bud Rogers. "I showed up really regularly," Arnie laughs today, "I don't think I was ever turned down."

There was a thrilling episode in 1947 when 13-year-old Arnold and 14-year-old Bruce Gifford became NW's Sunday all-night record men while regular Lew Fox was away on vacation. "It is the first time in the history of B.C. and maybe even Canada," The Province reported, "that two such youthful entertainers have completely taken over the operation of a major radio station." (Bruce Gifford later became an Anglican priest.)

Arnold went out on live shows with other NW stars, interviewed visiting celebrities, sang and played guitar regularly on various programs . . . then, when he was about 14, an alarming (but inevitable) thing happened: his voice broke. His days as a boy soprano behind him, Arnie added bass-playing and Hawaiian guitar to his repertoire of skills, and continued to appear on the Ranger's Cabin — now occasionally performing with two other teenagers, Ron and Doug Beckett.

When he graduated from UBC in June 1958 with a Commerce degree, Arnie was hired by IBM. Three months later, he married.

But his CKNW career was not over just yet. After Arnie left IBM in Toronto, he started selling national TV accounts there. Then, when the Rhythm Pals came to town, Arnie joined them in performing on CBC.

In the summer of 1971 he came back to NW as an account executive. "I had accounts like Woodward's, Lawson Oates, Smitty's Pancakes; I liked it a lot. Then Peter Kosick at CJOR asked me to come over and be sales manager there. Pat Burns was going so big I thought maybe it wasn't a bad idea.

"It was a bad idea."

When Arnie left CKNW the second time it was for good . . . almost. "When I left NW at the end of January, 1964 I had won the sales prize for that period. It was partly an accident of timing: General Electric had a big Christmas lights promotion on, and they bought $10,000 in one month. That was HUGE for those days. I was over working at CJOR when NW awarded me that prize. I always thought well of them for that."

"I was still in my air force blues . . ."

One of the major players in CKNW's future made a quiet entry into the story in the summer of 1945. He was a slim, Edmonton-born 21-year-old, an air force wireless operator. His name was Hal Davis.

Davis had been in radio a third of his life. At 14 he was acting in dramas on CKUA, encouraged by a friendly teacher. Later young Hal produced some of those plays, with casts drawn from local students or Little Theatre. He operated, too, cuing the music, bringing in sound effects, building skills that would help him in later years.

When he was 16 Hal won an announcing contest held by CJCA. Sandwiched between his announcing duties, he took elocution lessons from the well-known Bertha Biggs. The station saw something in this eager young fellow: he was hired for summer relief announcing. "I was a neophyte, opened the station at 6 a.m. Back then the night time was the prime time. I ended up doing lots of different things. I'd work all day, right into the evenings. I got $12.50 a week."

Later, as a liberal arts student at the University of Alberta, Hal worked at the campus radio station.

By May 1943, he was in the air force. They sent him to Vancouver to take wireless operator training, then on to Montreal. Hal graduated at the top of his class, was sent to Calgary to become an instructor.

"I started hanging around CFAC Radio in Calgary, and ended up doing a six-to-midnight shift. I'd read newscasts, introduce transcriptions . . . so I was getting my $1.50 a day from the air force and $65 a month from CFAC. Then in the spring of 1945 I got transferred to Tofino."

Tofino, on the west coast of Vancouver Island, was an isolation station. "When you wanted to go somewhere, you went in an army supply boat. I've been sick in more army supply boats . . ." His duties were not onerous; the war was winding down, and his job consisted of keeping

information about vintage recordings he'd made . . . and only Cullen had it! Sammy Davis, Jr., asked Jack to send a copy of their interview to him in the States because there was just so much good stuff on it. ∎

The 1948 Fraser Valley floods, and CKNW's instant volunteering of its services as an emergency flood control coordination centre, was a milestone in the station's history. The Canadian Army took over the studios. NW's decision to volunteer its services set a tone of intense and sincere community involvement. Because of its drama and the fact everyone in the Fraser watershed was affected, it was savvy programming, too! The station reported on the floods 24 hours a day, as transmitter in touch with the submarine patrols that plied the coast on the lookout for the enemy.

Another wireless operator there, Fred Darling, had met Bill Rea. When Fred heard Hal mention his radio experience he suggested Hal drop in to see Rea on his next leave.

"Well, I came down on a '48' to visit some Vancouver friends, it was the summer of 1945. I visited CKNW and introduced myself to Bill Rea. I was still dressed in my air force blues.

"Rea introduced me to Bill Duncan, and he auditioned me. Then he said he was going out for a coffee, and left me to do the next show! When he came back from coffee Duncan offered me a job at $1 an hour." When Hal was discharged he phoned Bill Rea and was offered a job. After a brief trip to Edmonton to see the family, Hal and his new bride Esther came back to Vancouver January 3, 1946.

"Bill Rea met us at the CN's New Westminster station and took us on a tour of the town. He took us past his house. It had a copper door. I never forgot my first sight of that house, and that door. It was a landmark." (Inside the house was a pink marble fireplace from the old Hotel Vancouver.)

"What's it cost for the bus . . .?"

"The reason I got into radio?" says Bill Hughes. "I was good at math."

We'll explain in a moment.

"The only thing I *ever* wanted to be was a radio announcer," Bill says. "But I was poorly equipped for it: I was shy, nervous, had a terrible drawl. I was terribly skinny,

When the Fraser River flooded in 1948, the station reported on the floods 24 hours a day and staff helped pile up sandbags.

light weight. But I still had this ambition. I learned to read by reading the newspaper aloud, just as an exercise. My mother thought I had a problem with bodily function: I'd go into the bathroom so much. But there was wonderful resonance in there. I'd reconstruct the hockey game of the day. I'd do the cheering, announce the lineup, it was all part of this dream. I didn't use a microphone, didn't *have* one."

He started with a more prosaic job: delivering newspapers. This skinny, ambitious kid built his route up to a point where the weight of the papers threw his shoulder out of whack. He feels the effects on that right pectoral muscle more than 50 years later — it affects his golf!

The $11 a month Bill made in his home town of New Westminster was important to his family; his dad's income at the time was $20 a month.

When Bill's army service time came, he was rejected during the physical. It was that pectoral muscle. "I'd graduated from high school, but I hadn't made any plans. I was shocked at not making it into the services."

What to do? A fateful conversation in April of 1944 with Joyce McKay, a fellow Grade 13 student at Duke of Connaught, brought a solution. (Grade 13 was equivalent to the first year of university.) "Joyce came to me in dire trouble. She was horrible in math, I was best in my class. She asked, 'What do you want to do when you're out of school?' I said I want to be a radio announcer. She said 'I already knew that,' and told me her brother, Stuart McKay, was production manager at CKWX. 'If you help me,' Joyce said, 'and I pass the exam I'll introduce you to him.' So I helped her. She made the exam by two points: 62 per cent.

"I got introduced to Stuart. I'd never sat in front of a mike. There was a script in front of me. The light comes on. Well, over the years I'd trained to read for *sense.* So they could tell I had potential, even though I was intensely nervous. They told me they couldn't take me on there, but they'd write a letter to CJAT in Trail. CJAT was part of the Taylor Pearson Carson chain, as CKWX was."

Bill sent an application, but couldn't wait. "The war was coming to an end. I thought, when the guys start coming back, I won't have a chance." He scraped together what money he could and, with his parents' blessing, hopped the train for Trail.

"I did my audition. I told Walter Dales, the manager, I had no money for a return ticket. He took compassion on me, put me to work in CJAT's record library. Very, very occasionally I got to go on the air."

CJAT was an excellent training ground. You had to learn everything. That helped Bill in later years when he was up for selection as manager of CKNW. He had done "a little bit of all of it."

(Bill's mother wrote him from New Westminster, all excited about a new radio station right in town. It was called CKNW, she wrote, and it played "funny" music, "cowboys and Indians" stuff. But it was right in their own back yard, and she hoped Bill might consider asking for a job there.)

When Bill's holidays came up, he decided to go back to Vancouver and try his luck in radio there. "My parents were really against it. I was making $80 a month. But I was determined to come back."

staff rushed around on low-lying Lulu Island piling up sandbags to keep back the rising waters, and the transmitter was hoisted onto pilings. NW gained a lot of new listeners as a result of its constant coverage. ∎

Bill Rea and the Rhythm Pals welcomed the famed Sons of the Pioneers.

During the '40s, NW occasionally went past its midnight sign-off if war news warranted it. After one of these late sign-offs, an NW engineer pulled out a record he'd just obtained, the famous under-the-counter Crepitation Contest. It described a farting competition, held in a huge arena, involving many contestants famed for their flatulatory skills. It came complete with impressive sound effects and excited commentary.

The engineer slapped the disc on the turntable and began to

Bill returned to CKWX, auditioned again, and got a job. His salary went up to $100 a month, for a news-reading shift, 3 p.m. to midnight. Then he became the voice of The Vancouver Sun with a major newscast at 10 p.m. Suddenly, it was Bill Hughes With The News, and he became known.

"Then, along about May of 1946 a guy named Bill Rea phoned me. He drove over to the house to talk to me. He brought his dog. My mother hated dogs. We had a cat. He brought his dog in. My mother didn't like him.

"He wanted me to come over to NW, to be *featured:* 'Bill Hughes With The News.' In some areas, he was not to be denied.

"I said, 'Mr. Rea, I don't like doing music programs.' 'Oh, Billll,' he said (and here Hughes drops his voice an octave or two), 'no waaaay. The Fiiiiive, the Eiiiiight, the Tennnnn O'Clock newscasts . . . you'd prepare the 12 Miiiiidnight news.'

"'Let me write this down,' I said. 'What are you making?' he asked. '$100 a month.' 'What's it cost for the bus to take you to work?' '$12 a month.' 'You see!? You're already making $112 a month! You won't need to take the bus! With the $100 *we* pay you, you'll be making $12 more a month!'

"I told him I didn't see it that way. 'OK,' he says, 'we'll make it a real $112 a month.' So, on September 1, 1946 I started at CKNW. I was 21. It wasn't long before I woke up to the realization that there was no money in announcing. The guys with the good suits who owned the cars were the *salesmen.*

"I went to Bill Rea, and said 'I want to get into sales. My house payments are $23 a month, and I'm having trouble meeting that.' He says, 'OK, but I want you to do a daily newscast and fill in on Roving Mike. You can have the *entire* Fraser Valley as your sales territory: White Rock, Whalley, Newton, Haney, Port Coquitlam, Coquitlam, Pitt Meadows . . .' They couldn't even *hear* us in the Fraser Valley!

"But, you know, before long I was billing $3,000 a month. That gave me $300 a month in my pocket. I'm making money! This was straight commission.

"But I'm also reading the 8 a.m. news for no pay!

"'Yes,' Bill Rea says, 'but it'll *make* you!'

"And he was right."

". . . we had a trio sound we wanted him to hear . . ."

The origin of the Rhythm Pals — Mike, Marc and Jack — is an illustration of how sheer luck can play a part in making careers. The unique combination of these three voices produced a beautiful harmony that made them major recording and personal appearance stars for decades.

When Bill Rea was at CKMO, he enjoyed the singing of a young fellow named Jack Jensen, who made guest appearances on Evan Kemp's show. "And," says Jack, "Bill Rea would give me a few bucks for singing on his shows." When Rea started NW, Jack and Evan Kemp would follow him. Member number ONE for the future group was in place.

A local dance band, the Pony Pals, fronted at first by Andy Fraser, was appearing at the time on Sunday nights on NW. One of its members was accordion player Marc Wald, just out of the army. Marc would soon become Rhythm Pals member number TWO. Number THREE, Mike Ferbey, who, like Marc, had once been part of a Saskatoon group called Sleepy and Swede, showed up in 1946 on his return from nine months of USO performances in the Philippines. Now the three men who would become the Rhythm Pals were all performing at the same radio station. But not yet as a group.

"What happened next," Marc Wald says, "is that the three of us got together sort of informally, and sang and played a Jimmy Wakely hit called Standing Outside of Heaven. We thought it sounded pretty good, so we went to Bill Rea and told him we had a trio sound we wanted him to hear. We did the song for him, and he said he really liked it, and put us on the air. Well, the phones started ringing from listeners, and the reaction was so good Bill made us a regular act."

Suddenly the boys were everywhere on the NW schedule. Marc Wald: "We were getting phone calls from Fraser Valley dairy farmers: 'You boys keep on singin' like that — our cows are giving more milk!'"

At first, the Ferbey, Wald and Jensen trio were known by their first names: Mike, Marc and Jack. "We told CKNW's listeners we needed a name for our group," Mike Ferbey recalls, "and of the suggestions sent in, Bill Rea picked the Rhythm Pals as the best." It was December, 1946.

"A nurse named Elizabeth Clarke had written a song called Bluebird On Your Windowsill, and she came on NW and sang it. She was just awful; Bill Rea was laughing. But the song was good. We recorded it, and it was a hit. We got tired of singing it! We taught the song to Tex Williams, and he had a hit with it. And lots of other performers did it." They also made a hit of North Vancouver composer Keray Regan's My Home By The Fraser.

Mike Ferbey: "Our break from CKNW came Christmas time in 1949. There was a Christmas bonus problem. We got $6 or $7 each. Jack was really mad — he gave his

play it for his colleagues' delectation. There was no fear of it going on air; it was 2 a.m., and the transmitter was off. Unfortunately, they'd forgotten the speaker on Columbia Street, installed to allow passers-by to hear CKNW. It was still "live."

Someone down on the sidewalk started banging frantically on the front door and pointing up, but when the horrified engineers cut the feed a small crowd of late-night revelers shouted in protest. ∎

Cowboy star Jimmy Wakely was a welcome visitor at CKNW.

Aubrey Price: "You could tell when a rebuke was coming from Bill Rea: he'd tweak his nose. And when he was angry he'd shift furniture around . . . move chairs back and forth, shove a desk. I remember one Saturday afternoon he phoned me and asked me to come in about some copy someone had written. He had a stack of it on his desk. 'Oh, say, Aubrey,' he says, 'the copy stinks.'

"And I said, 'Oh? What copy, Bill?' And he said, 'Oh, all of it,' and he picked up this stack and just threw it into the air, all over the room. He liked the dramatic gesture. This was his way of motivating the staff." ∎

bonus back to Bill Rea and said, 'I think you need this more than I do.'" Hal Davis still recalls the look of disgust on Jensen's face when he saw the cheque . . . and still recalls the sulphurous rage of Bill Rea, who took EVERYBODY'S cheques back.

As it happens, young Evan Kemp was performing at NW, too, and he had earlier overheard Bill Rea and the Rhythm Pals arguing about money. The group wanted a raise, and Rea wasn't going to give it to them. "You don't know what's involved in my starting this station, boys. I had to suck up to the politicians, and borrow a lot of money. You've only been here a year-and-a-half, and you want a raise." He turned to Jack Jensen. "Jack, let's say you were walking down Columbia Street and you dropped dead. You could be replaced in a moment."

Mike Ferbey: "Tiny Elphicke at CKWX had wanted the Rhythm Pals over there, so we went to WX. We started New Year's Day, 1950. But it was a good time for us at NW. They were good to us."

Jack Jensen elaborates on Mike's reminiscence: "Bill Rea fired us. But after we were at WX for a while, Bill Rea showed up at my place. We lived quite close to each other in New Westminster: 'Come see my new car,' he says. So we're driving around in his big blue convertible, and he says, 'It sure would be nice to have you guys back. Do you think you could work two or three months for Tiny, then come work two or three for me?'

"I said no.

"But, you know, I loved that guy. He got me my start."

"I got really excited about radio . . ."

Knowledge of the music got Joe Chesney through the CKNW door. Chesney, a native of Willowdale, Saskatchewan, had served as a wireless operator and air gunner in the RCAF during WWII, was stationed at Patricia Bay after the war.

"I had a friend, another RCAF type, Bud Rogers. He'd been invalided out, and got an announcing job at CKNW. I visited him there, and I got really excited about radio." Joe got a job as a trainee announcer in 1946 at CFJC in Kamloops. (One of his chores was to assist on a morning program hosted by an ebullient evangelist named Phil Gaglardi.) After a few months he moved on to CJAV in Port Alberni . . .and visited his CKNW pal Bud Rogers again. This time Joe talked to Bill Rea, who hired him. "A show I'd been doing on CJAV, Sagebrush Serenade, had been a big hit. We played records by performers like The Sons of the Pioneers and Gene Autry. It pulled mail really well, so Bill Rea thought I could handle *his* shows when he was busy or away. I started at CKNW in mid-October, 1947, at $100 a month. I was 28."

The Man With 6,000 Songs

During this book's preparation, a fine letter arrived from Isobel Morris, whose late husband Jimmy was an orchestra leader and CKNW's music director. Mrs. Morris reminds us Bill Rea brought in many western stars, like Hank Snow, Wilf Carter, Roy Acuff, Texas Jim Robertson, Merle Travis and Ernest Tubb. "My husband and his Radio Mountaineers played with them all, and Jimmy interviewed them on the radio. Jim sang on both the Ranger's Cabin and Bill Rea's Roundup, and knew so many tunes Bill called him the man with 5,000 songs. Bill started a contest for people to stump Jimmy: they called it 'Stump Jimmy Morris,' and he performed it live at many places. He also entertained at many Orphans' Fund picnics, and at hospitals."

While Jim was music director at NW Bill Rea had him make trips to Seattle to get the latest hits on records, so that CKNW could beat the other local stations. Listeners often sent in songs they had written, Isobel says, and if Bill thought they were singable he would have Jim learn and sing them.

The Morris family's contribution to CKNW didn't stop with singing, playing music and producing daughters: the station's first in-house staff letter (called ChucKles and NeWs) was published in the Morris home on a hand-run duplicator.

"He could be astonishingly kind . . ."

"Ladies, are your stockings on their last legs?"

That was the first line of commercial copy Aubrey Price wrote at CKNW. It was 1948. He eventually became copy chief. And although he left NW more than 40 years ago, Aubrey's recollections of the place are clear.

"Bill Rea was a big fellow," says Aubrey, "big in his stature, big in his voice, big in his ideas. His whole spirit was throughout the station. He was a hard taskmaster, a perfectionist, demanded so much. He'd often call the entire staff into the studio and give us pep talks. He'd seem to inspire *himself* with those talks, sort of a 'win one for the Gipper' style. We liked Bill, but he made all of us nervous. We felt we were always being monitored, and this, as he knew only too well, kept us on our toes. When he left on a business trip, a cloud lifted. But he could be astonishingly kind: a fellow came in off the street one day, looking for work . . . Bill sent him down to Gregory Price Clothiers, and had him completely outfitted head to toe, said he wouldn't get a job looking the way he did."

After Aubrey left the station in 1953 to work in England, he got a cable from Rea asking him to come back to NW as copy chief. "I thought, oh, oh, he's had a row with someone. He even offered to pay my fare back from England. But as I was quite happy where I was, I said no thanks, Bill."

"I need 20 announcements in one day . . ."

Al Klenman, an early CKNW time salesman (he started in 1948, left in 1955 to become the commercial manager at Victoria's CKDA), said one of the ways Bill Rea wrung more money out of commercial time was to sell, not 60 seconds of time, but 120 words of copy. The announcer would presumably read those 120 words in fewer than 60 seconds. That time could then be banked and, when 60 more seconds had been accumulated, that could be sold.

Al, who had been at CKWX from 1937 to 1947, sold CKNW's all-night show shortly after he arrived to Campbell Used Cars for $500 a month. "In my first year," Al says, "I brought in $44,000 extra revenue. That's not much in today's terms, but back then . . ." But the sale of which he remains proudest is to Woodward's Stores. He still has the original 1948 contract, the first Woodward's had ever signed with a radio station. "Jack Drain bought the time. Woodward's was fighting Wosk's back then for the top share of the heavy appliance market. Jack called me at 7 a.m. one day. 'We're having a big sale; I need 20 announcements in one day.' He got 'em."

NW staffer Gordon Reid was leaving the station, and Margaret Rea and Hal Davis were out getting a gift for him. Copy writer Aubrey Price saw them down on the street on their way back. "They were at the light, and I figured if I go downstairs now I'll just meet them. Well, I don't know what possessed me. At the bottom of the stairs I got down on my hands and knees as a gag, and opened the door onto Columbia Street. Hal and Margaret were there, but so was Bill Rea, talking to them very seriously. Hal and Margaret are trying hard to keep from cracking up. I began backing away still on my hands and knees."

Hal says Aubrey showed remarkable presence of mind. "He looked up at Rea and said, 'I seem to be a little short this month.'" ∎

Bill Rea worked hard at publicity.

"I'd hustle by day, broadcast by night . . ."

Come back with us now to those thrilling days of yesteryear . . . to be more specific, to Friday, November 15, 1935 in Vancouver.

A new movie opens that day at the Orpheum, a musical called Shipmates Forever. A 12-year-old boy and his dad have just come out of the theatre and are walking home past Woolworth's. In the window is a musical hit-parade display, including a shiny new 78-rpm record of a song from that movie — Dick Powell singing Don't Give Up The Ship. The boy turns to his dad and pleads for 35 cents to buy that record.

And that is how the record-collecting career of John Francis Cullen began. He still has that Dick Powell record nearly 60 years later.

Hooked on radio, Jack remembers being in bed with the mumps at 13, listening breathlessly on his earphones to the American networks. Radio drama, comedy, big bands, it was all manna to this kid.

But it wasn't until 1939, when he was 17, that young Jack first began thinking he himself might like being part of this exciting world. "I used to listen to CKMO, there was a show on called DX Prowl. DX was radio jargon for 'distance.' The DJ said he had a pet mouse named Jerry — and if the record skipped, he'd say, 'Jerry! Get off the turntable!'

"But my real inspiration was in 1940, with Phil Baldwin on MO. He had a show called Musical Grab Bag. 'At 1410 from 4 to 5, I have a yen to jam and jive.' He was the guy I really listened to." (CKMO was at 1410 then.)

The Second World War delayed Jack's entry into radio. He went into HMCS Discovery in August 1941, after three months was shipped off to Ste. Hyacinthe, Quebec. As a boy, he'd been interested in the technical end of radio, thanks largely to friendly advice from a ham operator named Elwood Siebold. Because of that skill, Jack became a 'sparker,' a navy radio operator. Two years' posting in Sydney, Nova Scotia was followed by sea duty. Later, Jack was at VOUS Armed Forces radio in Newfoundland, *and started collecting transcriptions.* (Transcriptions are records made just for play on radio, often for one-time use. They contained musical shows, comedy programs and dramas. You were supposed to throw them away after use. Jack didn't.)

During his service, Jack had been in Ireland a couple of times, was able to buy American records there. He'd keep shipping all this stuff home to his younger brother, Lorne. "In fact, instead of taking my rum allowance I used the money — 10 cents a day — to buy more records.

"And I got all the radio equipment off my ship, the Columbia, too. Back on civvy street I built a shack at the back of our house for the record collection. I had about 5,000 by now. And I started my own little illegal radio station with the gear off the Columbia. I picked

Jack Cullen brought to CKNW a little program called the Owl Prowl.

780 on the dial, that was KIEV in Glendale, Calif., and I'd go on the air with Bob Hughes as my one listener. The range was a few blocks. 'Hello, Bob, can you hear me?'"

Jack needed a high place to put his antenna, and the only suitable place nearby was the top of a church steeple, and so, late one night . . . "Well, I really didn't think God would mind."

He started taking courses at the Sprott-Shaw School of Commerce and Radio. "One of the owners was Kay Willis. She owned CKMO Radio, too. *And it was in the same building.* They'd use trainees to do the on-air stuff for free. I decided to get familiar with the engineers; they hung out at the York Beer Parlor. I began in engineering at CKMO in the late spring of 1946. The DJs were *always* asking me for information on the records. 'What picture did this song come from?' 'Who sang this back in . . .?' and so on. Gradually they came to realize the kid knew his music. Al Reusch was the program director back then. He said, 'Give the kid a chance on the air.'"

Jack got a midnight to dawn show called Pacific Patrol. "I used all my own records, *and* my own needles. You were supposed to change the needle every time you played a record. I'd rotate them a little, get three plays. They paid me $65 a month. Cheap bastards."

The tradition of people dropping in on Jack's shows began about this time: cops, ambulance drivers, ladies of the night, old buddies like Bobby Hughes, lonesome girls from the dance hall below . . . One morning the station's janitor found a box of beer on the fire escape outside the window and told the manager. The beer was Jack's. He was fired.

"Now I'm looking for a job. I called Bill Rea at CKNW. 'Jack, you're not right for us, but we have a station in Port Alberni, CJAV. We'll send you there.' Bill Rea's sister, Marg Chapman, was running it. There was a pulp mill at the back door. It was a muddy town back then. I stayed at Mother White's Boarding House. Marg told me I'd never be an announcer; she was right, too. I'd read news, and say things like 'Andrei Gromyko accused the UN of seduction . . .' or I'd refer to 'shitty council.' I became strictly a deejay.

"I had love sickness, so I quit and came back to the mainland. I'd met a beautiful girl at CKMO, Joy Scott, the receptionist. I married her in 1948."

Jack's life changed again when a new manager, Bob Bowman, came to CKMO. "I went to Bowman with a proposition he couldn't refuse: 'I'll do a show for you,' I said, 'for no salary. I'll sell my own commercials.' The station had *one* commercial after 10. One. It was for the Bamboo Terrace. They said, 'Well, we're not losing anything on this, it's free time. Sure, kid, go ahead.'

"I took over DX Prowl. I'd charge $1.50 or $2 for a spot. Frank Iaci and I came up with the name Owl Prowl. The show started October 15, 1947 on CKMO. It ran from 10 p.m. to 1 a.m. It was much more hit-parade oriented than today. 'For music with a smile, Leave us on your dial.'

"I was a movie buff, and I subscribed to all the music and entertainment papers: Billboard, Variety, Metronome, Downbeat . . . and I *used* all this stuff. I sold my own spots: I'd hustle by day, broadcast by night. The show clicked so quick. In six months I was laughing. Jack Scott plugged it in his column in the Sun, that was a big break. I was the hot new kid. I started going out to community centres, deejay hops . . . And I was *brash.*

"Owl Prowl was on CKMO for two years. I was making about $1,000 a month. In 1948 that was *good.* I had advertisers like Sid Harrison, Arthur Murray Dance Studios,

Dave Armstrong, 1944

CKRM in Regina; Bill Fox, the cereal-time announcer and Province newscaster and, at one time, with KBRO, Bremerton; Jack Jensen, original of the Rhythm Pals, who started as a solo artist with guitar and song; Evan Kemp, another strum and song man who began at the age of 12 and who is on the daily 'Ranger's Cabin' radio presentation . . . And, the loyal little lady, Rosalie Slater, of the accounting section who in those days was Rosalie Ontko." ▪

In July of 1951 a CKNW monthly magazine called Top Dog began. It was aimed at ad agencies and the food and pharmaceutical trade, to remind them regularly of CKNW and its popularity. Account executive Rolly Ford was first editor/photographer.

The covers illustrated Bill Rea's belief that three subjects were sure-fire: kids, pets and pretty young women. The women were frequently lightly clad. A few appeared to be not clad at all.

Top Dog showed NW's on-air people at work, took readers behind the scenes of the station, reminded them constantly of its high ratings, covered Orphans' Fund activities, introduced new staff, showed NW store displays — it crammed a lot into its miniature pages.

As time went by, the circulation widened, and when Mel Cooper took it over as part of his promotional duties, he arranged to have a smaller version delivered regularly free to 150,000 households in Greater Vancouver!

The October 1956 issue is typical. Lead story is the re-election

The little Top Dog magazine crammed a lot into its pages.

Gervais Jewellers, Ridley Ice, Bamboo Terrace, the Fairmont, Advance Taxi, the Barn on Granville, the Cave when Ken Stauffer and Bob Mitten ran it, Isy's . . .

"Then one night Bill Rea climbed up the fire escape outside the CKMO studio, came in through the window, and asked me to come work for him at CKNW. He said, 'I don't like what you're doing, but all my staff are listening to you.' I said, 'You've only got 250 watts.' 'Not to worry,' he says, 'we're going to 1000.' 'Well, call me then,' I said. Oh, I was *brash*.

"Rea *did* call me when they went to 1000 watts. I go to see him. *He* thinks I'm going to work out of New Westminster. 'No bloody way,' I say. 'Besides, my Austin can't go that far.' Rea says, 'I just purchased the Alexandra Ballroom. I'm going to rename it Danceland. You can do your show from there.'

"Okay. So now we have to come up with a gimmick for my first show. And I have a contract problem: my *last* day at CKMO, August 15, 1949, is the same day as my *first* day at CKNW. Here's what we did: I did my last show on CKMO live while my first CKNW show, a *recorded* version, ran on NW at the same time! So I fulfilled both contracts."

"John Francis Cullen, boy disc jockey" was, at last, at CKNW. He began as MC on the 1320 Club, a 3:10 daily show. And, more importantly, he brought along a little show called the Owl Prowl.

The Cow Left A Memento

Typical of CKNW's top-quality engineers was Calgary-born Doug Court. In September, 1952 when Doug (direct from 14 years in the navy) joined the technical staff, no fewer than three of his colleagues — Vern Wileman, Hal McInnes and Bob Macdonald — had been in the air force. Out at the transmitter, Clare Purvis was another ex-navy man.

Appropriately, the transmitter was in a military-style Quonset hut.

"We were out in dairy farm country on Lulu Island," Doug says, "and cows would wander around and lick the salt off our cars. One of them came into the building on a very hot day when Vern Wileman was outside on a brief 'sun break,' and the two of them stood there and stared at each other for a while. Getting the cow out without having her kick something and put us off the air was a ticklish problem, but Vern finessed it." The cow, as cows will, left a steaming memento of its visit.

Back then NW's all-night record man did his show at the transmitter, where there was a good collection of 78s. The all-night man also kept an eye on the transmitter — regulations required it to be manned. When that rule was dropped in 1953 Doug moved back to the main studio.

After Mac Mackenzie left, Doug says, NW needed another engineer. "Jack Gordon went to Ken Wheeler's class at Vancouver Community college, wandered through, and picked out a kid named Bob Vogt. He was good.

"On November 8, 1966, driving home after work Bob Vogt rolled his car and was killed. Jack found Bob's replacement the same way — got a young fella out of Ken Wheeler's class. His name was Dave Glasstetter, and he was smart as a whip."

Doug Court was eventually to become senior engineer. In 1978 he stepped aside to focus on administration. Jack Gordon retired and Dave Glasstetter became chief engineer. Doug in turn retired in 1981, but continues to work as a consultant on NW's NHL and CFL coverage. ■

of the W.A.C. Bennett government. The station boasted it had been the first, by 45 minutes, to predict a Social Credit landslide; first by five minutes to air the first election return; and the first by 15 minutes to have Premier Bennett's victory speech on the air. NW president Frank Griffiths came down to lend a hand, spent the evening keeping staffers well supplied with "steaming cups of coffee."

We're shown a new toothpaste called Gleem (it gets TOP DOG'S Bark of Approval!); meet NW's new Advertising Manager, Tom Huntley (who later became a successful B.C. artist); see Jim Cox interviewing the New Westminster Royals' new manager, Hal Laycoe; learn Woodward's plans a new-six-level parking garage next to its Hastings Street store; celebrate the opening of the PGE line from Vancouver to Squamish - and so on.

The little magazine would last for several years. ■

Bob Hutton and
family in Hawaii.

"He's Top Dog Now And All Grown Up"

THERE WAS MORE TO THE '50S THAN THE FIRST APPEARANCE OF Elvis Presley. The Korean War started, and Canada sent troops there. The RCMP boat St. Roch went through the Panama Canal, becoming the first ship to circumnavigate North America, and Alcan began to build its giant smelter at Kitimat.

In the U.S. they were enduring the Senator Joe McCarthy years, and the hydrogen bomb was tested. Alaska and Hawaii became states.

Queen Elizabeth II was crowned, and W.A.C. Bennett became B.C.'s premier. Canada's first TV station signed on in Montreal, an ominous event viewed with more than average attention at CKNW. Marshall McLuhan predicted the world would become a global village. The Canadian Labour Congress was born, and so was the Canada Council. In the Soviet Union Stalin died and the beefy Nikita Khrushchev succeeded him. The space age began with the Soviet launch of Sputnik I, and a technological advance was reached in B.C. with the destruction of hazardous Ripple Rock. NW was on the scene.

At home, John Diefenbaker became prime minister and appointed Ellen Fairclough to the cabinet, the first woman so honored. Lester Pearson won the Nobel Peace Prize.

Tragedy struck in B.C. with the collapse, while under construction, of the Second Narrows Bridge. Jack Webster rushed to the scene and described the tragic events for CKNW. And NW was there, too, when B.C.'s Harry Jerome set a world record for the 100-metre dash.

The '50s began for CKNW with a move to a larger home at 227 Columbia. "Reported by experts to be the most modern and best-equipped radio broadcasting studio building in western Canada . . . the new building has four studios, including one with seating accommodation for 50 persons . . ."

Jim Cox's newsroom was bigger, with reporters like Stan Moncrieff, Mike Giraud, Henry Shannon, Mauri Hesketh, Les White, Maury Gwynne and Bob Giles.

A station pioneer, Dave Armstrong, left for Victoria to open CKDA. Bill Rea pulled Bill Hughes in from the Fraser Valley to handle national sales. It was a job that made the shy Hughes so nervous, he admitted to a co-worker, that sometimes he threw up before important meetings.

The Rhythm Pals were a big hit on NW, but dissatisfaction over money developed and they hit the trail.

Bill Rea's Roundup ran every afternoon, and was described as a "request program

When Bob Hutton moved over to CKNW in 1955, in one of the most astonishing convulsions in the history of Vancouver radio, so did all of his listeners. Virtually overnight NW went from third in the morning to first. Hal Davis: "We got monthly ratings from Elliott-Hayes. They showed that, in one month, Bob Hutton was on top again — but this time on CKNW."

When Bob Hutton told CKWX's Tiny Elphicke he was leaving to go to NW, Elphicke snorted, "You're not going to a radio station, you're going to a circus." To publicize Hutton's arrival CKNW got a picture of him atop an elephant. It was purely coincidental, but Hutton cracked up. "Elphicke told me I was joining a circus. He was right!" ■

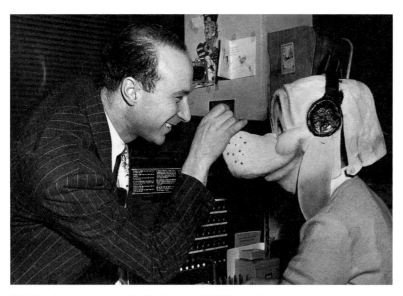

Hal Davis stops to chat with Top Dog at CKNW switchboard.

on a generous scale, featuring the rollicking songs of the rolling plains." Jack Cullen's Owl Prowl was on from 10:05 to midnight — "Clowning Cullen carries on with music and musing and much ado." On Saturday nights NW carried PCL hockey, called by Jim Cox. A September 1951 Bill Rea memo approvingly cited fights in hockey games as audience pleasers.

Every one of NW's major newscasts was sponsored. When a new sponsor showed up, asking for a newscast, Rea simply created a new one, at 12:30. Then he created an 11:30, a 10:30 and so on. Soon NW had news every half-hour all day long. And the station's reputation as *the* place to tell when things happened was indicated in July, 1955 when a bridge at Mission collapsed. The driver of the last car over the bridge, who had escaped by mere seconds, went directly to the phone to contact CKNW!

Morning man in the early '50s was a tall, jovial Saskatchewan fellow named Joe Chesney. 1951 began with huge-voiced Wally Garrett coming to CKNW after years with CKWX and CKMO. Teenaged Dick Abbott also started with the station in '51, is still with the company more than 40 years later.

A monthly magazine called Top Dog started July, 1951. Started as a trade publication, sent by NW to food, pharmaceutical and allied companies, Top Dog was eventually delivered to every home in the Lower Mainland.

In August of '52 a major figure in NW history joined the station — but Warren Barker's beginnings were somewhat humble: he filled in for Bill Rea on Ranger's Cabin, and was known as Ranger Warren.

Under Al Klenman CKNW opened a sales office in Vancouver to be closer to the money. And in 1953 Fiesta! started. This quiz show developed into a mail-pulling phenomenon of literally staggering proportions. Mail bags were stacked teeteringly high from floor to ceiling, spilling out into the staff lunchroom, hallways and adjacent offices. (In August, 1953, some 3.5 *million* outdated entries were put to the torch.)

On May 22, 1953 Bill Rea memoed: "You will be interested to know that our Vancouver audience has increased 21 per cent in the last year and our audience in the Vancouver Area (100-mile radius) is up 101 per cent."

Top Dog's April, 1953 issue said of NW newsman Bob Giles, "Giles is so hot at digging up hidden news facts that the Vancouver daily papers now monitor all NW newscasts." More than 40 years later, they still do. As busy as he was, news director Jim Cox added the title of sports director in 1953 . . . that same year lacrosse broadcasts ended at NW and Warren Barker transferred to the newsroom.

Some NW staffers, like night announcers and newsmen, began working a five-day week in late 1953 instead of the six to seven days they were used to. In January 1954 the rest of the staff also got to enjoy the privilege.

Into this rosy picture dropped a disaster: in May 1954 a fire in the Swanrite building caused havoc at NW; water damage was so extensive the entire staff packed up and moved into temporary quarters in Bill Rea's Vancouver dance halls.

Wilf Ray had been at CJOR, came to NW to do the all-night show on location at the PNE. "The Nash people," says Jim Cox, "had just come out with a car in which the front seats could be folded back down to make a bed. Wilf went to Bill Rea and said he had this idea: he would sleep in the Nash during the day at the PNE, then just walk over and do his show from whatever building they were using at night. He'd save transportation time, and so on. Bill says, 'That's a great idea, Wilf. Do it!' And Wilf says, 'Okay. Uhh, one thing . . . I'll need a Nash.'"

He got one! ∎

Patt McDonald, an American brought in by Bill Rea to manage CKNW, was fired and left for CKMO. Frank Walden, on the CKNW board from 1949 to 1955, remembers MacDonald. "He was a person of enormous inactivity. I never caught him doing anything . . . except file his nails." McDonald took Jack Cullen and a dozen others with him. "He was a very charming guy," Bill Hughes said. "He lured them away." McDonald was replaced in 1954 as general manager by NW veteran Hughes — whose suitability for the job was first questioned by Bill Rea on curious grounds: Hughes was too skinny!

An engineering crackerjack named Jack Gordon was brought in as a consultant in 1954, the same year Mel Cooper joined NW as promotion manager and Sir Michael Bruce was brought in as "public service director." Bill Rea's irrepressible spirit still dominated CKNW. "He wore a black shirt," Mel Cooper recalls, "and when he came into the station, you could hear the whisper, 'Black Bart's coming, Black Bart's coming,' and he'd be stomping up the stairs and giving orders as he came."

In November, 1954 a balding, boyish Jim Pattison signed a hockey contract with CKNW on behalf of Bowell Maclean Motors, and NW started carrying Friday night Canucks games. Earlier in the year, the station had won Mountie baseball broadcasting rights away from CKMO.

The fire, months of frustrating failure to acquire a television licence, then a financially disastrous foray into selling television sets, combined to work a terrible effect on Bill Rea. In May, 1954 he collapsed from exhaustion, and was hurried to hospital. A few weeks later, he relinquished day-to-day control of the station and in 1956, moved with his wife and daughters to California. Those who knew Rea said his failure to win a TV licence after years of trying had frustrated and disgusted him.

1955 was a major turning point for CKNW: there was a power increase to 5,000 watts, and Bob Hutton, the Lower Mainland's dominant morning man on CKWX, was hired away by NW. Hutton brought his audience along. "Bob Hutton," said Mel Cooper, "made CKNW Number One." That was good news for Cooper, just named national sales manager.

NW began using the slogan: By Every Survey B.C.'s Most Listened-To Station. CKNW was picking up thousands of new listeners and dozens of new accounts. Clothier Murray Goldman credited NW with doubling his business in one year, and a company called Richmond Oil actually requested suspension of its commercials: they were getting more business than they could handle! Comptroller Erm Fiorillo returned to CKNW in 1955 after several years away; also joining were newsmen George Garrett and Mauri Hesketh, and deejay Jack Kyle — who would spend a lot of his time in a new mobile studio, a glass-enclosed snuggery he dubbed the "Crystal Palace." Car radios were becoming a factor. NW did the first "road show" with Kyle in the Crystal Palace. Every Sunday night he'd park by the main roads, and tell listeners Say Hello by Honking. There was a lot of honking.

Even wise-cracking Monty McFarlane was at NW "for about 20 minutes."

A CKNW series called Education in Democracy sent students to Victoria to see the legislature in action.

A young Australian named Tony Antonias would join NW's copy department in 1955, would run the department by year's end and, a couple of years later, would write a jingle so insistently and instantly memorable that thousands of Canadians remember it to this day.

In February of 1956 the announcement was made that CKNW had been sold to

Bill Rea did well with his band and the dance halls he leased and would later own. The Town Hall Ballroom, in the Driard Hotel, 1025 West Pender, thrived during the Second World War. It was a long room, with entrances on Hastings and on Pender, and near the docks for visiting sailors to discover. They'd find local girls and dance the night away to the sounds of Harry Varcoe and His Melody Men.

Rea's other ballroom was the Alexandra, which he renamed Danceland. Bill Hughes says in the early days of the station Rea's income from the halls helped tide CKNW over rough financial times. The ballrooms served NW in another way: when the 1954 fire drove the staff out of 227 Columbia, Rea was able to move much of the station's operations into Danceland.

Rea kept ownership of the Town Hall for years, even after he and his family moved away to California. ∎

Hal Davis producing election coverage with well-known Victoria announcer Ed Farey who was hired in 1954 to run the Orphans' Fund.

At CJCA in Edmonton the dynamic young salesman and program innovator Bill Rea was always coming up with new ideas. He created a children's show on which he read detective stories . . . a program on which you might have heard enthusiastic commercials for OWR PUFFS, a breakfast cereal developed by Bill and patented by him in 1936! The OWR stood for Oats, Wheat and Rice and combined the three in puffed form.

accountant Frank Griffiths and the Dr. Ballard family. The Rea era — brash, tumultuous, exciting but unstable — had come to an end. Now NW would move forward with more solid purpose, more focused objectives, more stability. The new executive expressed their faith in NW's staff and in manager Bill Hughes — and gave Hughes freedom to make decisions, a freedom he had not fully enjoyed under the mercurial Bill Rea.

The rapidly rising Mel Cooper became general sales manager in 1957, Jack Webster was welcomed, and a new man was hired as night news editor, a short, pugnacious, iron-voiced dynamo named Al Davidson.

1957 was memorable for another reason: Jack Cullen came back.

NW is so associated with the 980 frequency it can be surprising to learn it had been on the air at other locations on the dial (first 1230, then 1320) for 14 years. The switch to 980 happened in November of 1958.

1958, too, marked the beginning of the expansion of the Griffiths broadcast interests: they bought CJOB Radio in Winnipeg, the first in a series of acquisitions in broadcasting that continues to the present day. A feature of the CJOB and later purchases was that key CKNW staffers were invited to participate.

A new man took over the station's burgeoning news department in 1959. Jim Cox had stepped aside to head sports full time. From the ranks NW plucked

Warren Barker, who would, over a remarkable 33 years, transform his newsroom into the best in western Canada, maybe in the whole country. Barker would set standards of energy, aggressiveness, ingenuity, fact-finding and sheer damned excellence that transformed radio news in this country. CKNW's identification with news was strongly established: once, a man in a burning house phoned the item in to NW's newsroom while he was still inside the burning building.

Mixing the light with the serious NW brought its listeners Bob Hutton demonstrating the hula hoop in live broadcasts . . . yes, hula hoop on radio . . . while airing events like Jack Webster's electrifying coverage of the Robert Sommers influence-peddling case.

In 1959 Joe Chesney left NW to start CJJC in Langley.

Fiesta! became a victim of a regulatory decision that disallowed radio contests of that kind. Hallways jammed with bulging mail bags magically cleared. But, retaining the same title and the same host, Wally Garrett, the show changed to a phone-in program of household hints and the like — and increased its ratings! "With this program," said one staffer, "CKNW for the first time became the *undisputed* leader in the ratings."

Little wonder, then, a catchy NW jingle of the time could claim:

Not so long ago he was a little pup

But he's a Top Dog now and he's all grown up!

"I became a nostalgia broadcaster . . ."

Vancouver had never seen anyone quite like Jack Cullen. On his very first day on NW he went up with an RCAF officer in his helicopter (using a portable disc-cutter to record the interview) for later use on his show. That was unusual enough in 1949 to get him a story and photo in the paper.

He did his show from a taxi; did weather forecasts from the roof of his studio; once did the Owl Prowl in the nude, swimming at the YMCA. He rode the Grouse Mountain gondola doing the show, fortified by hot rums at every stop, making for a somewhat unintelligible final hour. He dressed as the Easter bunny, hopped all over town, giving prizes to whoever caught him.

He did gag commercials, one for a car lot called Clinker's, "conveniently located right on the border," where customers were assured of models "hot" from the States. The RCMP actually called him in, and he had to explain it was a gag.

One young couple won Jack as a baby sitter. He did his show from their home, told what it was like caring for the kids, sang them a goodnight song. The parents heard the show and called Jack to ask why the kids were still up so late. He worked that into the program.

Jack and Joy Cullen did a Saturday morning show, Jack and Joy. They'd do chatter between records. Jack himself cut a record! With the late Chris Gage on piano, he sang There'll Be Some Changes Made. Today, the disc has been turned into a clock decorating one wall of his record-crammed studio.

Audiences loved it. Jack Wasserman wrote: "Jack Cullen's ratings are so high not even his bosses believe it. Even in radio, class will tell."

It's sometimes forgotten, but Jack quit NW five years after his first arrival. "Hockey was cutting into my revenues, and Patt MacDonald had left his job as manager of NW and gone

("The World's First MIXED PUFFED CEREAL — Dextrinized Puffs of Oats, Wheat and Rice!")

Bill's daughter Erin (born Catherine) still has a stack of labels from that old and long-forgotten cereal, along with one of the nifty and important-looking badges young listeners to the show could write in for . . . *if* they enclosed an OWR PUFFS label. Bill never forgot that the art was made possible by the commerce. ∎

Jack Cullen is welcomed back to CKNW in 1957.

The Town Hall Ballroom, like Danceland, was used after the 1954 Mothers' Day fire, too. Rea claimed CKNW's collection of 78s, deluged by water and smothered in smoke, was worth $1 million. He hoped the insurance company would see it that way, but they wanted confirmation of damage to the records. Music director Jimmy Morris was delegated to check them. The entire collection was trucked down to the Town Hall Ballroom, and Jimmy checked every disc. He'd wipe them clean, then play them. The insurance man dropped in now and again to see how things were going. Unfortunately for Rea's insurance hopes very few records sustained any damage. ∎

over to CKMO. He invited me there. Six months after I started they changed the call letters to CFUN."

Hal Davis asked Jack to come back. Cullen was dissatisfied with CFUN, anyway. "We cut the deal," says Hal, "in Jack's car in the White Spot parking lot at 6th and Kingsway." It was the spring of 1957. The station had new owners now, and Bill Hughes was the manager. Hughes had told Davis he was reluctant to bring Cullen back. "He spells trouble." "Yes," Hal said, "but he also spells ratings."

Jack's Danceland location was close to Isy's, the Cave, the Marco Polo, the Commodore. Jack started grabbing more interviews with visiting performers . . . and the flow of friends intensified as the show's fame grew. Jack Wasserman was a regular visitor, "Cyril Brandolini, Kenny Welsh, Jim Madden, singer Donna Leah, Al Davidson, Rene Castellani, Frank Iaci . . ." Not a few of Jack's droppers-in were accomplished drinkers. "Cullen's studio," Province columnist Bruce McLean wrote, "looked like the waiting room at a detox centre." For Jack, who had split with Joy in 1953, the '50s were a blur of "parties, broads and interviews." In 1958 he remarried, and he and Alma have been happily together more than 35 years. He got out of the act-booking business — one of his sidelines — about that time, too. "My last booking was Johnny Mathis at Exhibition Gardens." He made enough from that gig to take Alma on a honeymoon.

Jack told a Vancouver Sun interviewer in August, 1957 that kids had taken over radio, "and the result is murder, musically." Jack had opened his own record store by now, told the interviewer Elvis Presley's rock 'n' roll was the greatest single stimulant to the trade. "Cullen's already sold 700 of Presley's latest album at a cost of $4 each, even though the album has been released only three weeks. 'Junk sells,' Cullen finds, sadly."

"TV didn't bother me as much as the other late-night hosts in the beginning. I had such a good head start. But in '55 I started feeling it. The music was changing, too: Bill Haley didn't bother me; Elvis did: the lyrics were unintelligible. I never got to like Elvis until he mellowed out. A young whippersnapper named Red Robinson over at OR was playing rock, and really making it. I played a *very* little bit of rock, and bad mouthed the rest. That didn't endear me to the young audience, but it did to the older. And that was good: I became a *nostalgia* broadcaster."

"I took that as a challenge . . ."

On December 21, 1991 Dick Abbott marked 40 years with CKNW. "There was an eight-month hiatus, otherwise NW has been my life." The number of commercials, jingles, features, special programs, etc., etc., that you've heard packaged by Dick Abbott is beyond numbering. He's one of the best, most sought-after production engineers in North America. Ted Smith's evaluation of Dick appears to be universal among the staff: " . . . one of the finest, most genuine and dedicated people I know."

Dick's known for his speed and concentration. A representative of hockey's Seattle Totems came to Vancouver one day, told Dick the club needed a promotional campaign . . . and needed it *that very day*. Dick was collaborating with the talented David Hoole at the time, and the two of them put their heads together. Before the end of the day, they had packaged the entire campaign — and called it Blood, Sweat and Cheers. It was a smash.

Dick was born in Kamloops in 1935, moved to the coast with his family when he was six. He got into music in junior high, played alto sax, clarinet and flute

On December 21, 1991 Dick Abbott marked 40 years with CKNW.

("Stan Kenton was my idol.") And he was a jock, too, into all sorts of sports. At 16, he got a job in the CKNW record library.

Eventually, Dick began packaging commercials . . . then making transcriptions . . . ended up doing all the production at NW. "I learned to edit doing Gerber Baby Food commercials." Some of the programs he packaged (such as an Easter special with music and readings) are still being played on NW years after they were created. And he recalls, with a shudder, his first remote: it was at the Bowell Funeral Home, where organist Ed Reimer would play 15 minutes of sweet, solemn music. "There were bodies there in open coffins!" Dick taped the show, and left. Quickly.

Dick credits chief engineer Jack Gordon with being a tremendous influence. "He was so patient. And if I wanted to do something, and didn't have equipment to do it, he'd build it! He started calling me his 'production manager,' and I got a memo where he used that phrase. I took the memo into Hal Davis' office, and said, 'Does this mean I'm your production manager?' Hal grins, and says, 'I guess so.' So I took that title."

Dick has worked with hundreds of different people at CKNW over the years — but has a special regard for Hal Davis. "In my opinion, Hal has never been given credit for being one of the most innovative program directors in radio history. He was open to experimentation. His hirings, and his patience with talented, extroverted people has been taken for granted. I, for one, will always be grateful for his help." And he has a special left-handed regard for Hugh Wallace. "Hugh was assistant manager at the time. I hadn't been at the station long. We're coming back from an Orphans' Fund do; Hughie's driving, Arnie Nelson's in the front passenger seat, I'm in the back. Hughie says to Arnie, '*You'll* make it on talent.' Then he jerks his thumb over his shoulder at me. '*This* guy'll make it on personality.'

"Well, I took that as a challenge. After 40 years, I thank Hughie Wallace for that."

When Bill Hughes was promoted to manager of CKNW in 1954 he was, at 29, the youngest general manager of a major radio station in Canada. Two years later Frank Griffiths and Walter Owen guaranteed a loan to Hughes of $36,000, allowing him to buy a share of the station.

Erm Fiorillo: "In conversation one day with Bill Hughes and me, Griffiths turned to Hughes and said, 'Bill, one day I'm going to make you a millionaire.' The new owners needed competent management, and they knew they had it in Bill Hughes. His share participation in the station eventually did make him a millionaire. There's no doubt Bill was a taskmaster, but he was an executive: articulate, smart, knowledgable."

Bill Hughes stayed on as general manager until 1970, when he moved downtown and became the President of Western Broadcasting. ■

Engineer Jack Gordon was called in by CKNW after its 1954 fire. They needed technical advice, and they needed it fast. "I agreed to design a *better-equipped* station. The reason was the fantastic array of talent Rea had gathered. But I wonder now how many realized how much I was on their side.

"Back in the late 1930s, before I arrived in B.C., I had put in regular stints as announcer, newscaster and disc jockey, and as producer and talent-coach of live programs. So, while I wasn't in the special class of the 'naturals' in each area, I shared their exasperation with the limitations placed upon all of us by typical factory-designed equipment. Bill Rea offered me the opportunity to design facilities that could fully release such talent. There was inevitable conflict between the traditional 'Just hook it up somehow,' and the new imperative of doing it *right*. It created stress, but that was more than offset by my pleasure in the excitement of talented people when they could be shown what truly custom-designed new facili-

Dick still brings an infectious enthusiasm to the job, after 40 years of it, still tries new ideas, new equipment, new effects. The most fascinating part of the business, he says, is the "what if?" factor. "What if we speeded up the music here?" "What if we brought in this electronic sound effect?" "What if we . . . etc., etc."

At a 1992 barbecue party at Frank Griffiths' home, more than a hundred CKNW employees were gathered. Dick leaned over the boss' chair to say hello to him, and Griffiths, now in his late 70s, and frail, clasped Dick's hand and looked up, smiling. "I hope you have good memories of this place."

Oh, yes.

"I wormed my way back into his heart . . ."

"When you were a staff announcer at CKNW," says pioneer Joe Chesney, "you could do anything. I did news, music, and when Ferdy Baglo left I picked up the All-Time All-Canadian Hit Parade, playing standard pop tunes of the day. Then I was transmitter operator, did the midnight to 6 a.m. show from the transmitter site. The extent of my technical knowledge? Chief engineer Bill Collins told me one day, 'Chesney, you know just enough to be dangerous.'

Joe Chesney could do anything.

"I was fired once by Bill Rea. Rotary had a project where they put a barrel in the Fraser River, and ran a sweepstakes based on the best guess at the time it would go under the Pattullo Bridge. Bill was on the bridge, set to describe the barrel going under. I was at the station doing the Bing Crosby Show, and forgot to throw it to Bill. And of course he couldn't reach me out there on the bridge. He was *furious,* and fired me. Two weeks later he rehired me. I became the transmitter operator. But I wormed my way back into his heart again, and a few months later he pulled me back in to the station."

There were musical rules to follow. Joe recalls a Rea dictum that every third record was to be a hit. On the console were 50 hits of the day. Rea used to say, "Don't play anything you can't sing or hum."

Joe began doing CKNW's morning show in September, 1951, did it until Bob Hutton came over from CKWX. Joe moved into a variety of other programs, then got into sales in '57. "Then one day I told manager Bill Hughes I had an application in for a radio station in Langley, and he said my usefulness to CKNW had ended. I left NW, went to CJOR. In 1962 my application was approved and I started CJJC."

"I was meeting myself coming home . . ."

Wally Garrett is the perfect example of the announcer whose voice belies his appearance. That huge, resonant sound issued from a small, rather slender frame of 5'6." Born in Kamsack, Saskatchewan, in 1924 Wallace Alfred Garrett grew up mostly in Vernon. He had no special training to develop that voice. It was just there.

He started in radio at Kelowna's CKOV in 1943. His natural skills soon got him a job at CKWX, where he occasionally did the news in a tuxedo. That was on the nights he had earlier hosted a live Public Opinion show from the stage of the Orpheum. "Tiny Elphicke liked showing advertisers through when I was doing the news in a tuxedo. They were really impressed."

Wally Garrett at the mike with Bill Fox during the Orphans' Fund request show, 1957.

In 1947, Wally went to CKMO as program director — a step up, but to an unstable environment. "You'd get your pay cheque and dash over to the bank fast before the money ran out. I was there three years. Then I bumped into Bill Rea. We chatted, but, you know, it was a country-and-western station way out in New Westminster. Well, one day I came to a parting of the ways with CKMO. It was late in the morning. The grapevine must have been working fast — Bill Rea phoned me that same afternoon.

"I started at CKNW January 1, 1951. For the first year I took the interurban to work. I started doing the Vancouver Sun News, had to go down to the Sun building to do it, then rush back on the interurban for the 10 p.m. at CKNW. It was no sweat. Today they talk about pressure. You just did it. I did the morning show for a while."

Wally's excellence at a variety of tasks meant he was given a lot of work. (Warren Barker calls Garrett the most well-rounded announcer NW ever had: "He could do it all: soft sell, hard sell, news . . . and a great voice.") The predictable result was that his workload got heavier and heavier. Finally, it got too heavy.

"The day before the fire in '54 I was up to my *nose* in work. I was meeting myself coming home. I got a memo from Bill Rea adding more! Well, that finished it. I wrote a two-page letter of resignation. I was furious."

At home the next day, still fuming, Wally got a phone call. It was Bill Rea. "Oh, Wally, about this memo . . ." "It's all in there, Bill," Wally said, and slammed the phone down. Later the same day the phone rang again. Again it was Bill Rea. "Oh, say, Wally, the station is burning down . . ." Wally slammed the phone down again. "I thought he was drunk."

Then he turned the radio on, and heard Sid Lancaster excitedly describing the fire. "My God," Wally said, "it *is* burning!" So he and his wife Marge went down and watched it burn.

The fire eventually cooled off, and so did Wally. "A few days later I went back to NW for a lot more money and less work."

In March, 1971 after 20 years, Wally and CKNW came to a parting of the ways.

ties would allow them to do."

Jack Gordon's ability to see beyond the bare technical requirements shows up in every important engineering decision he made. When CKNW's staff moved back into 227 Columbia, four months after the fire, they found not only a repaired building, but a vastly improved technical operation. The crowning glory was a state-of-the-art 5000-watt RCA transmitter. Jack Gordon had insisted NW get the best. On November 5, the station jumped from 1000 watts to 5000 — and was delighted to hear from listeners that the signal was stronger, crisper, and more far-reaching. Later, the present 50-kilowatt plant was built to even higher standards.

Few thought to laud the engineers. Good engineering is invisible. ∎

How did Sir Michael Bruce ever get hired at CKNW?

"Over my dead body," says Bill Hughes, manager when Bill Rea returned from a trip to England in 1954 accompanied by this curiously inappropriate addition to the staff. Sir Michael was the brother of Nigel Bruce, famous as the amiably bumbling Dr. Watson in the Sherlock Holmes movie series that starred Basil Rathbone. Sir Michael, eleventh baronet of Stenhouse and Airth, and a clone of his famous brother, was hired as "public service director," likely an attempt by Bill Rea to bring some "tone" to the station.

It didn't work out. "Here we were," says a baffled colleague, "selling fish and playing geetars, and there was Sir Michael Bruce."

He seems to have come and gone rather rapidly, leaving behind dim memories of a frequently sozzled, constantly sleepy gentleman. Everyone who recalls him seems to have seen him sleeping somewhere — in chairs, on couches, on a park bench. Fin Anthony saw him on the park bench, got him a taxi home.

"I want you to meet a friend of mine . . ."

There is affection in the voices of CKNW staffers when they speak of comptroller Erm Fiorillo. It wasn't Erm's competence with a balance sheet that inspired the warmth people feel toward him. It was his thoughtful, compassionate and common-sensical attitude toward his co-workers.

Erm, born in Fernie in 1916, began his career in corporate finance early: as a teenager, he did the books at his family's grocery store in Fernie. He trained at UBC as a teacher, "but it was difficult to get a job teaching during World War II if you were of Italian descent."

He finally did get a job teaching (English, phys ed and social studies) in Coquitlam, but left it in 1942 to join the air force. The RCAF gave him training as a navigator, he was good at it, and was assigned to teach it.

During his air force service, Erm married Ellen Stradiotti. More than 50 years (and six children and 12 grandchildren) later, they're still together. Ellen's brother, Henry, whom Erm had met out at UBC, introduced the two.

Erm became business manager of the Stradiotti brothers' fishing and towing business. At the time the business' assets included one boat, and "an old shack on some rental property on the North Arm of the Fraser.

"I had to learn how to 'hang' nets at the Stradiotti company," Erm continues, "to buy and sell logs, and run a marine gas station." And he made a change that is still evident today: "I got the company to change the color of their tugs. At the time, every tug in B.C. was the same color. Today? Every company has a different color."

The Stradiotti firm thrived, acquiring waterfront property, building six more tugs, getting more business . . . and forcing Erm to learn accounting. It happens that another fellow Erm had met out at UBC was a commerce student, Frank Walden, who was to become a chartered accountant and auditor. "Frank came down and worked up a set of books for us. When I left the Stradiotti company after five years, I called Frank to tell him I was leaving and to ask his advice about finding a new job. I had a hungry wife, and four hungrier kids. Frank was the auditor at CKNW and they were in real need of a credit manager to clean up their bad accounts. 'What do you think of meeting with CKNW's owner, Bill Rea?' Before too long, the two of us were sitting in Bill

Erm Fiorillo, company comptroller.

Rea's office. One of NW's sponsors, Dr. Ballard, was sitting outside with his ad man but Bill took the time to interview me. Then he said, 'On the basis of Frank Walden's recommendation, and my personal evaluation, you've got the job. Your salary will be $200 a month.' We stood and shook hands, and then Bill opened the door and introduced me to Dr. Ballard. 'I want you to meet a friend of mine, Erm Fiorillo.'

"And that's how I got to CKNW."

"That's What Christmas is all about . . ."

The CKNW Orphans' Fund grew with astonishing speed in the 1950s. In 1949 the Fund collected more than $17,000, a figure worth comment then. But by the mid-50s more than $150,000 was being raised every year for needy children, and in 1953 NW won the Gillen award for the Fund's good work. The Orphans' Fund Picnic had by now become a famous annual event. As Bill Rea's workload increased, he decided someone should be placed in charge of the Fund, someone who could give it the care and thoughtfulness this special job needed.

A perfect candidate was waiting in the wings. A Victoria-born broadcaster who came to NW in 1954 would become as identified with the station and the Orphans' Fund as anyone. Ed Farey had been a well-known Victoria announcer and program director at CKDA, and, in addition, had done excellent volunteer work there on such efforts as a Christmas Party fund. He was named Victoria's Good Citizen of the Year.

Bill Rea put Ed in charge of the Orphans' Fund. It was an excellent choice; Ed's energy and empathy were the ideal combination.

What did operating the Orphans' Fund entail? Ed's daughter, Deana Proxa, grins. "Never seeing your family. It did keep Dad really busy. But I remember one Christmas Eve he got a call at home from someone at NW. After he hung up he said to me, 'Want to go for a ride?' He put together a basket of donated toys and clothing, and we drove to a part of Vancouver I never even knew existed. I went with him to this shabby apartment and a woman answered the door. Well, it was like a Grade B movie. She'd obviously been beaten, she was holding a baby and there was another child crying in the background. The mother looked pretty rough. But she smiled. And in the car on the way back home Dad said, 'Now that's what Christmas is all about!'

Ed Farey's energy and empathy were an ideal combination.

"She got me off the farm and into radio . . ."

From April 1959, when he was promoted to news director, until he retired 32 years later Warren Barker set a standard of excellence in radio news unsurpassed in the country.

His beginnings were modest: he was born in 1928 on a farm near Okotoks, Alberta. School was at the opposite corner of the farm, and Warren's earliest memories include being bundled up with his sister and carried to school in a wagon driven by his father. On cold days, and there were a lot of them, his father would heat a big rock and tuck it under the blankets for the kids to snuggle up to.

The Barker family put a premium on education: Warren got a scholarship in Grade 9 for having achieved the fourth-highest academic marks in the province. His sister Betty was number one!

"I didn't apply myself much in high school. It was in the 'big town,' Okotoks. I remember there were four kids in my Grade 9 class, and all four of us entered a high-school radio quiz show called Dollars for Scholars on CFAC in Calgary. We were up against four sharpies from a big Calgary school. We lost narrowly. It was my fault, too."

His exposure to radio at CFAC had interested 14-year-old Warren. Later, when his dad sold the farm and moved the family to Edmonton, he submitted some commercial copy to CJCA. At 18, he was hired.

"Dalt Elton, the program director, told me I'd never get a job on the air. He was quite right, too. I *mumbled,* didn't enunciate clearly. So CJCA sent me to Bertha Biggs, a voice coach. She managed to get me off the farm and into radio."

Al Klenman describes him as "destitute, but prestigious." "Sir Michael was a big phony," one colleague sniffed, "but he did have a lovely English accent."

Sir Michael's task was to deliver a nightly commentary (8:10 p.m.) on world affairs, a quirky addition to CKNW's daily schedule.

Al Klenman says Sir Michael, whose office was in the Danceland Ballroom, was on CKNW's books as a salesman, and recalls he was instrumental in getting the Money's Mushrooms account for the station.

He was at NW less than a year. No one knows what became of him. ∎

In January, 1951 he moved to CKDA, Victoria. "They had me doing a request cowboy show at DA. I *hated* country-and-western music: Hank Snow, Eddy Arnold, Kitty Wells. Hated it! But there were other shows. I did the commercials on Victoria Cougar hockey broadcasts. Bill Stephenson was there, he did the play-by-play."

Warren shared an apartment with another DA broadcaster, Ray Nichol. Early in 1952 Nichol got a job in the CKNW newsroom, learned there was a vacancy in the copy department, and told Warren. Warren went to New Westminster for an interview with Bill Rea and copy chief Aubrey Price, and was hired. "Part of the reason," he grins, "is that Rea knew of my experience jocking country and western." He started August 4, 1952. He was 23.

"I soon became the host of the late afternoon abortion, Ranger's Cabin. I was 'Ranger Warren,' and you'd find me on top of 'Big Mountain.' I opened the show as Rea had done, with the 'engineer's whistle,' It was a bicycle pump, with a whistle attached.

"Around the middle of 1953 I gave up my glamorous role as Ranger Warren, and went into news full time."

A remarkable career, spanning more than 40 years, took a bold new turn.

"He tells me I'd be a natural . . ."

Maybe Gerry Davies got his singing voice from his Welsh genes. CKNW's all-night record man for 20 years, from October, 1952, Gerry was born in 1926 in Tonypandy, in the Rhondda Valley of Wales. His dad emigrated to Canada in 1927 and, two years later, brought the family over. One day in late December, 1943 Gerry walked into the kitchen and his mother said, "Look at the Sun."

Ivan Ackery, the famous promotion-minded theatre manager, was, the paper reported, launching a contest to find "Our Own Frank Sinatra." A movie called Higher and Higher, starring Sinatra, was coming up and Ackery wanted to drum up some attention. Gerry, 17, who at the time fronted a band of eight members as young as himself, went down to the Orpheum with four or five friends. "There were about 150 kids there, all wearing Sinatra-style bow-ties, and those jackets. You could sing either with Ronnie Matthews at the pipe organ, or Dal Richards' band. I opted for the band."

On the last night of the contest there were two finalists . . . and Gerry was one of them. He won.

"Well, the theatre was packed, 3,000 people and the lobby was jammed. They had radios in the lobby so people out there could hear the contest. Ivan came out on the stage and congratulated me and the movie started. I won $50. There was another prize, a week's engagement at the Cave, but I wasn't old enough to get in. I did get to sing once, though, as a guest artist with Dal's Orchestra at the Panorama Roof in the Hotel Vancouver.

"About 1949 I became a dance instructor, taught ballroom dancing — fox trot, waltz, tango. I used to see Jack Cullen at Danceland, broadcasting for CKNW. He tells me I'd be a natural in radio. 'Go knocking on doors.' There was no BCIT to get training, you just went and looked around. I went to see Bill Rea."

Gerry launches into an impression of Rea's deep, hearty and sonorous voice as he describes how Rea offered him a part-time shift, a 1 a.m. to 6 a.m. Sunday record show. Location: out at the

A very young Gerry Davies won $50 for doing Frank Sinatra.

CKNW transmitter on Lulu Island. "I'd get there at midnight, Cullen's show went to 1 a.m., then I came on." After moving to CFQC in Saskatoon, then to CJIB in Vernon and Port Alberni's CJAV Gerry was seasoned.

"Then Bill Rea called. Finally, there was an opening. I started doing NW's all-night show October 1st, 1952."

"But you're so skinny!"

Bill Hughes: "Along about 1952 Bill Rea was turning a lot of his attention to TV. KVOS had signed on, CBUT was about to . . . he wanted a station. So, he said, 'I need a successor to run CKNW.' He picked three prospects from sales, and three from programming. I wasn't one of them. He brought in an industrial psychologist, who said, 'I'd like a seventh guy, someone not in this group. So I was added. We all went out to UBC and took extensive tests over two days. I was exhausted, almost drove my car off the road once.

"Later the psychologist came back and talked to Rea.

"I was unhappy with NW at the time. I was dickering for a job in Ottawa. Rea says, 'I want to be frank with you. I want you to be manager of the station.' I said, "Whaaaat?!" I was in total shock. Then Rea said, 'But you're so *skinny*. Are you strong enough?' I went to my doctor. 'Nothing wrong with you,' he says, 'a good challenge wouldn't cure. Take the job.' I put on 30 pounds in six months. I just needed to have that uncertainty gone.

"I became station manager in 1954."

"I became the first beat reporter . . ."

Marke Raines first went on radio more than 50 years ago. He slammed a book shut as a sound effect during a radio drama on CFCN, the sound meant to represent the angry closing of a door. He was in Grade 6.

Marke's experience since has been somewhat more varied and exciting. He was, for example, the first full-time beat reporter in Vancouver radio. But his route to that job was rocky. "I had a lisp and was nasal. So I taped myself and really listened to my voice, and I cured it.

"In 1951 I came to CKMO in Vancouver. I was in the newsroom, and doing some copywriting. CKNW was looking for a copy writer, but I had no interest at all in moving. Then Norm Pringle, the production manager, says, 'Eunice Hoffman's there.' I said, 'Is that the girl you once said was just the one for me?' It was, and he was right. Eunice was working in the NW copy department. So I went to CKNW.

Marke Raines on the job.

Bill Rea thought I'd been just a writer, then he heard me on air at MO. 'Oh, you're an announcer, too.' He sweetened his offer; he liked all-round people. I started in January, 1952. I'd hop the interurban to get out there. So now I'm half in the news department, half in copy.

"Eunice and I were married June 14, 1952." (A coincidence: Eunice had once worked as a reporter for the Edmonton Bulletin, Bill Rea's last employer before he got into radio. Her own radio experience was varied: she'd been at CFRN, CJCJ and CFRB.)

Marke Raines: "I lucked out on my very first call as a beat man. I thought, 'Where should I start this?' Aha! City Hall and the mayor! So I went to Vancouver City Hall, walked up to the third floor, and told the receptionist, 'I'm from CKNW, and want to talk to the mayor.' Mayor Fred Hume comes out, sighing. 'I know why you're here. I'm selling the Vancouver Canucks.'"

Instead of registering what he felt — total astonishment — Marke nodded gravely and interviewed Hume about the sale. "My first time out, and I get a scoop!"

Then he went down to the cop shop, got three stories there. "All three were leads! I remember Les White running up and down the halls, 'Marke Raines got three lead stories! Marke Raines got ...'

"The noon news had three headlines, and I'd done 'em all." ■

For a long stretch in the 1950s, a lot of the look of CKNW's advertising was the creation of a young guy named Stan Buchanan. Stan walked in to NW in 1953. He was 22. "Phil Baldwin, the assistant manager, said 'We need someone like you, who can draw *and* write.' I had been at CKMO, writing advertising copy. I went into promotion at NW, doing paste-up, camera-ready art, writing and voicing on-air promotions."

Mel Cooper came in to run the promotion department in 1954, and that was timely because Stan and Mel had worked together before in a small promotions firm of their own. (Even so, things didn't always run smoothly: Stan

With Jim Cox's help, Marke got into the NW newsroom full-time.

"Everything I ever knew about news I got from Bill Rea and Jim Cox.

"After I was there about two years, Rea got an idea: a *beat* man, someone who went out in a news car and covered stories out there. That was a new idea in 1954. So they sent me out in my '48 Plymouth, and I became the first beat reporter in Vancouver radio."

Marke Raines was a CKNW news "beater" for 10 years. He and NW made another step into the future when he got a car phone, and used it to call in some stories.

"I got a phone call from a legend . . ."

Born George Neldon Cooper in St. John's in 1932, Mel Cooper arrived in Vancouver in 1945, graduated high school in 1950. He went to UBC with an ambition to be a writer, worked nights at McGavin Bakery to pay his tuition.

"One day I was standing in a lineup for something, and the guy behind me started chatting. His name was Gary Pederson. He dragged me over to Radsoc, the Radio Society. Well, I'm not a joiner, but I went. A young lady greeted us, her name was Grace Amanda Eaton; everyone called her Gae, from her initials. I ended up marrying her.

"CKWX decided to put on a course for students. I remember I didn't 'win.' In fact, Gae beat me. We all sent out our tapes, and I got a job offer from CJAV in Port Alberni. Gae worked there, too, in copy.

"I did *everything* at CJAV. They offered me a permanent job, but Gae and I wanted to go back to university. We did, and I started working weekends at CKMO. I was 19.

"Then CKWX offered me a job. They trained me for the newsroom, and two weeks later Gae and I were married.

"I became one of the first beat reporters in Vancouver, did a lot of police stories. My salary was $165 a month and a bus pass. We'd bought a little house on West 22nd, and Gae got a job as a long-distance operator with B.C. Tel. But I had to make more money. Stan Buchanan and I had started a little company when we were at UBC called BC Creative Promotions. The BC was for Buchanan Cooper. I went to CKWX and told them I could do the same promotional things for them. So we started doing projects for CKWX.

"I'm still working in the newsroom. One day, in the spring of 1954, I got a phone call in the newsroom from a legend. I thought it was a gag. I said to someone, 'Fellow on the phone says he's Bill Rea.' The fellow asks, 'Are you the guy who's doing the promotion and news?' 'Uh-huh, sure, sure,' I say, 'That's me. Who *is* this, really?' Well, it *was* Bill Rea. Now you have to realize the broadcast establishment saw Bill as brazen, even a little nuts. And I *hated* country music. 'What time do you go to work?' he asks. I tell him. He says, 'I'll drive you to work tomorrow.' I had a whispered conversation with Bill Stephenson. 'What should I do?' CKWX, you know, hated Rea — so innovative, so aggressive. Bill says, 'Talk to the man.'"

On May 3, 1954 Mel Cooper (left) started at CKNW to run the promotion department.

For a long stretch in the 1950s, a lot of CKNW's advertising was the creation of Stan Buchanan.

Cooper talked to the man, and was hired. "He'd asked me what I was making. $165 a month. 'You'll start at $325 for me.' I told Bill Stephenson. He was stunned. He says, 'I'm only getting TWO TWENTY-FIVE!'

On May 3, 1954 Mel Cooper started at CKNW.

"Bill and I smelled smoke . . ."

"We shared 227 Columbia with a glass company," engineer Doug Court says. "They had an electrical device with a heating element for shaping auto glass. That's what started the fire."

It was Sunday morning, May 9, 1954. Mother's Day.

Sid Lancaster was in the news room, Bill Duncan was on the air. "Bill and I smelled smoke at 8:30 a.m.," Lancaster told the Sun the next day. "Bill went out to investigate, and when he saw smoke coming from a third-storey window he called firemen."

Sid Lancaster did what anyone in his circumstances in a burning building would do: he went on the air and began to describe the fire. Bill Duncan called the fire department, then hurried around to alert anyone else in the building that it was ablaze. NW staffers, alerted by phone or the broadcast itself, began showing up. They took out discs, technical equipment and office records as fire engines wailed and smoke billowed out more heavily.

Bill Rea drove up, took over the evacuation process, seemed almost elated by the excitement. "Call UPI," he told a newsman at one point, "tell them it's a million-dollar fire." Later he collared the same man running by. "Call UPI back; tell them it's a *two-million dollar fire!*" Accountant Rosalie Slater came running out with a box of files. "That's the last of the accounts receivable," she said. "Great!" Rea said. She looked back up at the burning building. "What about the accounts payable?" "Let 'em burn," Rea laughed. NW saved all the accounts receivable files, listing the names of advertising clients who owed them. It saved the station's life.

recalls one day throwing a bottle of rubber cement at Mel's head when Mel came in roaring he had to have something that very day. "Mel had a lot of ideas, but he was hard to work for." The bottle missed Mel, and broke a window.)

Bill Rea was really enthusiastic about Stan's use of NW's Top Dog character in newspaper ads. "'Those ads are great!,' he'd say, "They're GREAT! Those lines are marvellous!'" Rea was really good at getting free promotion, Stan says. "He'd send material plugging CKNW to other media — for example, he'd send pictures of NW deejays in the Crystal Palace to weekly newspapers — and they'd use them! He had the material made up into the mats papers used at the time, and that made it easy for them to use. So they did.

"After a while, Bill Hughes came to the conclusion we didn't need art work any more. He liked my art work, and design, and the ads, but wanted to go in another direction. So, after about three-and-a-half years at NW, I left." ■

When CKNW's building burned in May, 1954 newspaper reporters and photographers had, naturally, shown up. Bill Rea — not one to let any opportunity for promotion go by — clapped a fireman's hat on his head and posed for pictures with the burning building in the background, telling reporters NW was the hottest station in town. The Sun put damage in the fire at $500,000, and Rea claimed $300,000 of that. He said he was considering building his own studio. "In any case we won't be back in the Swanrite Building," he said. "I want fire-proof studios."

"The very next day," says Mel Cooper, "we had big ads in The Province and the News-Herald showing our Top Dog character, a little singed and hobbling on crutches, but saying 'CKNW is STILL the hottest radio station in B.C.!' That was Fin Anthony's idea." ∎

Lancaster's dramatic broadcast ended at 9:06 when fire ate through the building's electrical circuits and put the station off the air. Then fire chief Claud Highsted ordered everyone out of the building.

A crowd of onlookers had been gathering. It would swell to 10,000.

The order to vacate the building had been timely: just as the firemen thought they had the blaze under control, cans of paint stored on the third floor began to explode from the heat. The fire burst into new life, broke through into the top two floors, jammed with stored furniture and electrical appliances. This stored material began to burn. Then, with a muffled roar, the roof of the building collapsed. Not until the afternoon was the fire finally brought under control.

"More than a score of firemen," the Sun reported, "were given oxygen as they battled the choking fumes for more than six hours . . ." The fire gutted the third floor of the five-storey structure; CKNW's damage, which was extensive, had all been caused by water.

Engineers Clare Purvis and Mac MacKenzie had the station back on the air in one hour and 10 minutes.

Incidentally, in a heart-warming display of selflessness, both CJOR and CKWX came forward with help for NW in its hour of need. OR loaned a portable console, to set up in Danceland, and WX's chief engineer Charlie Smith spent a night at NW's transmitter helping to isolate and end a stubborn hum getting into the transmitter from the console.

"We're going to build a new studio," Bill Rea had said. "It's gonna be a honey." He'd spoken too soon. NW's insurance was nowhere near sufficient to cover the losses sustained by the station, and a new studio was not in the cards just yet. Most of the staff moved into temporary quarters in Danceland, one of Rea's downtown dance halls, from which Jack Cullen was already broadcasting, and began to adapt to uncomfortably crowded conditions. There was one telephone in the beginning, and receptionist Joan Johnston worked out a bell-ringing code — using a school bell — to summon colleagues to the phone.

The transmitter hut on Lulu Island became Studio "A" and a temporary newsroom. Warren Barker remembers catching a bus every day to go to work, and having to walk several blocks to get to the transmitter/newsroom site.

For four long, frustrating months these cumbersome arrangements prevailed. Finally, on September 6, 1954 CKNW moved back in.

The fire brought a benefit: the arrival of engineering consultant Jack Gordon, who put the station back into 227 Columbia Street with new equipment. NW now had a better, crisper sound.

Its owner was not as resilient. Not long after his gag photo with the fire hat, Rea went home and, before his horrified family, collapsed. He recovered, but another collapse was not far ahead.

"This thing hurt him . . ."

Bill Rea was obsessed with television and his obsession wasn't confined to starting his own station: he thought it would be smart to sell the sets, too. CBS, the American network, had a subsidiary that sold sets bearing the network's name. Rea set up a deal with CBS to be its western Canada representative.

The market looked promising. Only 10 per cent of homes in the crowded southwest corner of the province had TV sets. In April of 1954 Phil Baldwin, who'd been

In 1957 Dr. J.C. Ballard, CKNW's chairman acquired two bloodhounds to assist local police in missing persons cases. The station would win praise for its public spiritedness.

A van was bought, equipped with survival gear "allowing NW trainer 'Woody' Cushman to stay on the scene of emergencies as long as necessary and to participate in actual rescues.

"Cushman is spending extensive periods in parklands and bush areas with daily training exercises for hounds preparing for emergency tracking."

The dogs were actually used once or twice, but it was just too much trouble. Bob Hutton cracks that "they're *still* trying to clean the **** out of the van they carried those dogs around in." ∎

made manager of the new company, announced he expected to sell 5,000 sets in the next 18 months, and was lining up dealers.

Then disaster struck. The scene shifts to New York, where NW station manager Bill Hughes is all set to return from a business trip.

Hughes: "I'm sitting in the lobby of the Roosevelt, waiting for the bus to the airport. Two guys sit down behind me and start talking. I can't help overhearing. One of them tells the other that CBS is getting out of the television set business! I got on the phone and called Bill Rea. 'I just heard CBS is getting out of the TV set business at the end of this month,' I said. 'As soon as people hear CBS won't be making any more sets, they'll stop buying. If we get caught with our inventory, we're sunk.'" There were hundreds and hundreds of sets.

"Well, we still took a beating, but not as bad as it would have been if we hadn't sold them. We set up a huge tent at Royal Oak and Kingsway and *sold* TV sets. By the end, we were practically giving them away — and the TV retailers never let me forget it."

Three months after Phil Baldwin's confident prediction, CKNW was out of the TV-set-selling business. Jameson Brinkmeyer, the splendidly named account executive given the task of moving the sets, moved them all. "Brinkmeyer was right out of a Broadway play," says Mel Cooper. "The sales guy with the glossy ring, the sharp suit, the snappy patter."

Frank Walden said the TV fiasco hit Rea harder than the 1954 fire that heavily damaged NW. "This was one instance where he didn't display much acumen. He had mispredicted. He had endless enthusiasm, drive and optimism, but this thing hurt him." A Vancouver Sun story in the mid-50s says he lost $100,000.

"What is your biggest account?"

For years, Fin Anthony's face was seen on television in B.C. as much as anyone's. His ad-libbed ads for Woodward's were a tradition. Woodward's is gone now, but Finley Anthony continues to be active (and still connected, indirectly, with CKNW: he was involved in negotiating Rafe Mair's most recent contract with the station.).

After brief stints in broadcasting and teaching, Fin was working at CKMO when he realized it was the salesmen who made the money. "I called Bill Rea at CKNW. He offered me a job at the senior announcer level: $290 a month. I told him, "I want to be in sales." He called Al Klenman in NW's Vancouver office, and Al hired me. It was January 1, 1954. I was 24. I learned while doing. The 'draw' was $400 a month. If you sold $4,000 worth of time that month you made your draw. And you got 10 per cent of everything over $4,000.

When CKNW defector Patt McDonald started CFUN (the former CKMO), he was joined by about a dozen other NW staffers — including one of its stars, Jack Cullen, and one of its star salesmen: Fin Anthony.

Fin's recollections of Patt McDonald's days at NW are interesting. "I remember this big Texan couldn't believe Canadians' use of the word 'hockey' on the air. Down in Texas, 'hockey' was what cows left behind in fields.

"Some of the people at NW didn't like the way Patt ran the station. I didn't have any problems with him. Patt had a sidekick, Jameson Brinkmeyer, also from the States. This guy had a different watch for every day. I remember at the first sales meeting Brink attended he asked Hughie Wallace, 'Would you be kind enough to tell me: what is your biggest account?' Hughie tells him it's Trapp Motors and mentions a figure. Brink says, 'Hmm, that's a pretty good expenditure for a month.' Hughie says, 'That's a year.' From that point on, things sort of went downhill."

"You'd better get down here . . ."

In May, 1954 Bill Hughes was in New York on CKNW business. "Just before I left NW, I had told Hal Davis, 'Call me only if the station's on fire.'

"I was staying at the Roosevelt Hotel. The phone rings. It's Hal. 'You told me to call you only if the station was on fire.' 'That's right,' I said, 'That was our understanding.' 'Well, it's on fire.'

"I told him I'd come right back, but he said, 'No, Bill Rea wants you to go to Toronto. We'll need replacements for some transcriptions, etc., that have been destroyed or damaged.' So I go to Toronto. I did my work there, and then I get a call from Bill Rea. He's flying to Ottawa, and wants to meet me there. There's a meeting of the board of governors of the Canadian Association of Broadcasters, and they're putting on a dinner for the prime minister, Mr. St. Laurent. Bill was one of the governors.

"We got a small suite in the Chateau Laurier, so that we could be together for our talks. That evening was a nightmare. I had never seen Bill in so much turmoil. He couldn't sleep, he was under great pressure, he wanted to be talking all the time. And a lot of it didn't make sense.

"The next day was the St. Laurent dinner. Because we were hosting the prime minister, we were to wear tuxedos. I'd rented one and I was sitting in the suite that afternoon waiting to go to the dinner, and the telephone rang. It was Tiny Elphicke of CKWX, calling from the CAB suite. 'You'd better get down here,' he said, 'Bill Rea has collapsed.'

"I ran down. Bill was on the floor, looking as if he'd had a massive heart attack. So white. I thought it was curtains for him. He took his watch off, gave it to me. 'This is for you,' he said. 'I'm going.' I said, 'Bill, I think we should pray.' Tears were streaming down my face. 'No,' he says, 'get Tiny. Get Tiny Elphicke.' I found Tiny, brought him over. Bill looked up at us. 'Tiny, come close. Bill, come close. Give me your hand, Tiny. Bill, put your hand on top of Tiny's. I'll put my hand on both of yours.'

"So we all had our hands together. We bent closer. Bill said, 'Tiny, I want you to promise Bill not to oppose CKNW's application for a power increase to 5000 watts.'

"As God is my witness, that's what he said. We just gaped at him. Of course, Tiny agreed. Then they took Bill off to Ottawa Civic Hospital."

Bill's wife Marjorie flew in the next day. Hughes visited Rea, and started reading a news release he had prepared: "'Bill Rea was taken ill at . . .' 'No!' he says, 'tell them I was *stricken*.' So, he was 'stricken.'

"That effectively ended Bill Rea's relationship with CKNW. He would never again have the same influence, and not long after he took his family and moved to California."

Bill Rea had been through the NW fire, through the financial fiasco of the CBS-TV set sale, and through years of frustration trying to obtain a TV licence. He was also extremely active outside CKNW: president of the B.C. Public Halls Association, president of the B.C. Association of Radio and Television Broadcasters, and a director of the Canadian Association of Broadcasting. Perhaps it was surprising his collapse had taken so long.

Bill Rea's choice of Santa Barbara as a place to live had the happy and haphazard quality of much of his life. In 1951 he and the family were driving through on their annual trip to Palm Springs when the car radio died. Says his daughter Erin (formerly Catherine), "Dad would not go on. The car radio had to be on. So he went into a radio shop. The fellow who fixed the radio, George Brooks, insisted on showing us around town. Mr. Brooks was a tiny little man, and so was his wife, like little dolls. They had been dancers." The two men became friends, and in 1953 the vacationing Brooks traded his home in Santa Barbara to the Reas for the summer, while he and his family stayed in the Rea home in New Westminster. A couple of months in Santa Barbara, and the Rea family was hooked. They became Santa Barbarans. ∎

The show indelibly associated with Wally Garrett is Fiesta. It's difficult to describe the impact that show had — and with such modest resources. "It was a one-man deal," Wally says. "Operating, announcing, playing the music, writing the questions, opening mail . . . I did it all. If the newsroom had tapes to play, you were the guy playing the tapes, too.

"There would be an object picked, and clues would be given to the object. It could be anything: The North Shore Lions, a famous building, a kind of car . . . There was no other input into Fiesta: I made up the questions. It had to be that way to keep it honest."

Over one stretch of two years an *average* of 9,800 letters arrived

Tony Antonias wins international award from the Advertising Association of the West.

"CKNW was, technically the lowest of the low . . ."

"Good engineering is invisible."

Jack Gordon means technology should be adapted to people, not vice versa. "No one should be conscious of the hidden complexity that ties all the parts of a station together, and assures its reliability, only that what they need is there when they need it."

Even now, 15 years since his departure, the staff speak of Jack Gordon with respect. He was prickly, occasionally hard to work with, but that arose out of a ferocious insistence on quality and the highest standards. This man knew his stuff. "As far back as I can remember I had a knack for looking at almost anything and understanding how it worked. Or, if it didn't work, why not." He tumbles a Rubik's Cube around in his hands. "I love puzzles, love working things out. In the early 1920s in Calgary it was the crystal set that first grabbed me, then tube radios."

The 1929 Wall Street crash and the depression that followed disrupted Jack's education. In 1930 he began work as an unpaid apprentice at General Electric. That paid off when GE backed him with test equipment to set up a radio-service business serving the Crow's Nest Pass. He worked at CFAC Calgary. Then came the Second World War. "I joined the RCAF as a pilot officer, and was posted as commanding officer to a 100-man radar station on the east coast. Nothing worked there, so I threw out 'the book' and made it work. That got me a transfer to Air Command, Halifax, a flight lieutenant in charge of the chain of radar stations from Maine to Labrador.

"After the war, I came to Vancouver as chief engineer of CKWX, and completed their new 5000-watt transmitting plant. I trained a replacement and resigned. I could no longer work for a manager who publicly described engineers as necessary evils, and who considered that quality didn't matter since the public had tin ears.

"I got into consulting work: echo sounders, auto pilots, high fidelity systems and the like. In 1954 CKNW had its fire. They called me in. CKNW was, technically, the lowest of the low. It had grown like Topsy. The engineers were hard-working guys, but not designers. I was reluctant to do the CKNW work, but Bill Rea wouldn't be defeated.

"I enjoyed working with Bill Rea. He was a hard-headed son-of-a-bitch; he'd pound the desk, but I'd pound right back. We fought to prove what was right, not who was right, and we both enjoyed it. Then he went to California, and started operating the station by remote control.

"I refused to get involved in routine technical operations at the station, because I'm no frigging good at it. I want to know where we're going. I'm in trouble if I have to focus on trivia for a long time. I wouldn't hire me as a chief operations engineer at a station. I'm the world's worst administrator!"

"Jack had a shop beneath 227 Columbia," Dick Abbott recalls, "where he worked out the details of equipment we'd have in the new building. He was actually using ergonomic ideas, shaping the controls, getting them to feel right for the people who'd use them. He'd be calling us down there all the time to sit in this chair, use that control, work that switch . . . and he ending up designing equipment that people could use *easily*, and learn *quickly*."

"I had the most beautiful dream . . ."

"I knew at 15 what I wanted to do," Tony Antonias says. "I couldn't get enough of American magazines — LIFE, Look and so on. I'd rewrite the ads. I'd do the same thing with radio. There was a station I listened to in Adelaide, South Australia, 5DN; they played the popular music of the day. I'd listen to their ads, rewrite them. I used to play 'radio announcer'."

Tony, born in Port Pirie, Australia, learned 5DN was looking for a mailroom clerk. "I woke up my mom and dad, told them about it. They were not amused." Tony presented himself at the radio station to be interviewed, and was promptly asked, 'Why, with your education, would you want a job in the mailroom?' He told them it was a leg in.

"What's that under your arm?" the man said. "Oh, some commercials I've rewritten."

The man read them, and called in the station's creative director. They asked Tony if he would like to join the station in the New Year as a copywriter. "I think I had an orgasm," Tony laughs. "I'm from Mediterranean stock, Greek, we're great interpreters of dreams. In late December, 1947 I said to my dad, 'I had the most beautiful dream: there was a dove on my shoulder.' My dad says, 'You'll get good news.' A few *minutes* later we heard the postman's whistle. I ran to the mail box and there was the letter appointing me junior copywriter. I was to start January 12. That was my 18th birthday."

In February, 1953 Tony came to Vancouver on holiday. "It had been a blisteringly hot summer in Australia, and I really *liked* the Vancouver climate. I decided to stay." He went to CKWX and spoke with copy chief Nina Anthony. "She looked at my portfolio, seemed impressed, then found out I was from Australia. 'Oh, I couldn't possibly touch you!' she said!"

Nina had been born in Australia. Maybe she thought two Aussies would be too much for one station!

So Tony worked elsewhere. Shamelessly exaggerating his hotel experience (which was non-existent), he got a job at Harrison Hot Springs Hotel, but wasted little time writing to CKNW. Hal Davis interviewed him and, on January 31, 1955 he started in the station's copy department.

"As I was leaving the station Bill Hughes, the manager, saw me. He said to Hal, 'Who's that?' and Hal said, 'That's your next copy chief.'

"I was copy chief by December."

"Move aside, fellas!"

Bob Hutton has lost none of the vigor and humor that made him B.C.'s top radio personality from 1955 to 1973, when he was morning man on CKNW.

Asked if a youthful bout with tuberculosis left lasting effects, Hutton, 72, quaveringly places a hand over his left chest. "This lung," he croaks, in a raspy wavering voice, "is all gone with consumption." Then he claps his hand on his right side.

daily. (Of course, Wally didn't open *all* those letters! Just one each segment.) The show was in 10-minute blocks, each with a different sponsor, a couple of records and a different clue. The jackpot built up each time a wrong answer was opened . . . and when that jackpot topped $1,000 the mail exploded. One astonishing week saw 320,000 entries come avalanching through the NW doors. One winner got $3,710 in a day when you could buy a house for $15,000 .

"We ran WX's Casino into the ground," Wally says. "We had to convert one room into a mail room just for Fiesta — and it spilled out of that. I developed ulcers over that show. It ran for about 15 years. Over the life of the show we gave away about $300,000 . . . in 1950 dollars." ∎

Bob Hutton, morning man on CKNW, has lost none of the vigor and humor that made him B.C.'s top personality from 1955 to 1973.

"I listened to the other morning guys . . . Ross Mortimer, Dorwin Baird, and so on . . . and I said, 'Move aside, fellas! Bob's in town!'"

When radio contests like Fiesta! were disallowed, the show appeared doomed. But NW kept the name, and the host (Wally Garrett), and turned the show into a combination of music and phone-in. The ratings went higher!

There was a single question of the day, say, "Should we have cocktail bars?" The talk portion of the show was confined to five minutes of each half hour. Manager Bill Hughes put in a buzzer

"BUT THIS ONE," he bellows, "IS FINE!"

Hutton was born June 29, 1920 in San Francisco. His Canadian parents were there temporarily, and Bob was in Canada before he was seven months old. His father, a railroader with the CN ("the good road"), brought the little family to Rocky Mountain House in Alberta, where Bob spent his first 10 years. "I got my first taste for the spotlight there, a boost to the ego. I played Santa Claus in our Grade One play. Loved that applause."

When Bob was 10, the family moved to Vancouver's Grandview district. Five years later CN moved his father to Kamloops. "That was *the* place to grow up. Small town, everybody knew everybody, skinny-dipping at midnight. I got heavily into high school drama. We wrote Jack Benny once for a script, he sent us one. We played all the parts; I was Jack Benny."

Then CFJC Radio in Kamloops formed a Radio Drama Society. "They had courses in elocution: arrround the rrrugged rrrocks the rrragged rrrascal rrran! I got hooked on radio. There was a guy behind the glass, *he* was getting paid. Hey! There's a step to Hollywood!"

About 1941, Ian Clark, CFJC's manager, offered Bob a job as an announcer. Salary: $15 a week. "I'll take it," I said, and my dad said, 'You don't have a job, kid, you have a disease.'"

The station's music library, Bob cracks, had about 40 records. After four or five years there Hutton met Vancouver radio man Laurie Irving, who told the young DJ an upstart new station in New Westminster, CKNW, had hired away Bill Fox, the morning man at CKWX. WX needed a new morning man.

In the spring of 1945 Bob went down to Vancouver. (His free CNR pass came in handy!) "CKWX was big time. Big double doors on the studios, a light that showed ON AIR. I was impressed. By now I was making $80 a month at CFJC. I told Tiny Elphicke, the manager, I didn't want to go back to $70 a month. No, he said, we'll give you $120 a month. Hmmmm. OK.

"I listened to the other morning guys . . . Ross Mortimer, Dorwin Baird, and so on . . . and I said, 'Move aside, fellas! Bob's in town!'"

Then, disaster! Bob developed TB. He had to go to the provincial sanatorium at Tranquille. CKWX, on the understanding he would return, sent him $75 a month."Tranquille was quite a place. There were more blankets *under* the girls' building than in it. I used to tease the other patients — put Epsom Salts in their urine samples."

Two years later, his tuberculosis tamed, he returned to CKWX. Bob would be there for 10 years, a hugely popular morning show host. His ratings were high and solid. "We didn't even count CKNW. The top guy to knock off was Colin Fitzgerald, 'GG' on CJOR; we got him within six months. I beat Monty McFarlane on OR, too."

Eventually, it came Bob's turn to be wooed away. "I had a couple of parking lot and gas station meetings with Bill Hughes."

In 1955 Bob moved over to CKNW.

". . . pass them on to the other fellows . . ."

CKNW has always been an aggressive cultivator of its advertisers. Right from the begining, NW got extraordinary results for a lot of its clients.

Anne Bolton recalls Bill Rea holding a regular Wednesday meeting. "He'd read a piece of commercial copy, and then he'd ask, 'What's wrong with this?'"

In the summer of 1953 NW was crowing that Jack Cullen's Owl Prowl show had doubled the sales of one of its sponsors, Ward Music. A big reason for success in the early years was Rea's indefatigable pursuit of opportunity. He kept a close eye on advertisements placed in newspapers by CKNW advertisers, and was alert to their increasing their ad dollars at radio's expense.

A June 26, 1951 memo from Rea to Al Klenman and Hugh Wallace of his sales staff nicely catches the flavor of his relentless whip-cracking:

"1. The golf driving range in New Westminster, behind the Catholic Church, opened up without our selling an opening campaign.

"2. Reddi-Whip is the only summer product we have sold.

"3. The man who is in charge of a territory should clip the newspapers daily for prospects and pass them on to the other fellows if unable to cover them personally."

In another memo, just three days later, Rea tells of driving past a potato chip factory the night before, "and I could tell by the smell of the chips they were working overtime." The message was clear: there was a potential sponsor in that aromatic little factory!

Even in his brief time at NW, copy writer Lyndon Grove was struck with two indelible thoughts. "One was, I couldn't believe NW was so good. It was a superb operation. But there was also something almost religious about the devotion to the station of many of its people. When someone left, it was seen as a kind of apostasy:

that alerted Wally — and his listeners — that time was up. Wally fought the five-minute dictum. His instincts, which were good, told him listeners liked the talk portions, wanted them longer.

They got longer. And eventually they turned into a new kind of program, with a new kind of host. Here again CKNW was lucky: It had, right in its own building, a man who would take this new kind of show and make it his own.

Jack Webster. ■

'How could we have been so *wrong* about so-and-so?' It was like being the son of the rabbi in a Jewish musical. There was an intense competitive spirit, like a hockey team, especially when it came to CKWX. It was a great triumph for us when we produced the Dueck car commercials, and WX had to run them."

"My name is Little Miss Sunbeam . . ."

For a textbook example of how to win over a reluctant client, look at Mel Cooper's 1955 pursuit of Weston Bakeries. Through his contacts in the food industry, Mel learned Weston was soon to introduce a new product onto grocery shelves in western Canada: Sunbeam Bread. It was an American innovation, and had been franchised to many bakeries south of the border. It was still unknown in Canada.

"We were on the outside looking in with the Weston people. I couldn't even get my calls to Jim Johnston answered. He was the key man. I went down to Seattle, where the Hanson Bread people had a Sunbeam franchise. I saw the drawing of the Miss Sunbeam girl on the package, and that gave me the idea. I came back to Vancouver, had an outfit made identical to the one on the package, the frilly little blue dress, then I hired a little girl and drove her to Weston Bakeries at Kingsway and Broadway.

"Now, remember, only Jim Johnston and his sales manager know anything about the upcoming launch of Sunbeam Bread into this market. I sent the little girl up to his office, and I waited in my car outside. The girl is carrying a little package. The receptionist says, 'Well, who do we have here?' The girl says, 'My name is Little Miss Sunbeam, and I'm here to see Mr. Johnston.' The receptionist bounces up and into Johnston's office. 'There's someone out here you just *have* to see.' Johnston comes out, sees the little girl, and he's instantly charmed. He takes her into his office and she hands him the pretty little package.

"In it is a letter from me: 'Dear Mr. Johnson, my name is Mel Cooper, and I represent CKNW. We think we can sell a lot of Sunbeam Bread for you in this market, etc., etc. I'm parked out on Broadway hoping to see you.'

"Well, he came down, invited me in, and we got that account."

Early CKNW Sports History

Bill Rea was not a sports fan, but he knew there could be money in sports broadcasting. Since the mid-30s, Bill's good friend Leo Nicholson had been bringing many dollars to CJOR through his broadcasts of Box Lacrosse. He would buy the air time, then go out and sell sponsors in what was known in the trade as 'bootlegging.' Lacrosse was the big sport at that time, eclipsing baseball, and the ill-fated pro hockey league of 1936.

Bill sensed that Leo could be persuaded, through a better deal, to bring the broadcasts to CKNW. In the spring of 1945, just eight months after going on the air, CKNW became the voice of Box Lacrosse. Nicholson was the consummate radio play-by-play man, building excitement even if a team was only killing a penalty. But Leo was a little hard of hearing, and did not always get the scoring and penalties from the public address system. He needed an assistant to record the goals and penalties in written form. 16-year-old Jim Cox (a lacrosse fan) was dragooned for the writing job, and to conduct interviews between periods. This was before the days of a 'color' commentator; the play-by-play man did it all while the play was in progress.

The following year, Leo died suddenly. The reluctant Cox was forced to become a play-by-play broadcaster, a position he held at CKNW for the next 36 years!

Jim Cox (above and below left) was a play-by-play broadcaster at CKNW for 36 years.

Bill Rea realized that sports not only made money, but inexpensively satisfied another broadcast requirement: live programming. Every station had to air a required number of hours of live programming each week. Most stations did so with live musicians. Rea found that by, using an engineer and an announcer, he could fill two-and-a-half hours with lacrosse a lot less expensively than with musicians.

In 1947 the Pacific Coast Hockey League was formed with both New Westminster and Vancouver entering teams. CKNW negotiated the rights with the owner of the New Westminster Royals, and the station's long association with hockey was born. After the league turned professional and became the Western Hockey League, NW broadcast both Vancouver and New Westminster home games.

High school basketball was hot as the B.C. Provincial Championships were originated in 1944 in New Westminster. CKNW's broadcasts of these games helped build a Vancouver audience, as Vancouver College always seemed to reach the final. Senior 'A' Men's Basketball began play about this time, with the great Cloverleafs, Oilers and Thunderbirds playing at UBC. NW got the rights to these broadcasts, and because a local girls' intermediate team was sponsored by the station's landlord (the Fraser Cafe), Bill said we'd promote the team with live broadcasts. (An aside: one of the players, Louise North, had been recruited from the Fraser Valley champs, Haney High, and won a job as secretary at CKNW. She is still Mrs. Jim Cox.)

By now CKNW was *the* sports station, CJOR still had Jack Short's horse races, and CKMO was dabbling in baseball at the new Queen Elizabeth Park Stadium (later named after Nat Bailey.) Sports promoters were now seeking out the station that appeared to want to broadcast anything that moved.

Al Principe was busy promoting pro boxing on a regular basis, so CKNW worked out a deal to do his main events from Exhibition Gardens. Al just about lost his barber shops in the very risky fight game, and finally sold the rights to I. J. 'Jack' Fox. NW continued boxing broadcasts for five years.

A giant in B.C. broadcasting history, Monty McFarlane, once worked for NW. "I can't remember exactly how long it was . . . about 20 minutes, I think." It was in 1955, and one of his shows was a nightly program called Sandman Serenade, a phone-in request show. Monty was at NW less than a year, but manager Patt MacDonald made an impression. "Bill Rea brought him up from the States as a TV consultant, at a salary of $25,000 a year. He was always immaculate, with alligator shoes and gabardine suits. You'd see his desk, absolutely clean, and he'd have his feet up on it. When Patt left NW he went over to CKMO and changed the name to CFUN.

"I do recall something else quite vividly from that time. Jack Cullen and his first wife Joy used to bring their little baby in when they did their show, and they kept it in a filing cabinet." ∎

In 1952 Mauri Hesketh went to see Bill Hughes at CKNW. "He auditioned me; I did my best Wally-Garrett-in-the-bathroom impression. Hughes said I was good, but I needed experience. So he gave me a list of stations in the interior. I bought a round-trip bus ticket that took me on a loop through all those places. At Penticton they told me, 'You're good, but you need experience.' At Kelowna they told me, 'You're good, but . . .' and so on. On the bus coming back from Kamloops I was feeling really low. Four stations, four rejections. The bus is going through Chilliwack, and I see CHWK on a sign. That's got to be a radio station! I begged the bus driver to let me off there, and I went in. I started working at CHWK in October, 1952." ■

At the same time Cliff Parker became the promoter of professional wrestling in Vancouver. Now, Jim Cox was a bit of a purist about sports. He felt it was serious business for the athletes, and should be presented as such on the air. Wrestling just didn't fit that mold. Bill Rea, however, thought it would be a hoot. By this time Bill had bought a television set, and with a massive roof-top array was able to bring in KING-TV from Seattle. He believed wrestling would be big. So, with plenty of money supplied by the promoter, NW did 30 minutes live from 9:30 to 10 on Wednesday nights. Amazingly, the main event would end at exactly 9:57, leaving ample time to 'plug' next week's card, which would star the villain who had just won the night's main event. Ahh, showbiz! (Hal Davis has a funny memory of a bout he and Jim covered, in which something went wrong: one of the wrestlers whose head was being banged against a corner post actually started bleeding real blood. Promoter Parker leaped up behind Hal and shouted into the ring at his wrestler, 'Don't bleed on the mat! Don't bleed on the mat!' "Parker had just had the mat cleaned," Hal says, "and it was an expensive operation.")

Things moved quickly from 1950 to 1954. Would you believe play-by-play golf on radio? CKNW did the Canadian Women's Closed at Capilano, and the Men's Canadian Open at old Shaughnessy.

UBC had a hot soccer team; so they did the Canadian College title game at the old UBC Stadium.

Automobile racing on radio? Why not? The Digney Speedway on McPherson Avenue in Burnaby was a quarter-mile track that ran stock cars every Saturday night in the summer. They begged CKNW to come in, and even found the sponsor to pay for it.

Lacrosse was beginning to lose its mass appeal as the postwar automobile boom changed people from being indoor spectators to outdoor participants in the summer months.

In 1953 CKNW dropped lacrosse and picked up pro baseball, in games featuring the Vancouver Capilanos, who the following year became the Mounties. Hal Rodd had been doing the games, both live and re-created (for road games) on CKMO, and came over to NW as a newsman and stats and interview man for Jim Cox. NW did the Western International League games for three years, finally dropping them when football came on the scene.

The British Empire Games were now upon us, and CKNW's one-man sports department got busy. Some newsmen were seconded as NW covered every venue from the track-and-field events at Empire Stadium, cycling at the Clark Drive velodrome, swimming and diving at UBC, rowing at Chillwack's Vedder Canal, boxing, wrestling, and weight-lifting at Exhibition Forum and Gardens. When possible they did live coverage, and for Jim Cox the Miracle Mile race between Roger Bannister and John Landy will always be a career highlight.

The B.C. Lions became a reality in 1954, and NW rival CKWX aggressively went after the rights. Bill Rea was not too interested in getting into a bidding war, and in fact was not sold on the viability of football in Vancouver. However, in 1955 the team begged NW to get behind it and offered to let BOTH stations broadcast the games!

That lasted for two seasons, but when their play-by-play man Bill Stephenson left for CFRB in Toronto, CKWX soon dropped out of the football picture. (But not before a rare event: for at least part of the time the two stations shared the rights, you would have heard Jim Cox on CKNW, and Jim Robson on CKWX!) Except for two brief periods, CKNW has held the B.C. Lions broadcast rights ever since.

One major radio sports promotion came in 1968 when efforts were being made to form a North American Soccer League. Many international teams spent their summer as representatives of North American cities. Vancouver's rep was Sunderland, of the English First Division. This was perhaps the hardest-drinking gang ever to descend on the city. The whole exercise was just a vacation for this rowdy bunch. Their on-field performance was just as undisciplined as their off-field hi-jinks. The season was a disaster, but it did give the NW sports crew a chance to broadcast games from such famous stadiums as the Los Angeles Coliseum, Kezar Stadium in San Francisco, Comiskey Park in Chicago, the great JFK Stadium in Washington, D.C., Varsity Stadium in Toronto, and Wayne State University Stadium in Detroit.

From 1944 until 1956 play-by-play sports on radio was big business. The advent of television reduced the impact, particularly in the peak evening viewing hours. Only the best of events would draw a radio audience, as witness NHL hockey and CFL football today. But in that 12-year period CKNW did play-by-play broadcasts of FOURTEEN different sports: lacrosse, hockey, basketball, golf, boxing, wrestling, stock-car racing, swimming, weight-lifting, track and field, cycling, curling, soccer and football . . . and Jim Cox did them all!

"I must have gone to every two-car wreck in town . . ."

George Garrett remembers well his first day on the air as a 17-year-old disc jockey at CJNB in North Battleford. He started: "Here's T-T-Tony M-Martin to sing T-T-Tahiti, My Island."

First-day nerves are normal — in fact, they're expected — and it wasn't long before George was comfortable sitting in front of a mike.

By the 1990s he had become the best dig-and-report radio newsman in British Columbia, a man who has broken so many stories on CKNW over the years that the station has made him essentially self-assigning. That's a natural tribute to a man who has been a news reporter in five decades.

George — not related to the other famous NW Garrett, Wally — was born in Mortlach, Saskatchewan, in 1934. He did pretty well at school, skipped Grade 7, then got to Grade 11, at which time his interest in girls exceeded his interest in science and geography, and he didn't pass.

Next stop: CJNB and T-T-Tony M-Martin. "I wanted to get into radio," George says today, "but not news. I wanted to be a disc jockey. I hitchhiked to North Battleford and applied for a job. The fellow who hired me said, 'I didn't hire you for your voice, kid, but because you had the initiative'."

A year later George was at CHAB in Moose Jaw, and a year after that returned to CJNB as program director! No slouch, he!

On February 1, 1956 George joined CKNW. Bob Giles, in the newsroom, had worked with Garrett at CJNB and told him NW was looking for people. "I started as a desk man, 4 p.m. to midnight. Marke Raines was a day guy at the

George Garrett on the scene of the Pines Cafe holdup, 1959.

CKNW's 1954 fire caused a lot of damage — none by fire!

"Rea had had some kind of muddy acoustic plaster put on the studio wall," Doug Court says. "It was a cheapie job meant to save the cost of real acoustic tile. The stuff stayed soft! This gunk started sliding off the walls in huge gobs with all the water pouring onto it during the fire. It was a terrible mess." Geoff Theobald, a well-known Vancouver TV producer today, remembers that mess. As a kid, he got a temporary job at NW cleaning it up! ∎

Gerry Davies, NW's all-night man, who succeeded Wilf Ray in October, 1952 has a vivid recollection of a bathtub race in the early '60s . . . not from Nanaimo to Vancouver, but in Kitsilano Pool. "Hal Davis was the emcee. There were three racers: Jack Cullen, Bob Hutton and me, and there was a hell of a crowd on hand. NW found some tin bathtubs and delivered them to our homes, and we could decorate 'em any way we liked. I chose a Hawaiian theme, with garlands on the boat, and I was tastefully attired in sarong and gumboots.

"Cullen had a 'secret weapon.' Hutton and I are racing legally, with a paddle; Cullen had a scuba diver under his boat. Bob and I are rowing furiously, Cullen's lolling, examining his fingernails, then he hollers, 'Okay, Charlie,' and the scuba diver kicks in his tank. But something goes wrong, and now Cullen is sinking. But he stands up gallantly, saluting as he sinks beneath the waves.

"Hal Davis started making cracks on the p.a. at our expense, so we picked him up and dumped

time, out on the beat in his '53 Ford. He had no radio, no pager, it was all done by pay phone."

A young woman named Joan McIntyre came in to NW one day to leave a request for a record to be played. George got talking with her, one thing led to another, and they'll celebrate 38 years of marriage in 1994. The Garretts have four grandchildren.

"Mel Cooper was sales manager when I started, and he had the idea to sell the news cruiser — in other words, sell the idea of a news cruiser to a sponsor. So we got the Sunbeam Bread News Cruiser. The first night guy assigned to it was Bill Fox, 'Barometer Bill.' After a few months I got it, and I worked the night beat for years.

"I must have gone to every two-car wreck in town, but over the years I made a lot of contacts." And he still laughs over the young competitor in a soap-box derby at Sapperton, roaring down the slope on his rickety vehicle shouting, "I'm George Garrett in the Sunbeam Bread News Cruiser."

"Then I bought some daffodils . . ."

"Frank Griffiths," says former NW chief engineer Jack Gordon, "is the most completely honest person I've worked with. I've never had him go back on his word on anything. He thinks about people."

Griffiths' name first became familiar to NW staffers (and the rest of B.C.) in February of 1956, when it was announced Bill Rea had sold the station. "Major shareholders in the new management," said a Vancouver Sun story, "are the Dr. W.G. Ballard family of Vancouver. Their representative is Frank Griffiths of Griffiths & Griffiths, chartered accountants, 1292 West Georgia. Minority stockholders are the Southam Co. Ltd., and a holding company, Muro Investments."

The name of veterinarian Dr. Ballard was already known to the public as a result of his thriving pet food business. He had recently sold that business to Standard Brands. Public interest in accounting companies being what it is, not many knew about Frank Griffiths, or that he and his father were partners in the largest firm of its kind in British Columbia.

"The specialties at Griffiths & Griffiths were municipal accounting and taxation. Dry, but regular. I grew up in that firm. I was busiest keeping people happy that my father made *un*happy. He'd come stomping around — it was my task to calm them down. I retired from the firm in 1967."

He recalls the beginning of his relationship with CKNW. "We were friends with the Arthur Moscarella family. He was publisher of The Province (and a Southam director). We're hospitable people, always had boats. We invited the Moscarellas for a boating weekend. We were sitting around one evening, after a day of fishing, and I said to Mr. Moscarella, 'There must be something you want to achieve.' He said, 'I'm interested in that radio station, CKNW.' They were vying with CKWX at the time for top station. Southam had owned a radio station at one time, but sold it.

"I offered to represent Southam, and go to see Bill Rea. I called on Rea, whom I did not know, and put Southam's proposal to him. My opinion of Bill Rea? Jumpy . . . impetuous . . . which you can't afford to be.

"We went before the CBC board of governors — that was the procedure then — and Southam were denied the purchase. The ruling was one company could not own radio stations and newspapers in the same market.

"I let a whole year go by. Then I went back to Mr. Moscarella. 'Want to try again?' 'Sure.'

"I went to see Bill Rea again. He was agreeable, but he wanted a deposit of $50,000. Non-refundable. If the application was turned down again, he would keep that money. I made an agreement: if Southam was not to be permitted to buy, *I* be permitted to buy.

"My partners in that application were Bill Murphy and Walter Owen, both lawyers. The CBC heard the application again, and again they turned Southam down, but gave it to us: Griffiths, Murphy and Owen. The announcement of that approval came to us out at Pitt Lake. My wife Emily and I and Jack Christianson and his wife were out there relaxing. I heard on CKNW itself that the sale had been approved, so I chartered a seaplane and flew from Pitt Lake to Vancouver. Earnings would accrue from that day, so I wasted no time. I went to the lawyers' office, Owen Bird, and signed the necessary papers. Then I bought some daffodils and flew back to Pitt Lake. I can't remember how — or if — we celebrated the approval.

"Bill Rea got his money, and went cheerfully off to California."

"Bill . . . have you sold the station?"

Some 40 years have passed since the transition from the Rea years to the Griffiths years, but Bill Hughes' memory of the time stays with him.

"When I was managing and he was still owner, Bill Rea used to phone me on Sunday nights from Santa Barbara. I never got to know who Ed Sullivan was! Bill was trying to make decisions from 1,500 miles away — but he didn't know the people now, didn't know the shows, didn't know the situation. I'd get irritated. 'Bill, if you don't like the way I'm doing things, come back and do it yourself.'

"I went to New York on one selling trip, and Bill Rea called me there. 'Skip some things on your trip,' he says, 'and come back via Santa Barbara. I'll pick you up in Los Angeles.'

"Rea picks me up at the train station in L.A. This is the middle of December, 1954. It's the *old* Bill Rea, expansive, big cigar. We're off to Santa Barbara. Had a great time, driving along the highway, into the house, talking, talking. Then he says, 'What are your plans?' 'Bill,' I replied, 'you invited me. I want to be home for Christmas. What do *you* want?'

"He got around to talking about the sale of CKNW to its senior employees. I told him it was a great idea. The staff had worked under enormous pressure since the fire; they had gone through a lot, and they should benefit.

"Well, I was amazed. He didn't have any real thoughts. He'd summoned me, but nothing was organized in his mind. I told him if there was nothing further to discuss, I wanted to go home. 'Don't want to stay another night?' 'No.' He took me to the train station, and I got the train home.

"Along about the middle of January, 1955, it was a Saturday afternoon, I get a phone call at home from Bill Rea. He's in the Hotel Vancouver. 'What's up?' I ask. He says, 'I want you to come over and see me.'

"That's when I met Arthur Moscarella and Dick Diespecker from the Province. Bill Rea told me he had sold the station to Southam. I was floored. I said, 'Bill, I can't

him into the water, clothes and all." (Hal, years later, cracks up when he remembers this goofy race. "I remember Gerry, up to his neck in water, because his tub sank, too, and he's STILL PADDLING!") ∎

Gerry Davies in the main control room, 1954.

Frank Griffiths became the new owner in 1956.

From the August 16, 1956 edition of Canadian Broadcaster comes a story of an early experiment by CKNW. Despite the up-beat tone of the piece, Hal Davis recalls the event with a slight shudder. It wasn't repeated.

"Radio station CKNW recently turned over its complete operation for three weeks to an eager group of students from the University of British Columbia. Termed 'Operation Holiday,' the scheme gave 11 members of UBC's Radio Society an opportunity to get some first-hand practical radio experience while filling in for vacationing CKNW staffers.

"A skeleton staff of experienced radio men guided the tyros

believe this. A few days ago you talked to me about helping the staff — they *rescued* CKNW.'

"There was an upcoming CBC board of governors meeting. In those days, the CBC regulated private broadcasters. I was asked to support the bid to the CBC board. I would have been subordinate to Mr. Moscarella *and* to Dick Diespecker. I told them I didn't like the situation, and needed time to think about it."

It wasn't long before Hughes got an indication of what life would be like at CKNW with Southam at the helm. He had engineered a deal through his various connections in the Western Interprovincial Football Union (a precursor to the CFL) for radio rights to all WIFU teams. His bid for $22,000 was successful. News of the coup made the papers. "Arthur Moscarella phoned me. 'What's this I hear about you paying $20,000 for *rights* to buy football broadcasts? We in the newspaper business don't pay for *rights* to cover games! From now on, you are not to spend another dime on this sort of trivia.'"

Amazingly, Moscarella did not understand the distinction between a radio station presenting a game live, as it happened, and a newspaper reporting on the game after the event!

"I could tell my wings were going to be clipped," Hughes says. "Moscarella had stressed that I report to him and Dick Diespecker."

Hughes did not appear at the CBC hearings in Ottawa. Bill Rea went.

"Between March 1st and March 31st I prayed a lot that this sale would not be approved. I literally *prayed*. First, because the newspapers would control us and, second, because it would stifle us. But never before had an application for a radio station been turned down. They presented it, and my prayers came true; the CBC board of governors said 'no.' Southam already owned a newspaper in town and this was too much of a concentration.

"Bill Rea told me, 'The station is not for sale. If I ever sell it again I will give you and the senior staff the opportunity to buy it.'"

In the next stage of this drama, Hughes and his family went to Santa Barbara for a six-week holiday, while Bill Rea came up to B.C. to look after things at the station. (Incidentally, while Rea gave the Hughes family the run of his home, he asked them not to pee in the pool.)

"Now," Hughes says, "Bill Rea starts phoning me in *California*. Finally I said, 'It doesn't sound as if things are working out.' 'No,' he said, 'I don't think I'll do it anymore. I'm coming home.' He came down, we talked again, and he reiterated: the station was not for sale, he was going to get into TV, and he was happy with the way I was running things.

"Okay, now it's January, 1956 — almost exactly one year to the day since Rea's call about Southam. The phone rings. It's Bill Rea. He starts talking, and after a moment I ask, 'Bill, have you sold the station?' And he said, 'Oh, Bill. Bill, Bill . . .'"

Rea asked Hughes to come in to Vancouver and meet the prospective buyers. That's where Hughes first met Frank Griffiths, Walter Owen and Bill Murphy. "They announced they had come to an agreement to buy CKNW. It was an interesting meeting. Then Bill Rea left. The others asked me what I thought. I told them I thought it was a betrayal of the staff. No staff, no station had been through so much hell, had served the community so well.

"Frank Griffiths was the spokesman. He asked me to think about it, and said we'd have another meeting. The arrangement was that if the CBC board turned Southam down again, then his group — Griffiths, Owen and Murphy — would go ahead with a bid. 'We don't want to make any promises,' Griffiths said, 'nor should you. But give us six months. See if you like us, and we like you, and if we decide to continue our relationship, we'll offer you a portion." He went further. If Hughes wanted to invest in the station, Griffiths' group would provide backing, and guarantee any bank loan he made to finance the deal. What did Hughes think of that? "I think that's fair."

They asked him to go to the hearings in Ottawa and represent them in the bid. And they had him introduce the group to the station staff. Later, Frank Griffiths told Hughes he thought he had done a great job at the hearing. "He said, 'Here,' and handed me tickets to Miami for a holiday. That started the relationship well."

The CBC decision came down in June of 1956: the Southam bid had again been rejected, the Griffiths/Owen/Murphy bid approved.

CKNW now had new owners.

And Hughes soon got an indication of the new boss' style.

"In early October 1956, I was on my way to Chicago, then to Toronto and Montreal on a sales trip. I was manager, but I also handled a lot of sales business. I went out to the airport and met Frank Griffiths out there. *He* was flying to Chicago! We flew down to Seattle together to make the connection, but at Seattle Frank said, 'Bill, I'm going to New York. And so are you! We've had three months working with you, and we're very pleased. So we asked around: what would Bill Hughes most want? And the answer was: tickets to the World Series. So that's where we're going.'

"Well. There were *beds* in the plane, a DC6-B; they had sleepers in them then. And we got to New York and went to Yankee Stadium and on October 8, 1956 I saw Don Larsen pitch his perfect game. And then Frank Griffiths told me they were giving me a share of ownership.

"And that's where everything started."

"Ohh, anyone can do that!"

"When I was about 15," retired NW newsman Mauri Hesketh says, "I had a little 'radio station' in the basement. I had a wall full of records down there, and a record player, and I built a microphone. My father thought it was nuts for me to be down there talking to myself. I wrote my own newscasts. I'd take stuff out of the newspaper, rewrite it; my teachers used to tell me I should write.

"My real desire in life was to be an airline pilot or a lawyer or both. One day just before VJ Day in 1945 — I was 14 — I was building a little bomb with my chemistry set, and it blew up. I lost the sight in my left eye. That put me out of the running to be a pilot."

In October, 1952 Mauri got a job at CHWK in Chilliwack. (The unusual story of how he got it appears on page 54.)

Mauri's girlfriend Lenny (who preferred that to Lenora) was living with her parents in Burnaby — and they could just barely hear CHWK when the wind was right. On one visit to Lenny's home, Mauri was really pleased when Lenny's grandmother praised his voice on the radio. But he was puzzled when she said he sang so well. "Grandma," Lenny explained, "that's not Mauri singing. He's the one talking between the records." "Ohh," Grandma said, with a contemptuous wave of her hand, "*anyone* can do that!"

in their announcing, news editing and writing duties. CKNW's program director, Hal Davis, who organized the project, reports that a number of promising radio types were uncovered.

"Davis also reports, however, that the neophytes did not carry out their broadcasting chores without the occasional fluff. One of the announcers blandly told his listening audience that, 'On the weather scene the outlook for *money* is clear, becoming *Sunday Tuesday* afternoon . . .' Other boobs committed by the sophomores included: 'In a weather, the moment, but first . . .'

"Letters and phone calls from listeners indicated that they were solidly behind the university students."

One of those "tyros" went on to become a CKNW staffer. Today, "Big Daddy" Dave McCormick is still active in radio in Vancouver. And the fellow who took over Bob Hutton's morning show, young Don Kalmakoff, would go on to become a CKNW engineer and launch a technical innovation that changed broadcasting. ∎

Mauri and Lenny were married in March of 1953, and by September he had a job at CKOK in Penticton. The Heskeths fell in love with Penticton, but not with CKOK. "I quit. I started painting houses, and we moved into Lenny's parents' place. Then I got a call from Hal Davis, CKNW's program director at the time. They needed someone to work three nights a week in news and two nights as a DJ. I'd been feeding items to NW from CKOK, and Jim Cox recognized my name. I went into the CKNW newsroom. It was 1956."

He would be there for 20 years.

"The typewriter went 'ding ding' . . ."

Come with us back to December, 1957 and the copy department at CKNW. Tony Antonias is copy chief. "I was using a manual Royal typewriter on my copy, but the keys were so sharp they were cutting through all the ribbons. When I asked for more from the accountant I was reminded they cost $1 each. 'Press more lightly,' I was told. That didn't work. 'Call the typewriter people, have them file the keys down.' Didn't work. The typewriter thing was annoying. My work day was spent at the damn machine. Finally I went to see Hal Davis. 'It's time for my holidays, and I'm going to Australia. If I don't get a new typewriter I'm going to stay there.'

"I came back from holidays February 14, 1958. There in my office was a brand new Olympia. Well! This was the cat's meow of typewriters then. The very best. I was pleased. Then the phone rang. John Donaldson, the station's retail sales manager, wanted to see me. He wanted me to do something for Woodward's $1.49 day.

"I became highly incensed. I was *copy chief.* This $1.49 copy could be nothing more than a mere listing of goods, nothing creative at all! I came down the stairs and stormed into the copy office. Iris Tickner's in there, she's puffing on a cigarette. 'Tony!' she says. 'What's wrong?'

"I blew up. 'This ****ing $1.49 day thing for Woodward's. I'm supposed to write ****ing copy for the ****ing thing!' I slammed my new typewriter in anger. It went *ding ding.*

"I stopped, and looked at the typewriter. Then I hit it again. *Ding ding.*

"A little tune popped into my head. '$1.49 day, ding ding.' Within 20 minutes I had it in my head: *$1.49 day, Woodward's, $1.49 day, Tuesday.*

"I don't write music. I rushed into Dick Abbott's office. 'Dick, please, quickly, write this down.' I hummed it for him. The NW Trio recorded it Easter Sunday, 1958. It worked. It tells you *what* it is, *where* it is and *when* it is, and it tells you *how much* it is! Suddenly, it was everywhere. It's been recorded in French, in Italian, in Chinese. Eaton's called, The Bay called, can you do one for us?"

It became as familiar a tune as any ever heard in Canada.

"George Patey's *mynah bird,*" Tony laughs, "learned to whistle it!"

Tony Antonias and his typewriter had written a standard!

"I went straight for the jugular . . ."

In 1953 a pugnacious 35-year-old reporter for the Vancouver Sun named Jack Webster, who had honed his skills in the cutthroat world of British tabloid reporting, quit The Sun to work for CJOR. John Edgar Webster, born in Glasgow in 1918, brought a new style to the ears of Canadians: "I went straight for the jugular," he writes in his autobiography, "Inflection was paramount. I wanted to sound tough even if I wasn't asking the world's toughest question. I sat leaning forward, giving the impression that I was ready to pounce. Really hard-nosed radio reporters were a scarcity in North America then, so my technique stood out."

Webster's relentless daily reporting on CJOR on the Mulligan police scandal made his name in Vancouver. The commission on the scandal lasted months. Oddly, a skill he had learned at 14 contributed hugely to Webster's success. Because recording devices had been banned at the inquiry, Webster took shorthand notes of the testimony, was able to quote juicy portions word-for-word on his broadcasts. Often, he read directly from his shorthand. The whole city listened . . . a phenomenon that did not escape CKNW's attention.

Not long after the commission's labors ended, Hal Davis approached Jack about coming to CKNW. But Webster had decided — reluctantly — to move back to Scotland. His wife was suffering bouts of deep depression, and they thought a return to Scotland might help. Sadly, it didn't.

In 1957 Jack Webster came back to Vancouver.

In the spring of 1957 Webster got a phone call in Glasgow. It was CKNW again. "They were offering me double the money I had been getting at CJOR, and the use of a company car." Webster and his family came back to Vancouver.

Jack was originally hired by NW to do City Mike, his daily report on various local malfeasances, a lunchtime program called Spotlight, and 10 capsule comments every weekend. But in an explosively dramatic way his role changed overnight. The scene was the B.C. Penitentiary.

CKNW was about to have its investment in Webster pay off. Big time.

"We had two cans of soup at home . . ."

No one who ever met CKNW sportscaster Al Davidson forgot him. Tough, smart, sarcastic, pugnacious, loyal, reckless, sentimental, opinionated — he brought all these qualities to his broadcasting. And he added what was, for radio, a priceless ingredient: he was impossible to ignore.

"Al Davidson didn't agree with everyone," his widow Pat says. "That was part of his charisma." She laughs wryly. "He didn't always agree with *me*. Why should anyone else be any different? He was never wishy-washy. He said what he thought."

Pat and Al had seven children in their 42 years of marriage, years in which the Davidson family moved a lot: those seven children were born in five cities.

Al himself was born February 18, 1926 in Yellowgrass, Saskatchewan, near Estevan. At 16 he joined the RCAF and served overseas until the war ended. It was in Port Arthur (now Thunder Bay), in about 1946, that Al first got into radio. "He was a disc jockey, and did news, sports," says Pat. "He'd had voice training, so that helped. He did play-by-play for the Port Arthur Bruins, and met a lot of players who went on to the NHL."

In 1948 Al got a job at CKCK in Regina. Pat worked there as traffic manager. "I didn't know who he was. I was too busy to notice much, anyway. It was a busy station, number one in the market. Al would be in the newsroom, checking the teletype. He hadn't been hired yet, but he wasn't waiting for anyone to teach him. In those days you didn't take courses, you just jumped in and learned on the job." Al and Pat were married in Regina in 1949.

"We moved to Toronto in 1951 when Al got a job at CKFH, Foster Hewitt's new

Hal Davis recalls going down to the transmitter one night, when the all-night show was being done from there, to find Wilf Ray, wearing a green eyeshade, and jumping around doing his show. "Wilf never sat still; he'd be pacing back and forth between the turntables, whizzing around finding things to play, a real ball of fire. He had an odd system of playing music: he'd drop the needle down part-way through the record, always exactly where he wanted, and play only that part of the song. He had a fantastic memory."

Jim Cox said Wilf Ray was the best operator he ever saw.

Wilf later became involved in religious broadcasting, is now head of a thriving real estate firm in the Fraser Valley. His daughters are partners. ∎

Bill Fox and Hal Davis out front of the first CKNW newscar, 1958.

One of the most well-known sounds in western Canada is the three-tone introduction to CKNW newscasts. It sprang from the fertile mind of production whiz Dick Abbott. "In the mid-to-late-50s the openings to the newscasts seemed as long as the newscasts themselves. Hal Davis decided to do something about it. He asked me to give it some thought, with a suggestion it be 'something like NBC.' I recorded on disc the

station. He did some news, some fill-in, a bit of work on Argos' games, color on wrestling and boxing from Maple Leaf Gardens . . . but we never made quite enough money. Al explained he *had* to look for a better-paying job. The contract said you couldn't do that. They fired him on the spot. In fairness to Foster, he gave his manager a free hand in decisions like that. Al had no bus fare, and we had two cans of soup at home.

"We moved back to Port Arthur, and Al got a job at CFPA. He covered sports, news, everything." It was at CFPA Al began to develop his famous style. By 1955 the Davidson family had moved to Winnipeg, and Al was covering news for CKY. But now he was itching to get into sports.

Al struck up a friendship at CKY with salesman Clay Hawkins, who became a kind of mentor to Al. "Clay went to CKNW to be their national sales manager." Pat recollects, "and he wanted Al to come to the coast, too. But then Clay died just about the time we moved to Vancouver.

"Al started in news at NW, in 1958, then he began helping Jim Cox with color on football, some lacrosse, WHL . . . He wanted to do play-by-play, but Bill Hughes had said, 'As long as I'm manager, you'll never do play-by-play.'

"But when Al re-created a boxing broadcast, Bill Hughes complimented him, gave him a box of cigars, etc., etc. I never understood that."

Al Davidson's reading style — it would become even more well-known later when he started in sports — was unique. "I'd never heard that *style* of delivery before," Warren Barker said. "I was puzzled by it. He used the pause far more dramatically than anyone else; he'd make a fender-bender sound like the explosion of the Hindenberg. His newscasts were more dramatic, more hammed up."

Al got into serious trouble a couple of years after starting at NW News, and it came about because of a conversation with another mighty mite. Phil Gaglardi, highways minister in the W.A.C. Bennett government, the famed 'flying Phil,' had been taking a lot of political flak over his work in that portfolio. Davidson got him on the phone to talk about it . . . and taped the conversation. "Twice during the conversation," says Bill Hughes, "Gaglardi asked if Al was taping, and twice Al said no." Al casually asked the ebullient highways minister if he'd ever wanted to just throw in the towel. And Gaglardi sighed and said, "Yeah, I'm thinking of quitting."

Gaglardi left for a trip to Japan . . . and Al ran the "thinking of quitting" clip. All hell broke loose, and Davidson was fired. He would later claim he was reading the news on CKLG within an hour of his sacking.

Was this the end of Al Davidson's connection with CKNW?

Stay tuned.

He drew big crowds . . .

Jack Kyle, whose unruffled, knowledgeable and friendly on-air presentations made him an NW favourite for 26 years (in two stretches of seven and 19 years), started in radio in his native Victoria by literally pushing his co-host into the studio. Jack, and Alan Pratt, who was in a wheelchair, co-hosted CJVI's Saturday Jazz Review show from 1942 to 1947. "I was a record collector," Jack recalls, "Louis Armstrong, Ella Fitzgerald, Jack Teagarden, Duke Ellington . . . all sorts of jazz. In July of 1943, I was 18, CJVI decided to hire me full time."

Then Jack was transferred to CKWX. His departure eight years later was not amicable . . . "So when Hal Davis talked to me about coming to CKNW I went right over. It was February, 1955. Jack Cullen had left, and I was brought in to replace him with a show called Sandman Serenade. Two months later Hutton came over. When Hutton arrived the morning ratings went way up. Bob put a little pencil mark on the wall every time WX got a new morning man. By the time Bob retired from his show 22 years later there were 30 marks on that wall." Kyle arrived at NW when on-the-spot "remote" broadcasts from business locations were catching on. Engineer Jack Gordon designed a totally new mobile studio, and it wasn't long before Jack virtually made it his home away from home. His breezy, amiable personality was just right for broadcasts in which he'd be seen by and meet thousands of NW listeners. Jack dubbed the studio the Crystal Palace. "They didn't like that name at the station, but other people started picking it up, and that's what they call their mobile studios to this day. I think I opened every damn supermarket, gas station and hotel in the Lower Mainland in that thing." Photos show he drew big crowds, too, sometimes extending for *blocks*. And Jack and the Crystal Palace were a PNE fixture for years. ■

electronic tone that marks every half-hour on CKNW, and with the aid of one of the first variable-speed turntables raised and lowered pitches until I had a number with which to work. Out of the whole bunch I edited together three that appealed to me; I even altered the rhythm slightly. These are the same notes, rhythm and all, you hear today before every newscast on NW, although they have since been reproduced on a synthesizer." ■

Jack Kyle came to CKNW in 1955 to replace Jack Cullen.

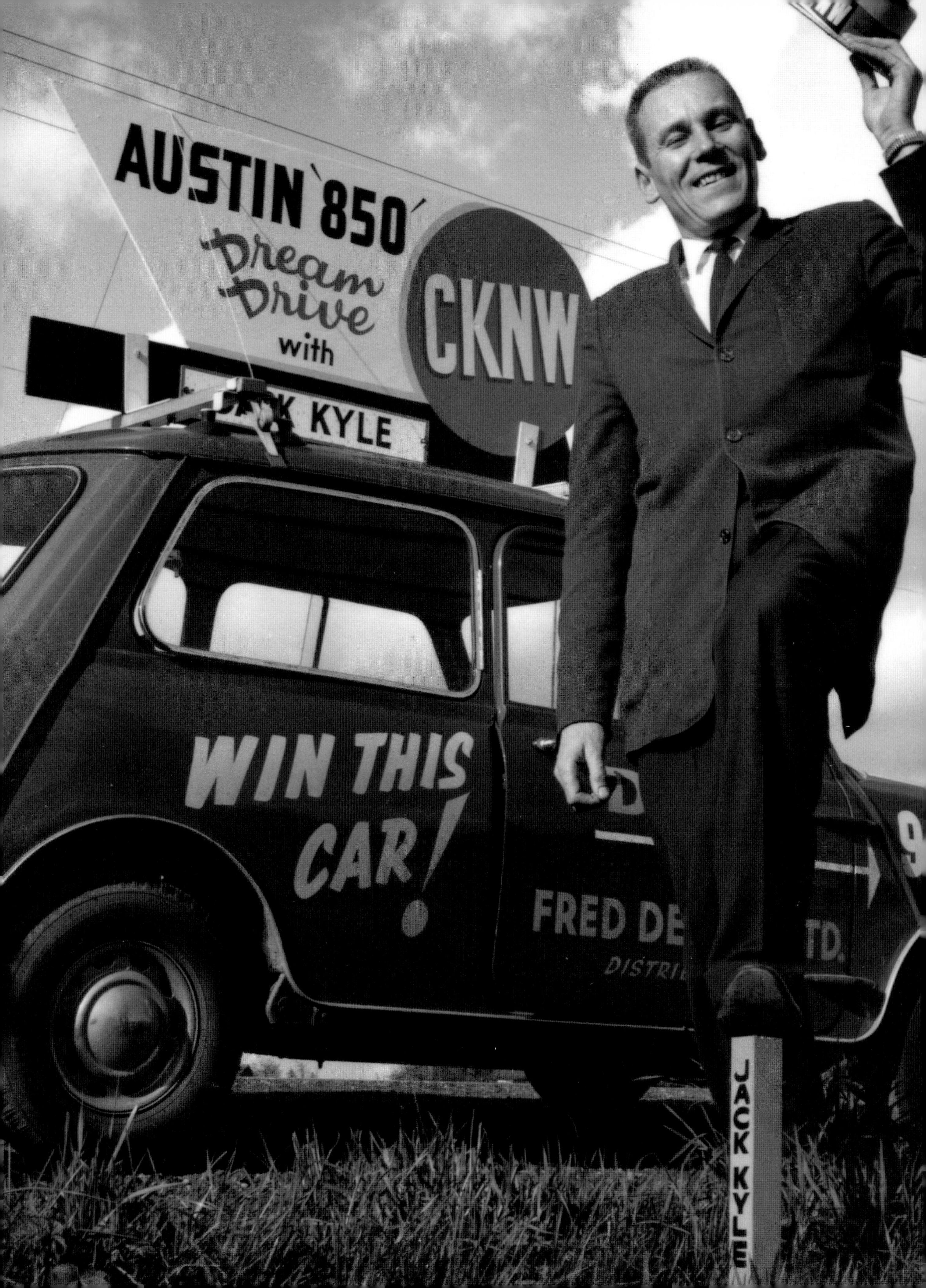

AUSTIN 850
Dream Drive
with
CKNW
WIN THIS CAR!
JACK KYLE

"You Say You Want A Revolution . . ."

CKNW STARTED THE '60S WITH A POWER BOOST TO 10,000 WATTS, evidence the station was growing in influence and coverage.

The station was there for the big (and little) news stories of the decade, would itself be involved in one of them. The W.A.C. Bennett government startled the country in 1961 by taking over the privately-owned B.C. Electric Co., a decision that would have seemed more likely to come from a socialist government. This decade saw the birth of the modern environmental movement, with the appearance in 1962 of Rachel Carson's book, The Silent Spring, and the creation at the end of the decade of Greenpeace. We got a new Canadian flag, a new bank in British Columbia, and celebrated the country's Centennial with a wonderfully successful world's fair in Montreal. Nancy Greene brought fame and glory to the province with her skiing triumphs, the Bennett Dam was completed in the interior, and something called Trudeaumania swept the nation.

Television had vaulted into a leading role in entertainment by the 1960s, but its effect was minimized at CKNW. The performance of the station was now so solid, with such an effective staff, even this disturbing new force didn't slow it down. "In 1960," says NW newsman George Garrett, "our competition fell away. You used to see five or six radio stations at news events, now it was just television . . . and us." CKNW, never slow in identifying and reacting to new trends, would eventually join in a partnership of sorts with the local outlet of a new television network, CTV, formed in 1961.

How well was NW doing? Let the Vancouver Sun's Jack Wasserman tell the story, from his column for Sept. 11, 1965: "The owners of CKNW, the 'top dog,' recently turned down a reported $5 million for their holdings, which include a station in Winnipeg. Informed radio men insist NW nets more than half a million a year and is the third most lucrative station in Canada."

Hurricane Frieda smashed into coastal B.C. in October of 1962 . . . and actually did NW good! It was the only coastal station north of Oregon to stay on the air. A team including Gerry Davies, Hal Rodd, Shervin Shragge and Jack Webster kept listeners informed of new developments.

A seemingly ordinary event that same year, 1962, was the hiring of a night-time receptionist named Adelaide "Lolly" Miller. Lolly would soon play a part at CKNW in a hurricane of quite another sort.

And, speaking of hurricanes, yet another began gathering force at CKNW in

The 1960s CKNW transition to a more contemporary sound and atmosphere was not without its awkward moments: colleague Dick Abbott laughs recalling David Hoole's complaint to Mel Cooper about the office he'd been given. It was too pristine, too sterile. Can I personalize this space, David asked Cooper. Sure, sure, Cooper said. Not long after, Mel hurried up to Dick, his eyes bulging in alarm. "Dick! Dick! Have you seen what David has done??!!" The "personalized" office was a blaze of psychedelic color, with a startling mauve carpet on the floor, on which squatted a massive, gleaming, ebony-black desk. "CKNW," says Dick Abbott, "was regimented at the time. David Hoole loosened me up. He loosened us all up." ■

Bobby Hughes was at NW "from 1960 to 1963 1/2," and again from the end of 1967 to 1970, in the copy department. Bob's been Jack Cullen's best friend for more than 50 years. They were both students at King Edward, but didn't actually become friends at school; it happened at Murray's Record Store. "I was in there one day boosting records," Bob says, "and I heard this tap on the glass. It was Cullen. He'd seen me. I thought I was in trouble, but no, he just wanted to tell me 'That's not the way to do it,' and he showed me his system: shoving them down inside your underwear shorts. We started working together after that. We were 16, 17, somewhere in there."

1963: Al Davidson was appointed sports director. Hurricane Frieda lasted one night. Hurricane Al would be around a lot longer.

Flashing hotly across the radio waves at this same time was a man who changed the nature of broadcasting in B.C., Pat Burns. His "Hot Line" show at CJOR, debuting May 13, 1963, had such a convulsive effect it's startling to look back and realize he came and went in just over one year!

Burns' corrosive and angry show was pulling down such high ratings CKNW began to pursue him — literally doubling its offer every time it talked to him — more to remove him as a disruptive force than for any keen desire to have him at CKNW. Fighting toe-to-toe with Burns was NW's own Jack Webster, back in the fold and given his own talk-show studio in the Hotel Georgia.

While the station agonized over whether to play the songs of a new British group called the Beatles, it had no difficulty deciding to air the funny and often bizarre telephone calls of a new staffer named Rene Castellani. Castellani, billed as the Dizzy Dialer, pretended to be someone else and would phone unsuspecting people with outrageous requests or questions — like the time he called a pet shop owner and asked if he was doing the right thing in cleaning his pet budgie with a pencil eraser. The Dizzy Dialer was hugely popular. But Castellani had a dark side. It would lead first to adultery (with Lolly Miller playing the real-life role of "the other woman"), and then to murder. The death by poisoning of Esther Castellani and the ensuing murder trial was the hottest news event of its kind in B.C. in the mid-60s, an uncomfortable and frustrating time for CKNW.

The murder and the trial that followed cast a pall over a period that should have been upbeat and positive: the station's power had been boosted to 50,000 watts in 1965; a clever and hugely energetic new staffer named John Plul had come aboard; and Western Broadcast Sales had been formed to create and enhance new sales opportunities for the station. In December CKNW became part of a public company for the first time as Western Broadcasting Co. Ltd. was started.

Rod Gunn, who would come to and go from CKNW several times over the years, and eventually become its president and general manager, arrived for the first time in 1965, the same year John Plul was moved over to the job he was born to do: director of promotion. Pioneer NW broadcaster Jim Cox moved over to national sales at Western Broadcast Sales.

The station was back on track now, and looking ahead: plans were made to move to a bigger location from the famous 227 Columbia building. Jack Gordon, whose acumen in keeping NW on the air in 1962 during Hurricane Frieda was still a fresh memory, was given the task of designing the new layout. He had a lot to work with: a deal with Canada Safeway, which was vacating its big store at 8th and McBride in New Westminster, gave NW a space judged more than sufficient to accommodate a growing staff. (It proved difficult to disguise the original use of the building, prompting the irreverent Bob Hutton to crack:

Al Davidson, here at Empire Stadium, became sports director.

"They spent thousands of dollars to make that Safeway store look like a Super-Valu.")

"I'm not going to be beaten by these guys . . ."

Lloyd Bray came to Vancouver from New Zealand in November, 1948 on the *Wairuna,* working his passage over as a "peggy, the lowest form of life on a ship. A peggy served food to the firemen and the rest of the crew."

While selling cars at Vancouver Motors Lloyd decided to get into radio sales. "I wanted to work for CKNW. No other station. The NW rep, Peter Kosick, visited frequently. The station tended to its accounts. NW's sales manager at the time was John Donaldson, a big man with a big ego, and a high IQ. I was subjected to abuse by Donaldson on the phone. This was his technique. 'What gives you the right to come in here and just . . .' and so on.

"Well, I monitored other stations, noted accounts NW *didn't* have. I made up a list, then when I finally got to see Donaldson, I said I don't *need* CKNW. I showed him my list of 'accounts.'

"Well, I started. One of my first accounts was BowMac, Bowell MacLean. Jim Pattison was the general manager, very young, very good. At one point, Pattison phoned Donaldson to complain about my youth and inexperience."

Time passed and then sales for Lloyd started slipping. Adding to his concerns: he had just been married. "I went down to Los Angeles and Las Vegas on a trip with my new bride, and while I was down there I considered my position at the station. I said to myself, 'I'm not going to be beaten by these guys. I'm going to make it." When I came back I began a morning run, a 12-block run, this in the days before it was fashionable, then I came back and took an ice-cold shower, so cold it nearly stopped my heart.

"I'd hit the road at 7 a.m. and start selling. At night I'd lock myself into my den at home and sit writing out innovative sales presentations.

"It started working. Sales started going up again, then I sold a big co-op account, Rootes Motor Cars, and that impressed John Donaldson. Then I got a call from David Catton and Bill Bellman at CHQM. 'We want you to be QM's sales manager.' Well, we had an agreement at NW that if we got a job offer from elsewhere, we were obliged to mention it. I told John Donaldson, 'I've got to be honest with you, I've had this job offer from CHQM.'

"Not long after, someone mentioned he had seen John Donaldson talking with the QM people — and then the announcement was made John Donaldson was the new man at CHQM!

"At that moment CKNW offered me the job Donaldson had held: retail sales manager." In later years, Lloyd did very well in the stock market, made enough to get himself a car dealership. That's Middlegate Honda on Kingsway.

"He was a listener . . ."

What the Griffiths-Murphy-Owen triumvirate purchased in 1956 was the International Broadcasting Co. Ltd., doing business as CKNW.

By the beginning of the '60s, three years later, NW had paid for itself. The purchase price was about $850,000. "It was a hell of a deal," former NW comptroller Erm Fiorillo reflects, still shaking his head in astonishment. "The station was number one

Jack Cullen doing the Columbia Dodge Show in 1963.

Today, at a vigorous 70, Bob Hughes, whose career includes many years as a club singer in Vancouver and elsewhere, works as an advertising model, does some commercial work . . . and still gets together with old pal Jack Cullen. ∎

An annual Orphans' Fund tradition is the Herring Sale. "Reg Banfield and Richie Nelson of Nelson Bros. Fisheries," says Erm Fiorillo, "came to NW and talked to Bill Hughes. The boat would go out, catch herring, they'd sell it on the dock, 50 cents a bucket. People were lining up to buy the herring; if they didn't have a bucket, they'd use something else. I've seen shoe boxes used, one woman used her upturned umbrella. The B.C. Pen sent a vehicle, and they were buying truck loads of herring."

Jack Kyle recalls selling herring for the Fund from the boats, with hands freezing, "and there was Frank Griffiths, working right alongside us." The first year five tons of herring were sold, now it's more than 100. And none of this costs the Orphans' Fund anything. All services and goods are donated. There are 40 fishermen involved now, and the same number of NW staff. ■

Norm Grohmann couldn't stay out of the studio long. He started at CKNW in 1961.

in the market, and there were more than $300,000 in receivables that I guess Rea forgot about. The house was already built, and nicely furnished. The new owner walked in and had it."

Contrary to traditional belief, there was no Ballard family money in CKNW. All of the capital put in by Inglewood Investments (co-purchasers with Muro Investments) was Frank Griffiths'. Shares in Muro were split evenly between Walter S. Owen, Q.C., and William Murphy, Q.C.

Was there a change with Bill Rea's departure? Jim Cox: "Yeah. It became a hell of a lot better place to work." Bill Hughes: "Bill Rea had become an anachronism. After he left, the station became less of a seat-of-your-pants operation." Erm Fiorillo: "I couldn't help but be struck by the startling contrast between Frank and the previous owner. Here we were, once working with a bombastic, outgoing, eccentric, great showman . . . and now here was a seemingly very shy, very quiet, reserved and totally unassuming individual with no broadcasting experience whatsoever. Frank was very nervous when he talked to staff gatherings; his hands would shake. He needed Bill Hughes as his rock.

"It didn't take long to discover that Frank was not about to make any staff changes. He showed from the very first day he took over that he knew what buying and operating a business was all about, even though that business was completely foreign to him. He knew that if he was going to learn about broadcasting, and how to operate a highly profitable number one station in the market, he was going to learn it from the staff that had made it so. He was a listener. I think what impressed most of the staff was Frank's way of inducing us to talk to him, so that he could listen and learn. In less than three months he was asking questions that made it obvious he had learned very well.

"You got the feeling he had no intention of changing the structure or foundation of the station, that he was going to give Bill Hughes free rein to make decisions, but you were never without the feeling he was in charge.

"Griffiths not only continued the basic benefit policies Bill Rea had set up for the staff, he insisted management upgrade the profit-sharing plan, the pension plan, and all the other benefits already in place. He wasn't the hands-on kind of owner Bill Rea had been: he had confidence in his manager, and the department heads and their staffs . . . and he *always* knew what was going on in the operation of the station."

Erm Fiorillo believes Frank Griffith's quick understanding of programming, production, on-air personalities, the value of strong news and sports departments, CKNW's family spirit, and the station's very heavy community involvement, guided his future expansion into the broadcasting world.

"He laid the foundation for the biggest broadcasting empire in the history of Canadian radio."

"I quit to go to the Caribbean . . ."

Norm Grohmann's buddy Tony Sibbald got him into radio. "Y'know what I did last week, Grohmann?" "What?" "I auditioned at two radio stations in Vancouver." "Well," says Norman, "I thought, hey, if Tony can do it . . ." But he went east to Chilliwack and CHWK. They hired him to write copy. He was 19.

Norm, the prototypical class clown, couldn't stay out of a studio long. He debuted as a guest on Alec Moir's kids' show on CHWK, reading kids' stories. "I was Uncle Sven Svensen from Sveden. I read the stories that way. No matter what the story was, I read it as Uncle Sven." (Norm did impressions even as a kid, entertaining classmates at Haney's Maple Ridge Junior High with Walter Brennan's thoughts on the education system, or Jimmy Stewart's opinion of the teacher.)

Next came CKWX, where Norm hosted an all-night Top 40 show for a couple of years. In 1959 he went to CKLG; then, on January 1, 1961 started at CKNW.

"NW had moved Jack Kyle out of the Road Show, the 4 to 8 p.m. slot, and I went in. It was middle-of-the-road music, traffic reports, news by Carl Waiz . . . I operated, too. I was Jack Webster's first operator when he did his evening talk shows. I did the 4-8 show for four years, from 1961 to '65. Then I quit to go to the Caribbean and sit around for four months." When Norm got back to town, he visited NW and Hal Davis asked him to come back. He took over the noon to 3 p.m. show and, again, did that for four years, six days a week.

Norm had been doing voice-overs for commercials and station breaks on BCTV, and in 1971 they asked him to do the on-camera weather on their evening news. Off and on, Norm has been doing the weather on BCTV for more than 20 years. In 1972 he took his weather lore onto Frosty Forst's morning show. Naturally, these guys can't leave the weather alone — so Norm has been Andre LePuque, a dim-witted and heavily-accented hockey player; the Swami, who dispenses ancient wisdom of an alarmingly weird kind; Byron Steeldrum Banana, of the West Indies; and Cecil Stoke St. Gregory Watt, a veddy proper Englishman.

Norm has a myriad of other voices; don't be surprised if you hear a very excited Porky Pig warning you of an approaching storm.

As a boy Al Davidson had a beautiful soprano voice, once travelled south of the border into North Dakota and sang with an orchestra led by a young fellow named Lawrence Welk. His vocal training helped in the development of his famous style. "There was a *dynamism* in his style," says Pat Davidson, Al's widow. "He loved the sports he covered, except for wrestling. He really got into it. He admired the quality of Lorne Greene's voice, really admired Foster Hewitt's style — that resonance was always there. There were people he admired, not for their public image, but for their work and integrity. If he had role models, it wasn't based on a voice, but for a professional attitude. He appreciated Howard Cosell — a real showman. He created excitement in his coverage." ∎

Former CKNW general manager Ted Smith had trained as an RCAF pilot, and after leaving the air force decided to pursue a career as an airline pilot. He was to go see Air Canada in six months. "Well, in 1963 'folk music' was very big, and while waiting to talk to Air Canada I became part of a folk trio out of Winnipeg! We were called the Wayward Singers, billed as 'Canada's Peter, Paul and Mary.' I played guitar. We were having a great time, playing coffee houses, universities and special events. But we all knew we had other ambitions. We played a lot at the Fourth Dimension, a big, successful Winnipeg coffee house.

"A fellow came up, introduced himself, said he was from Radio CJOB in Winnipeg. The station did a show called Folksay, did we want to do an interview? Sure. I'd never been in a radio station

John McKitrick in the studio.

"Second is never acceptable . . ."

John McKitrick's grandfather ran a small town newspaper, and that inspired him to want to be a journalist. But he was still surprised when, at 17, he was called "out of the blue" by the manager of CJNB Radio in his native North Battleford, Saskatchewan.

"I began as a general announcer at CJNB in 1953. It was strictly rip and read. After two years there, I went to CHAB in Moose Jaw. I started as a general announcer, hosted a woman's show, did a Sunday show with sweet music and poetry. In all too short a time, they made me news director. I was too young to be a news director."

John visited Vancouver one summer, and NW's George Garrett recommended him to Hal Davis. "I came back to CHAB and George Price there says, 'So! When do your start at NW?' I was flabbergasted. He knew.

"I started at NW in the summer of 1957. I was always in the newsroom there. I tried a few shots at the beat, but I always wanted to be inside. I was there less than a year when the copy chief, Tony Antonias, came and asked me to do some commercials for Dueck, the car dealers. I did, and Dueck really liked them . . . and that led to CKWX hiring me away. I was at WX two years, then went to CJCA in Edmonton. But after a couple of years there, I felt CJCA was moving toward rock 'n' roll, and news was becoming secondary.

"One day in 1961 Hal Davis phoned me. Warren Barker was now news director. I came back and started working as the daytime 'pilot.' "

By this time, the Jim Cox/Warren Barker dream of having CKNW News set its own pace, rather than follow the lead of the newpapers, was in full flower. And the system of rewarding callers with cash for news tips was paying off big time. "People who would never have dreamed of phoning a newsroom would call us with stories."

John was assignment editor, and acting director when Barker went on holidays. There were no bad times at NW, he says. "The years Webster was on OR were rough for the station, but not in the newsroom." For the last 20 of his years at the station, John was assignment editor.

He retired in 1990 and starting teaching broadcast journalism at BCIT in the fall of 1992. "Yvonne Eamor, another CKNW alumnus, was teaching there. She called me and suggested I might want to join them." His years of experience in the newsroom, and his seasoning in the Barker system, were invaluable experience . . . and shape his lessons. "I get anywhere from a dozen to 20 students, get 'em one night a week for 12 weeks. There are three semesters. I teach them how to write, how to broadcast."

Helping the focus of his lessons, too, is the credo developed in the CKNW newsroom: "Second is never acceptable."

". . . a comfortable bedspring as an antenna . . ."

Even Mother Nature seemed inclined to help CKNW in its growth and development. On October 12, 1962 and into the early hours of October 13, the west coast of North America was battered by Hurricane Frieda. In Eric Nicol's words, the coast "took the last, angry flick of the tail of a great typhoon that swept out of the Pacific and, totally unexpected, raced up the coast from California, devastating Oregon and Washington shoreline before hitting Vancouver with howling fury a little after midnight." A huge swath of the Pacific northwest lost all electrical power, and every coastal radio station north of the California border was knocked off the air.

Every station, that is, but one. Long before Frieda arrived, NW engineer Jack Gordon had assembled a useful little box, a cabinet on wheels, containing an amplifier, a battery-operated tape-playback machine, and a plug-in for a microphone. The box sat waiting in the control room for just such an emergency. A supply of pre-recorded tapes (containing music of the day) was also on hand. The box could be plugged into the still-working telephone lines. The phone line connected this versatile little console to a standby transmitter on Lulu Island.

With no electricity available, CKNW was on the air. No one else was.

Gerry Davies brought Hurricane Frieda to Vancouver by candlelight.

New-fangled transistor radios, and battery-operated radios, and radios in cars could hear just *one* station. As it had done in 1948 for the Fraser River floods, NW became a source for coordination and information.

One of Doug Court's souvenirs is a copy of a tape made off-air by a CKNW listener, W. Levett, living at East 30th Avenue and Windsor Street in Vancouver. Mr. Levett had picked up the signal on a "Miller crystal tuner . . . with a comfortable bedspring as an antenna," and had put the broadcast onto a battery-operated tape recorder.

Gerry Davies told of roofs blowing off, and signs careening down city streets. Barns in the Fraser Valley were collapsing. Hal Rodd of NW's news staff reported most streets were impassable, the Lions Gate Bridge was blocked, there were power lines dangling over roads and some looting was going on from downtown stores.

Newsman Shervin Shragge called in with the identities of the storm's two fatalities, one of them a woman who had died when a tree fell onto her car on the Stanley Park causeway. Light planes at the airport were being blown around and smashed to pieces. Jack Webster was roving the North Shore for NW to pick up what news he could from there.

When the storm had passed, many of the people who had stayed up to listen to CKNW's reports on damage stayed with the station. Once again, in a time of emergency, its hard-working news staff, technical excellence and community-mindedness had worked to the station's benefit.

Jack Webster at the Pen

"It was nearly 10 p.m. on April 19, 1963," Jack Webster writes in his autobiography, "when Tom Hall, warden of the B.C. Pen, telephoned me at my West Vancouver home." Hall told Webster there were prisoners who wouldn't go back into their cells. "They want to speak to Prime Minister Pearson or Webster. We can't get Lester Pearson so we're calling you."

Webster alerted CKNW, picked up his tape recorder and headed for the penitentiary. He got there in 20 minutes. Warden Hall told him three inmates were holding guard Patrick Dennis as hostage, and were demanding Webster act as a go-between in negotiations with the authorities. The men and their hostage were in the prison's gymnasium shower room, there were 15 other convicts locked by guards in a tunnel

before. I met Steve French there; he was sales manager. We got talking about careers. And I said, 'Oh, folk singing's just for fun, I'm going to be an airline pilot.' We talked about a career in sales. Well, I learned some of these time salesmen were making a lot more than I ever could as a second officer on a DC-8. I went out on some sales calls and confirmed it! We decided I'd try it for three months. I was given the Yellow Pages and told not to contact any accounts the other salesman had protected.

"Within 19 months I was the top salesman." ■

connecting the gym to the main prison, and more than 200 other prisoners milling about in the main part of the prison refused to go back into their cells.

Ward said he didn't know what the inmates wanted and was not allowed to let Webster negotiate. "I can only ask you to talk to them." Webster took his tape recorder, but the warden protested. "If I do not take my tape recorder along," Webster fumed, "I ain't going. That's my insurance policy." Tape recorder in hand, and escorted by guards through the prison, Webster walked straight into the mob of prisoners still refusing to go back to their cells. "The prisoners crowded round," Webster said, "wanting to talk to me."

He'd gone to bat on behalf of convicts before, had an empathy with them, and many of them knew it. It took Webster and his guards 20 minutes to get out of that room. One of the men locked in the tunnel watched the guards carefully. Webster learned later that, if the guards had attempted to rush the tunnel, this man would have shouted a warning to the hostage-takers and they would have killed Patrick Dennis.

Dennis was trussed with copper wire and a knife was being held at his throat by inmate Gerard Caissy, 28. Caissy, whose face had been burned when a home-made gas bomb he'd tried to use in the escape attempt exploded in his face, held one end of the copper wire in his hand and kept jerking it as he screamed to Webster. The wire was cutting into Dennis' neck.

Webster interviewed the three desperate hostage-takers until the 15 minutes on his tape ran out. They wanted, for reasons detailed in his book, to be transferred to another institution. "I told them I was going upstairs to talk to the warden, after which I would telephone a broadcast over CKNW, giving their demands and the officials' answers. They could listen to it over a radio that would be brought into the washroom.

"Warden Hall agreed to relay the prisoners' demands to the commissioner of penitentiaries in Ottawa, and I went on the air via telephone to CKNW: 'I am authorized to announce that the commissioner of penitentiaries has been asked to approve the transfer to other penitentiaries of three men who are now holding a guard hostage at knife-point. I have agreed to act as personal escort to the three convicts until they are transferred later today.'"

It's impossible in the space here to describe the tension and terror of that April night. It's vividly re-created in Webster's book. The prisoners loose in the main building began a destructive riot, guards battled them with tear gas, the guards in charge of Webster retreated, the tear gas panicked the three hostage-takers who screamed out threats to kill the guard *and* Webster, and Caissy was becoming more and more irrational in his demands. Webster learned later Caissy and the other two convicts had discussed letting the guard go and holding him as a more valuable trade.

When they finally set him free to continue negotiating for their release, Webster emerged from the hell below to find an army of prison guards and RCMP officers surrounding the loose prisoners, amid news that a detachment of soldiers was on its way.

"The front office of the prison was jammed with radio, television and newspaper reporters, all hungry for information — and some of them pretty annoyed that one of their number had been on the inside."

More complicated negotiations followed, but finally, 13 exhausting hours after it had begun, it was all over. The convicts' demands had been met, and the guard and Webster were released unharmed.

Marke Raines and Jack Webster at the B.C. Penitentiary. The prisoners wanted Prime Minister Pearson or Webster. They got Webster.

Webster, exhausted, headed to CKNW, "downed a couple of quick Bloody Marys and began broadcasting the tapes I had made during the ordeal. I was on air continuously for the next two hours."

Mel Cooper still shakes his head in amazement about that day: "He went on, did it extemporaneously, every quote, every incident, color, the drama . . . it was an incredible performance."

"Every radio was tuned to Burns . . ."

In early 1964 broadcaster Pat Burns was making waves. CJOR was pulling in thousands of new listeners with a stable of talk-show hosts. Burns was the undoubted star. His Hotline show on CJOR was getting CKNW right where it hurts: in the ratings.

"If you can't beat 'em, buy 'em,' program director Hal Davis said, and got together with Burns. He offered him $900 a week to come to CKNW. That was exactly twice what he was earning at OR. Burns said no, and told Davis he had a certain loyalty to CJOR. He was staying.

In March, with Burns showing no signs of slowing down, NW manager Bill Hughes invited him to a room at the Royal Towers Hotel in New Westminster, and upped the ante. He told Burns CKNW would give him $1,800 a week, plus a car. This was double the previous offer, with a car as a perk. Burns told Hughes he didn't want to work in New Westminster, so far from his home. Hughes said a studio would be built for him in the Hotel Georgia.

their mayonnaise. "But there's a lot more to discover," thought Tony. And that led to the line There's a Whole Lot More to Discover in the Flavorful World of Kraft . . . the line followed by another of those insidious little tunes that stick in your head and rattle around all day: Kraft is Quality, Kraft is Quality, Nothing Says Quality Quite Like Kraft. Even read aloud as prose, you can hear a catchy beat. ∎

Every radio in town was tuned to Pat Burns.

When engineer Don Kalmakoff started at NW they were at 227 Columbia, but planning a move to a bigger location at 825 McBride. "Jack Gordon called me, and said 'What's the state of your dissatisfaction?' They were looking for someone to ramrod this move. They asked 'How'd you like to build a radio station?' We went down and looked at the place. It had been stripped bare, looked like an airplane hangar. It was exciting. Most of the stuff we put in was designed by Jack Gordon; he's one of those genius types, did all sorts of innovative things. CFRB in Toronto was installing stuff in 1992 we put in in 1967. A lot of the equipment for what we wanted to do wasn't available, so we

Burns told Hughes he would think about it and get back to him. The next day he telephoned, again cited his loyalty to CJOR, and told Hughes OR had increased his salary, anyway. The answer, again, was no.

Day by day Burns was gaining more and more audience for CJOR. Marke Raines, who would leave NW to go to OR, remembers: "Every radio in town was tuned to Pat Burns. I took in my dry cleaning, they were listening to Pat Burns. I went to the cop shop, Pat Burns. I had a guy working on the dry-wall at my house, with the NW News Cruiser sitting out front, and *he's* listening to Pat Burns."

Something had to be done.

There was a third CKNW meeting, and at this one the heavy artillery was brought in. Burns was invited to a meeting in Frank Griffiths' office. With Griffiths were Bill Hughes and Hal Davis.

Burns was now offered $3,600 a week — again twice what he had been offered in his last conversation, and eight times what he had been making two months earlier. "Well, y'know," Burns said years later, "there comes a time when loyalty becomes stupidity. This was a very attractive offer."

Burns thought about it intensely, then went to see CJOR owner Marie Chandler. She was original owner George Chandler's widow. Burns told her what CKNW was willing to pay him. Mrs. Chandler, an emotional woman prone to tears, countered with an astonishing offer: if Burns would stay with CJOR, she would give him a 23 per cent share of the station!

"I opted for that," Burns said.

There was, he later learned from a lawyer/friend acting for him, a snag in the offer: she might not have the 23 per cent to give him.

Mrs. Chandler kept insisting Burns would get the equity, but the status remained quo. In August of 1965 Pat returned from a holiday in Alabama, and met with Mrs. Chandler and board member Allan Williams, a lawyer, expecting to talk about the new contract. Instead, Marie Chandler handed him a letter. It read, "Your services are no longer required by CJOR."

Burns could get no explanation for his dismissal. In a way it could never have predicted, CKNW's "Pat Burns problem" had come to an end.

There's a postscript: Burns' departure from Vancouver to Montreal talk-radio after the above-described events was as sensational as anything he accomplished on air. The Queen Elizabeth Theatre was packed with his fans for his farewell, with thousands more outside.

The rent for the QE had been paid for by CKNW! "We were so happy to get him out of town," Hal Davis remembered.

"Oh, oh, the Oatmeal Savage."

In 1963, CKNW's Jack Webster was "dragged kicking and screaming," as he put it, into the talk-show business. "I had the usual journalistic attitude and sneered at the first Talk Radio programs."

Then Pat Burns came along. Burns had been doing news until CJOR's Peter Kosick groomed him to be a talk-show host. Overnight, Webster says, this "gruff-voiced, well-informed, first-class demagogue" exploded onto the Vancouver radio scene. Alarmingly, his show began to eat into NW's ratings.

A worried NW brought in radio consultant George Davies from Winnipeg. "Davies was tremendously aggressive, a hard-nosed type," says Mel Cooper. "He listened to us, and he listened to the opposition. He said, 'There's only one guy who can beat Burns, and he's right in your building: Jack Webster.'" It took a lot of persuading to get Webster to do a talk show. He hated the idea!

Webster was earning good money for the time: $1,500 a month. NW doubled it, and Bill Hughes promised that as his audience grew so would his income.

"We had just two lines in the Georgia Hotel studios," says Webster, "but it was a great place . . . There was room service, you got to sit at a table at coffee break, Sun columnist Jack Wasserman would drop by, so would Simma Holt and all kinds of passersby. That hotel was a comfortable place to do a show. I always vaguely *resented* working in the basement of the Grosvenor.

"'Y' know, in those days people looked down their noses at talk shows."

In a little over a year Burns was gone, Webster's ratings were great, and sponsors were piling on. Everything was going swimmingly.

Until 1972.

Webster's lawyer, Jim Boughton, Q.C., phoned Bill Hughes and politely informed him of his client's salary request for the next season. It was in six figures. Hughes went ballistic, began screaming at Boughton on the phone. He told the lawyer they'd talk again, and rang off.

Webster, who'd been sitting in Boughton's office, hearing only his lawyer's end of the conversation, was depressed. It looked like the big raise he'd been hoping for wasn't going to happen. "Hughes always had the capacity to upset me," he writes in his autobiography, "usually by complaining: 'Oh, Jack, did you have to do that program on such and such?' He always did it on the day before I went on holidays so I'd have a miserable vacation worrying about his next complaint."

Hughes showed up at Webster's studio that night, five minutes before Jack was due to go on. He was enraged. "How dare you have your lawyer phone me and ask for that incredible amount of money?" Webster took a deep breath. "Bill, do you want me to go on the air tonight at half-past six or do you not want me to go on the air?" Telling him he had to go on, Hughes turned and left. "I used to annoy him," Webster said in a 1992 interview, "irk him."

Webster phoned his lawyer, told him what had happened. Boughton told him to sit tight. He called back a few minutes later: he and Webster were to meet with CJOR owner Jimmy Pattison at eight that same evening in the William Tell Restaurant. Pattison told Webster he was ready to cut a deal with him on the spot. Webster said he wanted $110,000 for a nine to noon program, Pattison countered with half-past eight to noon. "I want eight weeks holidays then, too," Webster said. Pattison replied, "You got it."

Webster told the author Pattison suggested the 8:30 start time because he wanted Webster to "go up against Hughes," whose CKNW Roving Mike show started at 8:45.

"My contract with CKNW," Webster continues, "required me to give thirty days' notice. The following day I went to the Bentall Centre and saw Hughes. He could hear me greeting the secretaries and bellowed from his office, 'Oh, oh. Here comes the Oatmeal Savage.' I smiled obsequiously as I entered his office and gently placed my resignation on his desk. He stared at it as I turned and walked out."

customized: The consoles were customized, the switching . . . there were no computers . . . we put in miles of wiring and lots and lots of relays.

"CKNW gave us engineering carte blanche — and autonomy. The production people would say, 'This is what we need,' and we'd build it. And Jack Gordon's style was 'The simpler you can make the operation, the better.' Now, with digital, it's technically easier to do a lot of this stuff.

"My own on-air experience was useful: I designed the newsroom in the McBride building; it had 10 times the space of the old one at 227.

"We really should have had another six months. An hour before the switchover to the new building we were still wiring the main controls." ∎

"Inventory"

Hal Davis remembers standing beside Bill Rea in the early days, as Rea watched his staff leaving after a day's work. Rea turned to him and said, "Hal, there goes my inventory." Acquiring, and even more important, keeping good "inventory," says Hal, was the secret of success through Rea's tenure. That skill was honed by successive management teams, encouraged by Frank Griffiths after he gained control of the station.

Good people stayed, and became fiercely loyal in an industry in which staffers commonly change jobs as often as they change shirts. People like Tony Antonias, Hal Davis, Bill Hughes, Erm Fiorillo, Jim Cox, Dick Abbott, John McKitrick, Pat McPherson, Shirley Drouin, Warren Barker . . . all made careers of 20 years or more at CKNW. The challenges and pleasures of working with other consummate professionals was part of the reason they stayed; another was the way they were treated.

From the beginning, Rea set aside a portion of the profits of the station, to be divided quarterly among the staff as bonuses. There was a fund pool for the executives, another for the rest of the staff. The biggest bonus came just before Christmas. (That system continued until the early '90s, and only the recession killed it.)

Hal Davis: "CKNW employees were the first in the industry to have company-supported health insurance. That was a novelty in the late '40s. Retired broadcast veterans are enjoying the benefits of a pension plan pioneered for broadcasters by CKNW in the early '50s. During those same years the forerunner of the COLA increases standard in union contracts today came into being at NW: everyone got an automatic $5 monthly increase every quarter to help them keep up with the increasing cost of living. Under Frank Griffiths profit-sharing continued. With the considerable growth of the station, it was not an inconsiderable amount."

Erm Fiorillo: "Bill Rea was years ahead of his time regarding staff relationships. He firmly believed that those who helped him become successful should share in that success. He made sure there were other benefits as well: insurance plans, health care, pension plans, even a grievance committee to handle staff complaints . . . and they could actually make decisions, and he didn't get involved. You know, in most pension plans a company will match an employee's contribution or even better it. Back then, when an employee left a company before his retirement the money the company had contributed on his behalf was returned to the company coffers. Rea changed that: when an employee left CKNW the money the station had contributed on his behalf *was redistributed among the rest of the employees in the pension plan.* What that meant was, when Bill sold the station he left the employees a real legacy: all the money the company had contributed on his behalf to his pension! And he, of course, was the largest contributor to the plan. So all that money was redistributed into the pensions of all the other participating employees."

"What about this kid at OR?"

John Ashbridge started "hanging around" CJVI in Victoria when he was 12, and by age 13 was unofficially (translation: the station brass didn't know) operating some of VI's shows.

John's rich and distinctive baritone has been an NW tradition for 30 years now, but you also hear it announcing penalties and lineup changes at games of the Vancouver Canucks.

"Ash" was born in Hastings, Sussex in England but left before the accent could

When Jack Cullen (left) started his on-air career, he had about 10,000 "items" (singles, LPs, transcriptions, etc.). Today, he has about 350,000. "I'd take all of this stuff home, and listen to it, learn about it. "

Since 1948, when he'd done his first interview (with singer Nellie Lutcher), Jack had amassed more than 400 talks with top recording stars, and they all came away staggered at his knowledge of their careers. In some cases he remembered their pasts better than they did! There was a famous instance in April, 1964 when Nat 'King' Cole vehemently denied on Jack's show that he'd ever made a recording before 1939. "Yes, you did," Jack insisted, and reached back into his bulging shelves, "and here's one." It was a 1936 Decca disc called Plenty of Money and You. Cole was flabbergasted, and hearing that early record brought tears to his eyes. ∎

Gary Bannerman's work at The Province was what first brought him to the notice of CKNW. Gary tells a story about his assignment to Victoria by that paper: "I got to the legislature, and befriended W.A.C. Bennett. He was originally from New Brunswick, as was I, still had cousins and such there, and I knew a lot of people he knew. Other reporters would see me deep in conversation with Bennett and assume he was the 'high source' cited in certain Province stories. In truth, he was asking me things like, 'Did you know Harry so-and-so in Alma?' At the end of this casual chatter, I'd ask a relevant question on some issue of the day, and he'd say, 'Splendid lunch, young man,' smile, stand up and leave." ∎

take: his family came to B.C. when he was five. "I got into Grade 1 at five by cheating on my birth certificate, so the little one-room school at Red Pass Junction could stay open.

"We moved a lot, tended to live around a Victoria-Nanaimo axis. After my CJVI 'experience' I got a part-time job at CFAX when I was in junior high, about age 14. I was mostly interested in production then; I started operating at CFAX, then announcing. I was at CFAX until the day I got out of school, then talked to Gerry Gawne at CJOR. I auditioned, and started at OR in late June of 1964.

"Along about the middle of 1965 NW needed a summer replacement newsman. I'd been doing some news from OR's McLennan Motors Mobile Newsroom. It was either Carl Waiz or Bruce Hood at NW who heard me, and said 'What about this kid at OR?'

"Hal Davis called me. 'Interested?' 'Oh, yes,' I said. So he hauled me out for an interview and an audition. Warren Barker had me write some copy.

"I started at CKNW 10th of May, 1965. I did announcing, operating, news . . . everything. I've probably done every shift. I co-hosted with Webster on Fiesta when Wally Garrett was away, I filled in for Cullen, for Grohmann, for Frosty . . . I couldn't get enough of it. Then the newsroom made a sickening discovery: one of their news cruiser drivers — me — was only 19. That presented real fleet insurance problems. So I came inside.

"I'd been here for about a year, then went to Hal, told him I'd really feel better concentrating on news. He said 'Leave it with me.' Before long I wound up doing mainly news.

"By the way, one of the other guys in the newsroom when I started was Maury Gwynne. His wife had been my cubmaster in Victoria!"

"This is W! Bennett guilty!"

If the amount of information coming into the CKNW newsroom was astonishing, its sources were sometimes unorthodox. "Every so often," alumnus Cameron Bell says, "we'd get mysterious phone calls. I'd answer, 'News,' and a voice might say, 'Tell Warren that R says Fred So-and-so is guilty.' I'd thank him, hang up, and say to Warren, 'That was R; he says Fred So-and-so is guilty.' Warren would thank me, slap a piece of paper into a typewriter and start doing the story.

"There was a famous case in 1965 in which a civil servant named George Jones was suing Premier W.A.C. Bennett for slander. The decision in the case was due to be handed down, and we were alert for it. The phone rings. I answer. A guy says, 'This is W! Tell Warren 'Bennett guilty'.' I hang up and say to Warren, 'That was W. He says 'Bennett guilty'.'

"Warren leaped up from his chair, jumped onto the table, reached behind on a shelf and brought out a sheaf of stories on the Bennett-Jones case. He jumped back down, put a piece of paper into the typewriter and banged out a one-sentence lead. One sentence. He read that on the air followed by the first line from each of the earlier stories. We had the news out long before anyone, and it had all the details.

"Who were R and W? I have no idea."

Cameron, who today produces CBC-TV's Front Page Challenge, reflects further on the pace in Barker's newsroom: "We answered the phone with the word, 'News.' It was one syllable. 'CKNW' was six syllables and that would have taken far too long to say."

Rene Castellani, here in his role as a visiting Maharajah, was a consummate actor.

Sentenced to hang Feb. 21, 1967

Rene Castellani had been at CKNW less than two years when he was told to resign, but his brief tenure there led to the most convulsive and traumatic period the station had ever experienced.

It began with Castellani starring in a popular and genuinely funny feature called The Dizzy Dialer, and ended in a charge of murder.

Hal Davis recalls how it all started. "CKLG had a promotion linked to the TV show, The Millionaire. We needed something to counteract it. So Bill Hughes and I came up with the Maharajah idea. The idea was this Indian prince was coming to *buy* B.C. We chose this fellow named Rene Castellani to be the character. He'd been running a night club, and performing there."

Mel Cooper: "We dressed Rene up like an Indian prince and registered him at the Bayshore as a visiting maharajah — fancy costumes, limousines, bodyguards, dancing girls. We'd send him to the Cave with his retinue, and he'd pick up tabs for every table around him. Everyone in town began talking about him. We had a star on our hands. Rene was a consummate actor."

His acting ability was needed on Dizzy Dialer, in which Castellani, pretending to be someone else, telephoned people and — in a perfectly deadpan style — made outrageous requests. He once talked by phone to a staff member at Harrison Hot

Joe Chesney happened to be looking out the window one day and saw Bill Rea emerge from his car, angrily slam the door shut and begin stomping toward the station. Chesney didn't know what was up, but he knew it was bad, so he crawled under a desk. Rea stormed in and fired everybody. Only the unseen Joe was spared. Of course, everyone was hired back the next morning, but it made for a turbulent workday. ∎

Rene Castellani was arrested for murder.

Dick Abbott has hundreds of memories of CKNW and its people. Some are funny, like the time Bill Rea decided NW's announcers were too pale, and installed a sunlamp in the studio. "Poor Wally Garrett was bald, and he got sunstroke." Some are plain silly, like the time Rea stared in innocent bafflement as his staff fell off their chairs laughing when he dedicated a record, live on air, to one Dick Ferkin "from Ruth,

Springs Hotel, explained he had just been entertaining a convention there, with trained fleas, and had left one of the fleas behind. The flea, he explained to the unsuspecting lady, would have taken refuge in the hotel's carpet. Following his instructions, she put the phone down near the carpet while he called out the flea's name: "Here, Pooky, Pooky." The Dizzy Dialer was a genuinely funny item, and Castellani handled it well. Even now, listening to tapes of his shows 30 years later, you may find yourself laughing out loud over his solemn silliness.

Frank Iaci, who had been his oldest friend and best man at his wedding, said Rene could "fix anything, *do* anything, act, play piano. He was outgoing, loveable, never had an enemy in the world." Newsman Mauri Hesketh remembers Castellani as "talented, a good writer, a funny man . . . a warm individual." On the other hand, Jack Kyle, who often bumped into Castellani on the ferries between the mainland and Vancouver Island, thought he was "weird," "crazy," recalls Castellani talking about getting a seer to help him find "buried treasure" in a Nanaimo hotel he had co-managed, and which had burned down under mysterious circumstances.

In January of 1965 NW manager Bill Hughes heard rumors of a romantic liaison between Castellani and Adelaide "Lolly" Miller, NW's night-time receptionist. Lolly, a widow, had been at the station since 1962, became a widow while at NW when her husband Don drowned. The newspapers later would mention often that Lolly was young (22) and attractive. Rene was in his late 30s. (CKNW alumnus Bobby Hughes went out with Lolly a few times himself. "She was pretty, but she had a broken nose. I remember when she got the insurance money after Don drowned, it was $25,000, I suggested to her she use some of the money to get her nose fixed, but she didn't.")

Disturbing to Hughes and others was that Castellani was married, with a 12-year-old daughter. He seemed careless of propriety: his station vehicle, emblazoned with the CKNW logo, was often seen parked outside Lolly's house. Challenged by Hughes, and questioned by Erm Fiorillo, Rene denied being involved with Lolly Miller. That was a bald-faced lie.

Castellani's wife Esther was a plump and jolly woman, but trial testimony later would indicate relations between her and Rene began to cool in 1964. She had, she told a friend, discovered a letter in Rene's pocket from a woman named "Lolly."

Hughes, determined to keep CKNW free from scandal, ordered the resignations of Castellani and Mrs. Miller. Lolly resigned May 5, 1965. But Rene stayed. When Hughes asked why, the staff told him Rene's wife was quite ill — it seemed unkind to drop him just then. As soon as she recovers, Hughes said, let him go.

Far from recovering, Esther Castellani became even more seriously ill, and on May 2 was admitted to Vancouver General Hospital. Her weakened condition, numbness, and other symptoms baffled the doctors. They suspected a toxicological cause, but more than 60 tests detected nothing.

Ten days after Esther's admission to hospital, Rene Castellani began his most well-known promotional stunt: he climbed to the top of the gigantic 20-metre-tall Bowell Maclean sign at 1174 West Broadway, famous at the time as the world's tallest free-standing sign. He climbed into a station wagon perched atop a scaffolding beside the sign, and vowed to stay there until every car in the Bow Mac lot was sold.

"I begged him to scrap the promotion," Mel Cooper said, "to spend his time with Esther. Rene said we had an obligation to the sponsor and that the show had to go on. I thought it was terribly callous . . ."

While he was up there, Rene broadcast regular reports. Passersby could see a little gag clothesline strung from the station wagon to the sign, with a pair of Rene's shorts swaying on the line.

Esther's condition was worsening. She lost all feeling in her limbs, was too weak to move, found it agony to speak. One of her doctors suggested to the family she might respond to food they brought in, rather than hospital fare. Rene began bringing in food, including milkshakes. The milkshakes would loom large in news coverage of the trial. NW's all-night man, Gerry Davies, recollects Rene would go to the all-night Knight & Day Restaurant on West Broadway and get hamburgers and chocolate shakes. "Esther loved chocolate milkshakes."

Nine days after he went up the tower, Rene came down. Later, at the trial, Gerry Davies would testify that on more than one occasion when he phoned Castellani up on the sign there had been no answer. Rene was to do regular reports, but sometimes he'd call Gerry and ask to skip a report. "The detectives interviewed everyone," Gerry recalls, "it was in Mel Cooper's office, and they asked me if Rene had done all the cut-ins. I had to tell them no. He'd missed maybe half a dozen in the week he was up there."

Castellani was visiting Esther in her room at Vancouver General. He visited during the day as well. (A nurse testified that he never came in if Esther's mother was visiting, but lingered at a distance until she left.)

While Esther lay in her hospital bed, Rene and Lolly applied for a mortgage. Lolly signed the application "Mrs. Adelaide Castellani." It was later learned Castellani and his daughter were living in Lolly's house.

On July 11, 1965 while being turned in her bed, Esther Castellani died. She was 40.

Mel Cooper: "The night his wife died, I went over to Rene's house, just to be with him and give him my sympathy. I walked in, and he had his feet up on the chesterfield, laughing at some comic on the Ed Sullivan show."

Two days after Esther was buried, Rene, with Lolly and her little boy, left for Disneyland. Rene talked to Wally Garrett before he left, asked him to arrange reservations at an Anaheim motel owned by Wally's brother, Marshall. They drove down in a borrowed CKNW-marked vehicle.

Esther Castellani's death might have remained an enigma but for her family physician, Barney Moscovitch. Hal Davis: "The possibility Esther was ingesting poison had never occurred to Dr. Moscovitch, or the consultants on the case. Barney attended her funeral, and when he got home from the ceremony he sat down and wrote on a piece of foolscap everything he knew about her case. As he looked at the list of symptoms they pointed to arsenic poisoning. He called the Vancouver City coroner, Glen MacDonald, and suggested she be exhumed and that further tests be done. When he said he

and Ron and the whole Ferkin family." Some memories are bizarre: on a blisteringly hot day Dick set up a fan to blow across blocks of ice at Jack Webster, doing his show in his underwear.

And some are dramatic, like an unexpected street encounter with ex-CKNW staffer Rene Castellani, who'd just finished a prison sentence for the poisoning murder of his wife. Castellani invited Dick to join him for a coffee. Said Dick, "Can I pour?" ∎

Lolly Miller, girlfriend of Rene Castellani.

wanted tissue tested for arsenic poisoning, MacDonald said, 'Isn't that a bit exotic?' Use of arsenic had been out of favor for half a century.

"Permission to exhume the body now had to be obtained from none other than Rene Castellani! He at first refused, but Bill Hughes convinced him to give permission, because withholding it might be a reason for suspicion." Jack Webster: "When Castellani started feeling the heat, he came to me for advice. I got him his first lawyer."

The tests showed there was more than enough arsenic in Esther Castellani's body to kill her. Coroner MacDonald ordered further tests made. These tests showed the arsenic had been administered to Esther over at least six months, perhaps as much as 13 months or more. The best indicator of the level and length of the arsenic intake: the dead woman's hair. Human hair grows about half-a-centimetre a month. Examining Esther's hair, it was possible not only to make good estimations of when the poisoning began, but even week-to-week measurements of the level of ingestion. The tests showed the level of arsenic intake had increased markedly during the time Esther Castellani had been in hospital.

In December, 1965 MacDonald called an inquest. The jury at that inquest found, after four days' testimony, that Esther Castellani's death was "unnatural, a homicide at the hands of a person or persons unknown."

The police searched the Castellani home, found a herbicide called Ortho Triox under a basement sink. The product label indicated it was 53.5 per cent arsenic. Some three ounces had been used.

On April 6, 1966 Rene Castellani was arrested for the murder of Esther Castellani. Two days earlier, he and Lolly had applied for a marriage licence. The trial was a sensation. It made all the papers, and all the newscasts. Oddly, CKNW news never mentioned Castellani's former connection to the station. He was described as a "radio promotion manager," or in similar terms.

The evidence, although entirely circumstantial, was damning: on November 12, 1966 Rene Castellani was found guilty, and sentenced to hang February 21, 1967.

An appeal was inevitable. The following March 10, the B.C. Court of Appeal unanimously ordered a new trial, finding the original judge had misdirected the jury. (He had told them Castellani was a bad character, and they might find him guilty on that basis.)

The second trial lasted 11 days, ended in the same verdict: guilty.

When the verdict was announced, Castellani rose and dramatically faced the jury of nine men and three women. "I've been asked three or four times if I killed my wife," he said in a flat voice. "I did not kill my wife. And may God have mercy on your souls." Some of the jury members winced.

A later appeal to the Supreme Court of Canada was unsuccessful, and Rene went to prison. Luckily for him, the federal government abolished the death penalty in 1968, while he was behind bars, and in May 1979 he was freed. He had been in prison 12 years, apparently a model prisoner. In fact, says Hal Davis, Castellani organized a prison band (The Hangman's Five). Hal met him one day, accompanied by a prison guard, and they chatted.

Rene was nothing if not resilient. Still shaking the prison dust from his shoes, he phoned Bill Hughes at CKNW and asked for a job. Hughes was flabbergasted. "You have to be joking!" he said. "After all the trauma you put this station through?"

Rebuffed by CKNW, Castellani found work at CFVR Radio in Abbotsford. Then, not much later, when Ted Schellenberg and Bob Adshead started CKEG Radio in Nanaimo, they hired Castellani as promotion manager. It was 16 years after Esther's death, and in a new city, and no one except Castellani and his employers knew the details of his troubled past.

Rene got married again, but not to Lolly. She had married someone else while he was in prison. He started a new Dizzy Dialer show, worked in CKEG promotion, and became good friends with Ted Schellenberg . . . even moved in with him and his family for a brief period.

To this day Schellenberg — who plans a book on Rene — is ambivalent on the question of Castellani's guilt: "The man I knew was a decent fellow, a good broadcaster, a decent friend. Rene Castellani was someone special."

On January 4, 1982 Rene Castellani, 56, died of cancer. To the day he died, he maintained he was innocent of the murder of Esther Castellani.

"You're coming to work for me at CKNW . . ."

John Plul wields as much influence — and often more — as any of the station's on-air stars. Plul is CKNW's vice president of marketing, and head of promotion, an awesomely energetic fellow who sees to it that NW's name is seen EVERYWHERE — and then adds a few more places.

He was born in Vibank, Saskatchewan in 1940; the Plul family moved around Saskatchewan towns until John was 14, then came to B.C.

Young John was in a hurry: he went to work at Dietrich-Collins, heavy equipment distributors in Vancouver, and bought a house. You read that right: he bought a house when he was just 14. "I hated school; I left when I was not quite 15 and got a job at Dietrich-Collins. I didn't have an education, so I started in the store room." Four years later he was made marketing manager, replacing a fellow named Bill Clancey, who went on to become a behind-the-scenes public relations force in B.C. politics.

John's circuitous route to CKNW took him through Sweden. John explains: "When I'd been with the company eight or nine years, Fred Dietrich called me in and told me about a program called the Rotary Group Study Exchange. Young business people from around the world were financed by Rotary to go to various countries — it was Sweden that year — and I had been nominated to represent Vancouver.

"I won, and went to Sweden for three months. The district Governor of Rotary sent someone to watch over things; it was Bill Hughes, manager of CKNW! We got along like a house afire. Hughes said, 'When we get back, you're coming to work for me at CKNW.' And I did, eventually. It was 1965."

It's probably best that John did switch from Dietrich-Collins. Not long after he'd started at CKNW, a tragedy occurred at his former workplace. Jack Dietrich, Fred's brother, walked into Fred's office and shot him dead.

"The first paper I read was Variety . . ."

General manager Rod Gunn's memories of CKNW go back to childhood. He learned to tell time on NW, still remembers the jingle: "When the big hand points straight up, The little hand tells the time: it's 2 o'clock! It's 2 o'clock! Listen for the chime!" He remembers bringing in his mom's Fiesta entries. And he was born just up the street from the station, about four months after it signed on.

"It's hard for anybody who never worked there," says Bell, "to understand the volume of work considered routine in the CKNW newsroom under Warren Barker. The amount of information that went through that newsroom was astonishing. And the pressure was tremendous. There were buzzers that went off at five minutes to and two minutes to the newscasts, because we didn't have time to turn around and look at the clock.

"One of the guys went to the doctor because there was something wrong with his plumbing. The doctor can't find anything causing it, but on a hunch asks him 'How often do you pee?' He says 'When I get into the station, around 7, and then again about 2:30, when I'm through.' The doctor says, 'Men aren't built like that. You've gotta pee every two or three hours.' And this guy shakes his head. 'I don't have time.'" ■

Tony Antonias' fertile imagination worked during a call on national agencies in Toronto. The people who produced Airwick, the room freshener, were concerned about the incursion into their market of new scented sprays. Airwick didn't spray; you just left it open in the room. Not too exciting. Tony got back to NW, and still had no ideas. The deadline for the campaign was fast approaching, and the account could be a lucrative one. Tony was sitting at his desk staring out the window when the idea came to him: Airwick Sits There Silently, *Taking It All In.*

Bingo. The client liked the line so much they used it in their national campaign, and put it on billboards all across the country. ∎

"I had an interest in radio early," Rod says. "My father was a drummer; the first paper I remember reading was Variety! I grew up listening to CKNW; by the time I got to high school my friends were telling me I should get into radio, I liked it so much. In 1963, I joined the Radio Society at UBC. I was hired that same year by Peter Kosick at CJOR. I could run a board so I was hired to operate, and later produce, for a fellow named Pat Burns. He was doing his Hotline show. They made me the music director almost as soon as I arrived, because I knew music well.

In 1965 I came to NW, got a salary of $400 a month for operating and helping Len Hopkins, the music director. I got married in '66, and went back to CJOR as production manager."

Since that day when he first came to NW, Rod has set what he believes is a station record for departures and returns: he left and came back five times.

"In 1970," Rod recalls, "I had an offer from manager Jack Teitelman to go to CFUN as program director. I talked about it with Bill Hughes. He says, 'You're not worth it. Not yet.' I called them, told them I'd changed my mind. Instead, I sold my house and took my wife and 15-month-old daughter to Spain."

On his return to Vancouver in November, Rod did go to CFUN, then rocking with on-air types like Terry David Mulligan, J.B. Shayne and Don Francks. Over at CKNW, meanwhile, a new FM station called CFMI had been spun off. Its program director/operations manager for the first couple of months was David Hoole. When Hoole left, Rod Gunn stepped in on January 15, 1971.

Six years later, he was program director at both stations. He was also given the job of acquiring and programming music for both.

In July, 1981 Rod left to manage Word Records — a company specializing in recording Christian music. That didn't work out, and in 1982 when Rod was offered the job as general manager of CHQR in Calgary, he took it. For the next eight years, he commuted *weekly* to Calgary to manage QR. The reason for that unorthodox work pattern is that Rod's son, Kristian, who is severely retarded, needed a level of care not available in Calgary.

Rod's experience at CHQR was invaluable: it would lead directly to his being offered the job in 1990 as president and general manager at CKNW.

"The pace was hot . . ."

Terry Spence, whose name became associated with CKNW's headline-making show, The Investigators, came to CKNW in the fall of 1966.

"Within a week of arriving, Hal Davis had me up in the air, doing traffic. I didn't know the city, so I'm flying around with four maps on my lap. The newsroom was a disaster: there was a rickety, noisy air conditioner, a hook for Warren Barker's red tie, a hole in the wall where Mauri Hesketh had thrown a typewriter — you could see the laths showing — hooks for wire copy, there were memos up on the wall from years long gone by, the teletype was in a closet, and it was dirty.

"The pace was *hot* in the CKNW newsroom. We phoned every police department in the Lower Mainland, every fire department, every RCMP sub-division. We called every one of them before 8 a.m., again at noon, at 6 p.m. and again later in the evening. So they'd get four calls a day from CKNW. You'd talk to some of these people for years, and never see them. I got to be friends with a lot of them on the phone.

"I worked inside for a few months while I learned how to pronounce local names, then I was put out onto the beat."

You had to be resourceful at CKNW news, Terry cackles, recalling the time he and a CKWX reporter were pursuing Ron Andrews, the mayor of North Vancouver District. "Ron had had a dozen coffees, and he had to go to the can. He went into the men's room at city hall, and I followed him in, recorder rolling. The WX reporter was a woman! She couldn't go in! I got the interview. You could hear the urinals running in the background."

"I was given a plunger . . ."

One day when he was 12, Dave Glasstetter saw a neighbor throw out an old Philco radio. He rescued it. "It didn't work, but by touching the tubes I could get a hum. That was kind of exciting. So I got an old phonograph, and converted the Philco into an amplifier for the phonograph."

Young Dave did all the things kids interested in electronics did: built his own crystal set, pirated speakers out of old radios he'd buy for two or three dollars, fooled around with electronic stuff, read Popular Electronics, "and got shocked many times."

But his first job was as a sheet metal journeyman. ("I replaced the old copper roof on the front of the old courthouse, what's now the Vancouver Art Gallery.")

He remembered from his school days a fellow named Ken Wheeler, head of the electronics program at Vancouver Vocational Institute, who had talked to Dave's class. "I went and applied at VVI. I didn't have Grade 12 math and physics, and the counsellor said I should have. But, he says, if there's space in the class we'll get you in. It's a 12-month course, with no breaks, and it's tough. Don't expect to pass.

"I started January, 1966. There were 20 guys on the course. In three months we

CKNW newsman George Garrett has chased news in New York City, Los Angeles, Israel, Toronto, Ottawa, Montreal and all over B.C.

But, in a curious way, he gives occasional work to local newspaper types. In a typical example, a reporter from The Vancouver Sun tries to interest his editors in a yarn. They say no. Frustrated, the reporter passes it along to George. George does the story on NW . . . and the Sun hears it on their newsroom radio. At which point they say to their reporter, "Hey, can you follow that one up?" ■

Terry Spence (left) came to CKNW in the fall of 1966.

There had been a radio station in the '20s in New Westminster. CFXC, The Voice of the Fraser River, had been started in the fall of 1924 by Fred Hume. Hume would go on to political fame as the mayor of New Westminster and, later, Vancouver, but in 1924 he was running a shop on Columbia Street that sold radios and electrical equipment. CFXC was on the air from the shop for an hour each night, featured soprano Miss N. Bradshaw, accompanied by Miss Mabel Knocker at the piano. Hume's newspaper advertisements were headlined: Have You Listened to a Radio Programme Yet? The program, alas, didn't sell as many radios as it was intended to do, and Hume signed the station off forever in July, 1926.

George Chandler bought it, moved it to Vancouver and renamed it CJOR. ■

were down to 15. At the end of the year one other fellow and myself were the top two students."

Dave had been taking math tutoring, too, and when time came after graduation to write the government exam, he earned — it was December 13, 1966 — his Certificate of Proficiency as a general radio telephone operator. That certificate hangs up on the wall of his office to this day.

A month before the awarding of the certificate — November 8, 1966 — a young NW technician named Bob Vogt had been killed in a car crash driving home after work. Jack Gordon, head of NW's engineering staff at the time, needed a replacement. He got around to Dave Glasstetter, interviewed him over the phone. "It was a real grilling," Dave recalls. Quickly, over the course of that phone conversation, it became obvious to Gordon that Glasstetter's knowledge was more than theoretical. He had built things, fixed things. One of the tasks Dave set himself at VVI was to fix an old 1K transmitter. He spent a month on it, keeping up on his classes at the same time, and got it working. Dave had purchased an old Roberts tape recorder, too, got that working. "And I was not unfamiliar with a soldering iron."

"Five minutes into that interview," Gordon recalled later, "I knew Dave had the makings of a top senior broadcast engineer. Nothing since has changed my mind."

On January 3, 1967 Dave Glasstetter joined the CKNW engineering staff. His first specific task? "I was given a plunger, and told to go fix a plugged toilet in the women's washroom."

Welcome to big-town radio!

No batteries needed . . .

"Jack Braverman," says a colleague, "is the Babe Ruth, the Hank Aaron, the Wayne Gretzky and Mario Lemieux of the radio advertising world. I'm so glad we stole him from CJOR."

Oddly, Jack didn't get into radio sales until his late 30s. He'd spent 17 years, from 1948 to 1965, as a film booker for United Artists. When he started, at age 21, he was the youngest man with that job in the film industry, booked UA films into theatres all throughout B.C.

In August of 1965, just before he got into radio sales, Jack married Doreen Turecki, a school teacher with three kids. (You know her as Doreen Braverman, president of the B.C. Liberal Party from 1972 to 1975, and the woman who made The Flag Shop one of the biggest operations of its kind in Canada.) "All of a sudden," says Jack, "I've got a wife, three kids, a mortgage, a dog and a cat with no balls. I had to get a better paying job." Doreen's job brought in $455 a month, $5 more than Jack was making.

Gerry Altman hired Jack at CJOR — where he had a formidable challenge: "CKNW had, for its 9 a.m. newscast, more listeners than OR amassed in a week!"

A little trick Jack picked up back in the '50s from Harry Woolfe, an old-time film manager, proved invaluable: he'd write tiny notes to himself, phone numbers, people to call, and so on, then push the tiny slips of paper under his ring. Jack does it to this day, after nearly 30 years in the business. The system works perfectly, and no batteries are needed.

CKNW's Mel Cooper started hearing about this crackerjack salesman. "I was with an account executive at J. Walter Thompson," says Mel, "and he asks, 'Do you know this guy Jack Braverman?' He started telling me about him, and I called Jack at his home. Lloyd Bray from sales went to see him." Bray met Braverman at Jack's tennis club, found him too casually attired and too casual in his demeanor. Bray was not impressed. He thought Braverman was a "playboy-type." Lloyd had, to put it gently, miscalculated. But Braverman was a force not to be denied. Mel Cooper looked at Jack's successes at CJOR — where he was selling far more accounts than the station's ratings justified — and said, "He's hurting us, Lloyd."

On May 1, 1968 Jack Braverman joined the CKNW sales force. He was 41. "They gave me an account list from someone who had just left the station. It wasn't a particularly strong list.

"But it just grew and grew." ■

CKNW listeners have been involved in news coverage from Day One. "If you see a newsworthy event, phone us. CKNW will pay one dollar for the best news tip of the day, and five dollars for the most newsworthy item of the week. If you see something newsworthy, call CKNW at . . ."

At one time that message ran on every newscast. As listeners became more used to it, the frequency was reduced. Now the only time it's announced (CKNW still pays for news tips — payments have increased to $5 and $25) is when the winners of the weekly prizes are announced on designated newscasts. But calls keep coming in.

When NW first went on the air, competing stations referred to it as the "dollar-a-holler" station. That was 50 years ago. As a result of the Rodney King incident in Los Angeles, TV stations are today importuning viewers to send videos.

NW was 50 years ahead of its time! ■

*Carl Waiz talked to Pierre and
Maggie on their honeymoon.*

"More People Listen To CKNW . . ."

CANADIANS RAGED IN THE '70S WHEN IT WAS ANNOUNCED WE'D BE going to the metric system of measurements . . . and CKNW's on-air people had to decide how to pronounce "kilometre." The Queen and Prince Philip visited B.C. to mark its centennial, and everywhere the royal couple went NW was sure to follow.

Quebec's terrorist FLQ provoked Prime Minister Trudeau to invoke the War Measures Act, and murdered the province's labor minister Pierre Laporte. A new Canadian hero emerged when Paul Henderson scored the winning goal in the deciding game of the first Canada-USSR hockey series. Hockey's Canada Cup was initiated, and the Toronto Blue Jays began. So did VIA Rail. Soviet dancer Mikhail Baryshnikov defected in Toronto.

The Watergate scandal convulsed the United States for the better part of three years. Chairman Mao died in China. The world's first test-tube baby was born. The first non-Italian pope in more than 400 years was chosen, and Margaret Thatcher was elected Prime Minister of Britain.

Pierre Trudeau led reporters from CKNW and elsewhere a merry chase as he married Margaret Sinclair in North Vancouver, and the Museum of Anthropology opened on the U.B.C. campus. B.C. Rail was extended from Fort St. John to Fort Nelson.

CKNW News had a busy decade. The W.A.C. Bennett government was defeated by the one-term Dave Barrett government, succeeded in turn by "Wacky's" son, Bill. Justice Thomas Berger conducted the Mackenzie Valley gas pipeline hearings. The United Nations held its Habitat conference in Vancouver. The restored Orpheum Theatre became the new home of the Vancouver Symphony Orchestra. And CKNW was first to report the details of a PWA crash at Cranbrook.

The 1970s at CKNW began with an ending, as long-time manager Bill Hughes left the station to become executive vice-president at Western Broadcasting, NW's parent company. Hughes was succeeded by Mel Cooper, the Newfoundland-born ball of fire whose promotional and sales abilities had been recognized and utilized for years by the station.

CFMI, tucked into a corner of the NW building, and on the air in 1970, repeated the older station's ratings success quickly.

The '70s began auspiciously for CKNW Sports: the station got broadcast rights to Vancouver Canucks games and got the right man to call those games. Jim Robson

If you'd been around CKNW in 1975, when the talk show studios were moved out of the Hotel Georgia into larger quarters in the Holiday Inn on West Hastings, you might have been perplexed by engineer Jack Gordon's behavior. For several days, Gordon sat behind Gary Bannerman as Bannerman did his talk show, intently watching the broadcaster. "He made me sort of nervous, actually," Bannerman says, laughing about it now, "watching how I moved my hands, turned on mikes, flipped phone switches, picked up scripts and so on. Then he went away and redesigned the whole layout." The transformation was remarkable. "Everything was right where it should be," Bannerman says, "right where my hands wanted it. It made the physical *flow* of the shift just so smooth. It was great." ■

Gary Bannerman was involved in three different prison hostage dramas.

In 1975 Gary Bannerman won an official commendation from the Canadian Penitentiary Service. The story of that honor is a dramatic one: Bannerman was involved in three different prison hostage dramas. The first involved an inmate, Michael Platko, holding a knife to the throat of a B.C. Penitentiary gym instructor as Bannerman stood beside the two men trying to calm the convict down. "Platko's hand was shaking, and he was cutting the instructor's skin. I'd take his hand, 'Hey, Michael, slow down now, you're cutting him.'"

The second incident was the famous 1974 prison drama in which prison social worker Mary Steinhauser died. There were

joined NW. For more than 20 astonishing years, Jim has been the voice of the Canucks.

Wally Garrett left CKNW in 1971, ending a 20-year affiliation that included an indelible association with the extravagantly popular Fiesta!

The early '70s mark a technical milestone for the station, thanks to imaginative engineer Don Kalmakoff. Kalmakoff conceived a new kind of tape cartridge while working at CKNW; it was such a great advance over existing "carts" it became an industry benchmark.

In rapid succession, the station won the Rogers Memorial Trophy for the new cartridge, a Radio and Television News Directors Association award for a special on a major oil spill, and a Billboard Magazine award to Jack Cullen as Disc Jockey of the Year. The H. Gordon Love Award for excellence in news followed, and in 1975 the B.C. Association of Broadcasters capped it all by naming CKNW the Station of the Year.

With Jack Webster's second and final departure, Mel Cooper conceived of a show to battle him. Called The Investigators, in its years on the air it made a lot of waves. Its biggest wave-generator was a young New Brunswicker named Gary Bannerman. Bannerman, a tall, intense, and intensely ambitious newspaper writer brought to his broadcasting the relentless pursuit of facts that had made his journalism so effective. CKNW had made a commitment to hard-hitting, investigative talk shows, and it found the ideal man to handle the job. As time would show, Bannerman's progress would not be entirely free of pain.

The energetic and jovially snoopy Earle Bradford came along that same year, moving from news to the role of 'man about town,' reporting to NW's listeners on Earle's Court on the doings (and misdoings) of local notables. If something opened in the Lower Mainland — a restaurant, a hotel, a major shop, anything — Earle "The Pearl" would be there to cover it, and tell us about it.

By the spring of 1973 CJOR's Jack Webster was third in the ratings, with CKNW's Ed Murphy in first place on The Investigators and Judy LaMarsh second at CKWX. Then Jim Pattison hired Murphy, giving OR a one-two-three punch of Webster, Murphy and Burns . . . and breaking CKNW's domination.

In 1973 Ted Smith, who would play an important role in the station's future, was hired by Hal Davis to be director of sales for CKNW and CFMI. Smith had been setting records as sales manager at CJOB in Winnipeg.

Mel Cooper left in 1973 to run his own station in Victoria. With three decades at CKNW, it was natural Hal Davis would step in to succeed Cooper. Hal was now at the helm of two thriving stations, both leading the ratings in their respective fields, and both making money.

Jack Cullen branched out, opened a record store. After two decades dominating the mornings, Bob Hutton retired. The transition to the new man had been planned for several years, (these things are not done haphazardly at this station). with NW's brash young musical director and afternoon DJ, Brian "Frosty" Forst, filling in for Bob when Hutton was on holidays or ill. By the time the switch was permanent, Frosty was seasoned in that time slot. For the 20 years since, he has been IT in the morning.

A sharp young fellow named Ron Bremner, who had been attracting a lot of notice at Standard Broadcast Sales in Toronto, was invited by Ted Smith to Vancouver for an interview. He arrived during the 1974 Easter holidays, and by May was part of the sales staff. Like Smith, Bremner was destined to rise meteorically in the organization.

Jack Stewart, NW's program director in the mid-70s, made a major contribution to the station's success when he worked out a way to keep Jack Cullen from being lured away by a rival station. "Buy his record collection," Stewart told NW, "then let him use it." It worked.

A February 28, 1974 internal NW newsletter had good news: "More people listen to CKNW than to any other station west of Toronto."

The '70s were made more fun for CKNW's listeners by a unique American import, a breezy San Francisco broadcaster named Art Finley, whose braininess and enthusiasm — and taste for unusual subjects — made for interesting and often funny programs. Art did a show on nudism once. His guests were from a local nudist colony and, Art told his listeners, were in the studio in the nude. Not wanting to feel left out, Art hosted in the nude.

1977 was an active year:

- John Plul left CKNW (but not for good, as it turned out) to exercise his considerable promotional capabilities in the provincial government's ministry of tourism; Linda Lee succeeded him.
- Dave Glasstetter became chief engineer, coming very highly recommended by retiring Jack Gordon.
- The peripatetic Rod Gunn became program director of CKNW *and* CFMI.
- Roving Mike marked its 10,000th broadcast, and host Bill Hughes was feted on air and in print.
- Hughes, who had purchased $36,000 worth of stock in NW in 1955, "six per cent of the company," sold the stock in 1977 "for a couple of million."
- Tom Larscheid, an ex-CFL star, joined the NW sports department as a color broadcaster for football. He would add hockey later.
- Hal Davis stepped down as manager, moved to Western International Communications in a new executive position: liaison between all the company's stations.
- Al Anaka became sales manager, succeeding Ted Smith, who was promoted to general manager in September.
- Erm Fiorillo added the title of assistant general manager to comptroller.

In 1978 CKNW set a record when it grossed $5 million for the year, and added to its laurels by winning the Charlie Edwards News Award.

Barrie Clark, a former Liberal MLA, joined NW in May, 1978 and took over the noon to 3 p.m. slot, once a musical show hosted by Wayne Cox. NW's commitment to talk shows had intensified, and it was one that was to pay dividends for years to come.

Al Anaka left the station to become involved in newspaper publishing, and his position as sales manager was filled in 1979 by the swiftly-rising Ron Bremner. Ted Smith's successes were rewarded by additional responsibilities and an additional title to go with them: in 1979 he became president and general manager.

It was a great way to end a decade.

more than a dozen hostages being held, and the three inmates were rough customers: Andy Bruce was in for murder, Doug Lucas had murdered a family member with an ax, the third man Wilson was a junkie. "Oddly enough," Bannerman says, "I didn't feel the same alarm as I had in the Platko incident, which was less serious. There had been 10 negotiators, but they were eventually winnowed down to two: lawyer Bryan Williams and me. We dealt with them constantly, sometimes going up hourly, for 41 hours. At one point Andy Bruce had a knife in my back, and I said, 'Hey, not so close,' and he *apologized*. We just kept 'em talking, got 'em tired, and never said no to anything they asked. It turned out that without any training we turned out to be pretty good negotiators. The Steinhauser case is now a textbook case." ■

Jim Robson at a Canucks game, 20 years and counting with an eventual induction into the Hockey Broadcasting Hall of Fame.

Terry Moore's working life could be described as motley. He has performed in plays and operas, ran a Dude Ranch ("It turned into a Dud Ranch"), was on TV in eastern Canada, studied voice at the Royal Conservatory of Music, attended Herbert Berkoff's acting school in New York's Greenwich Village, and was a short-order cook in a black bar in Harlem, the only white employee. He emceed comedy shows in New York's Catskills . . . where he introduced performers like Johnny Carson,

"My mother wrote to Bill Hughes . . .

"I was eight when we came to B.C. from Prince Albert, Saskatchewan," Jim Robson says. "It was 1943. My father was a penitentiary guard. I have two older brothers, and an older sister. I lived for a year on my uncle's dairy farm on Barnston Island. There was a little one-room school there, Mrs. Murphy teaching Grades 1 through 8. In 1944 we moved to Maple Ridge. My dad bought 10 acres two miles east of Haney on the Dewdney Trunk, and did mixed farming. My mother worked in a box factory.

"I auditioned at CKNW for Bill Hughes in May of my last year at school; I still have that audition, Aubrey Price gave it to me. It's awful, so slow and deliberate. Hughes gave me the names of seven stations, and who to apply to at each one. I got three replies; one was from Ken Hutcheson at CJAV in Port Alberni. Hutcheson was a CKNW alumnus. I started working at CJAV July 1, 1952, so on July 1, 1992 I marked 40 years in radio."

Jim wrote copy. The chief copy writer, Doris Jowsey, was, at 16, younger than he was! "I couldn't type; I'd been kicked out of typing class at school. I did a half-hour deejay stint on the air, following the 10 p.m. news read by Bob Switzer. After my show I'd sweep up, and dust.

"They had no sports director at CJAV. Then Bob Hall left and I started doing sportscasts. I was 17. It was mostly wire copy, some local stuff. I got into community sports fast, played basketball, badminton, soccer, baseball . . . Phil Barter and I did a half each of play-by-play of live basketball games with teams from Nanaimo and

Alberni. Then I ended up doing the play-by-play for the games, and Phil did color. They had excellent basketball on the Island; the Alberni Athletics won the 1955 Canadian Senior Amateur championship. That game was carried on CHUB in Nanaimo, and on CKUA at the University of Alberta. Hey, I thought, a *network*!

"Was it difficult doing the play-by-play? If you have the ability to describe something while it's going on, you'll do well. But you have to know the rules. Read the rule book! Throw me in a cricket game, and I'd be lost."

In the fall of 1956 Jim came to Vancouver and started working for CKWX. "I was the morning man at WX against Bob Hutton on NW. The sports director was Bill Stephenson, who had been at CJAV. We did B.C. Lions CFL football games, Vancouver Canucks WHL hockey, they weren't in the NHL yet, and Vancouver Mounties PCL baseball. Bill did most of the play-by-play; I did some. If Bill was east doing the Grey Cup, I'd do hockey here. I've called baseball, basketball, football, soccer and lacrosse.

"In 1960 Bill went to CFRB, Toronto, and my life got more complicated. In 1961 I did 230 sports play-by-play broadcasts, including high school basketball, and still had the morning show! Bea and I had three little kids at home. It was the toughest year of my life. I'd be up at 3:45 a.m., and out the door at 4:30. Bea and I got punchy; we'd start laughing over everything."

The pace eased in 1963 when the Mounties folded, but it was still sufficiently frantic. Jim found himself "screaming down to the Cock and Bull Restaurant on Granville, for a pre-game B.C. Lions show," then "screaming down to Empire Stadium for another pre-game program there." The game started at 8:30. When it was over he'd leap in his car and scream over to the Admiral Hotel to do the post-game show. "And the Lions that year were terrible: 2-13. A lot of the players would sit in their cars outside the hotel, waiting for the show to end. They didn't want to be interviewed after a loss. But guys like Norm Fieldgate, Pat Claridge, By Bailey, Sonny Homer . . . they really helped me out. Then in 1964 the Lions won the Grey Cup. Norm Fieldgate was crying, Joe Kapp was hysterical."

You're not going to believe how Jim Robson ended up at CKNW. He laughs when he recalls it. "My *mother* wrote to Bill Hughes: 'You should hire him.' And Hughes approached me. 'Would you come and do NHL hockey if NW gets the rights?' Sure, I said, love to. Then NW won the rights."

And in 1970 Jim moved to CKNW . . . and to 20-years-and-counting with the Canucks, and to eventual induction into the Hockey Broadcasting Hall of Fame.

"What is THAT in the hallway?!"

David Hoole was like nobody NW had ever seen before. It was the days of student rebellion, and long hair, and unorthodox clothing, and David looked the part . . . but it wasn't a role: he was the genuine article, a *hippie*. He even played in a rock-and-roll band. Hippies weren't rare, God knows, when David started at NW October 1, 1969, the day before his 23rd birthday, but the station had had no exposure to one. Bill Hughes, whose language was always circumspect and polite, gaped when he caught sight of Hoole one day. Hughes whispered fiercely to manager Mel Cooper, "WHAT THE F*** IS THAT IN THE HALLWAY? WE CAN'T HAVE STAFF MEMBERS WHO DON'T WEAR SHOES!" Hoole was kept on for a very good reason: his undoubted production skills. He read commercials in an easy, conversational, and intelligent style, unlike the stylized approach prevalent at the time. He knew music extremely well. He was a wizard at the control board. He was plugged in. He was brilliant.

Johnny Mathis, Buddy Hackett, Woody Allen and singer Enzo Stuarti, who liked Terry's lighting work so much he asked for him at repeat performances. "That stage-craft training came in handy later," Terry says. The New York phase of his career ended at WTFM Radio in New York City. ∎

David Hoole, like nobody before.

The acquisition of Art Finley for The Investigators was timely. "He was from the States," says Hal Davis, "and didn't want his kids drafted. He'd been with KABL, a 'good music' station in California, and had been brought up to CHQM by Bill Bellman. Six months later, Bellman fired Finley."

A former NW employee, Anne Bolton, was working at CHQM. Anne called Hal from QM, and told him a "very smart man" had just been let go. "You should talk to him" she said. Hal did, and hired Finley at once.

Art — whose frequent offbeat interviews were always lively — would nonetheless pack it in in August, 1973, telling NW management even if he stayed he wouldn't feel comfortable involved in a show in which "he would be advising Canadians on Canadian matters." ∎

The aquisition of Art Finley was timely.

"CKNW in the late '60s," David says, "was a bastion of respectability. I think they realized they *had* to do new things to keep up. So they pushed Brian Forst forward, Rick Honey . . . got younger sales guys. And they stopped playing really irrelevant music from the '40s and '50s: Frank Sinatra, Tony Bennett, Peggy Lee. They started going toward the softer end of what was then current: Simon and Garfunkel, Carole King . . ."

The station made David the first program director at CFMI when that FM arm opened, but, says David, "That was way too big a title for what I was doing. There weren't any humans to direct; the whole operation was automated. The machine even spoke the time."

David left CKNW December 1, 1973, just over four years after he'd started.

"I learned to be a professional at CKNW, to seek excellence, never to be satisfied."

For more than 20 years he has been running Westward Communications, which began as the Spot Shop Studio. It's one of the busiest production houses in western Canada. And not long before this interview, David Hoole wrote his 2000th jingle!

"I'm surprised they hired me . . ."

"Big Daddy" Dave McCormick got off to an early start: he was in radio in Ontario at age 14. By 1957 he was one of 'The Good Guys' at CFUN, a group that included Brian "Frosty" Forst, Brian Lord and Al Jordan. That lasted until 1962, when he went down to the States and spent 10 years in radio there.

"I came up to B.C. on a vacation in '71 and got to talking with Frosty, who was by then with CKNW, and before too long I was sitting having a chat with Mel Cooper, the manager. That meeting lasted six hours! I'm surprised they hired me: I had long hair, a Fu Manchu moustache . . . The atmosphere at NW was so different after my rock-and-roll days at Top 40 stations in California. It was so . . . antiseptic at NW. But soon I was in the Crystal Palace every Saturday doing shows, and I'd fill in on the drive home show and for Cullen. I became the permanent fill-in man for Cullen, when he was on vacation. In the earlier days, when Jack had his studio in his record store, I did the show from there. That was great fun: I'd have guests on the air, we'd play old records and tapes. Some people said, 'Dave's too contemporary!'

"I have a memory of HUNDREDS of Saturday mornings working in the Crystal Palace doing on-site commercial remotes. It was either too cold or too hot; I recall one Abbotsford Air Show where the records were warping from the heat! I did remotes from Wosk's, from Stacey's, car lots everywhere, hundreds of them. Jeff Gong was my remote engineer. He still is!

"A conversation I had with Rod Gunn evolved into a concept I invented and named: Discumentary." That became a CFMI perennial.

Dave has a knack for naming: during his Sunday stints on NW, he and John McKeachie developed the mini-sports reports that Dave would dub "Sporty Shorts." That name's still around CKNW today, even though Dave and John aren't.

Years after his departure, Dave's memories of NW are good. "Originally I could never figure out why NW worked! It seemed to do so much wrong, on and off the air. Then I discovered it was the people, who for the most part were treated well. That's what made it work for so long, and so well."

"Ed wanted to be the star . . ."

After Jack Webster's departure in 1972, program director Hal Davis began a hurried search for a replacement. Talk radio was now making an impact in the Lower Mainland, and competing with CJOR's masterful Webster would be tough.

"Ed Murphy was at CKWX," Hal says, "and was doing well. He was our ace-in-the-hole, but I went on a cross-country search for someone better. Whoever it was also had to know this market. I went with a list of talk-show people, and talked to them in Winnipeg, in Toronto, Ottawa, other places . . . but no one quite filled the bill. I phoned Mel Cooper. 'Get Murphy, I can't find anyone better.'"

With Murphy's arrival, the stage was set for Cooper's creation of The Investigators. The original team consisted of Murphy, Terry Spence and Art Finley. The concept: strong talk-show hosts in the studio, being fed items from strong reporters in the field.

Ed Murphy (left) from the original team with Mauri Heskith.

After Finley left, NW newsman Mauri Hesketh joined the Investigators team, which now included another excellent newsman, Scott Dixon. And somewhere along in here Hal Davis tried to make Sun writer Simma Holt a talk show host, but female listeners complained about her voice.

Davis describes the year or so of Ed Murphy's presence at CKNW as the worst year of his life as CKNW's program director. "He was drinking. He'd phone me, down in the dumps, and I'd go to talk to him. He'd buy a coffee and a brandy, and pour the brandy into the coffee and tell me he'd stopped drinking. Ed wanted to be the star, but I told him NW would never again be caught in a Webster-type situation, where the departure of one guy had such a devastating effect."

The Investigators began to make a genuine impact. In his Sun column for December 18, 1973 Jack Wasserman reported the ratings: they showed The Investigators first, with OR's Webster in second place. Says Terry Spence, "We were *burning*. The phones were ringing all the time; everybody who had a grievance against whomever. We did stories on a lumber-marking scam in Surrey, we bought drug paraphernalia at Kripps', we awarded a Slum Landlord of the Day title . . . I'd go down to a Powell Street flophouse, throw on an old ratty ski jacket I kept in the trunk of my car, and go in and talk to residents. I remember one fellow telling me his dive was one of the classier places: there was a can of Raid in everybody's room.

"Murphy anchored the 9 to noon slot, Finley did 6:30 to 8 p.m., I was mostly out on the road. My strength was in reporting. Judy Jackson was involved in the show. She was the call-screener, and sometimes played the wife in a husband-and-wife investigation. Ed or I might be the husband, Judy would be the wife, and we might visit a trailer park where we had heard a sales scam was going on. Judy was great at this stuff. Johnny Zwolak, we called him Johnny Zee, was creative and production director.

"It was *exciting*. Mel Cooper had a rule: no member of the sales department was allowed to talk to the investigative team. Advertisers kept cancelling, but Mel would say to the salesmen, 'We're going to let you sell ratings.' We did things like going to the White Spot and McDonald's and taking their hamburgers in for chemical analysis; we'd drain the liquid from canned peas: how much value was in them for your money? It was *terrific*.

Gary Bannerman: "Ed Murphy thought I was after his job as the 'star' of the Investigators. I was ambitious, all right, but ambitious for success in that job. We worked together in the Hotel Georgia studios for a month or so, but it wasn't a good situation. He'd sit in the host's chair while I stood there waiting to sit down, with the clock ticking toward my time on the air. He kept doing this, and finally he did it once too often.

"I said, 'Ed, if you're not out of that chair in 10 seconds I'll remove you.' He said, 'Like to see you try.' I picked him up and threw him across the room. Then, when I sat down and began my introduction he slammed the door loudly on his way out."■

Gary Bannerman (right) on the air with Bill Bennett (then premier of B.C.).

"We got all kinds of threats of lawsuits, and four actual suits, one from the Church of Scientology, another from First Memorial Services. That one was a real horror story, and we actually got the Funeral Act changed as a result of our investigations.

"Later, Gary Bannerman joined us from The Province and was added to the mix. Ed Murphy and Bannerman didn't get along." (As you'll read elsewhere, the animosity between these two resulted in a physical confrontation.)

Scott Dixon was disgusted with the internecine warfare, quit and went to work for the CBC. Hal Davis was at a remote at Wosk's one day when Mel Cooper telephoned to tell him Murphy had quit. Then Cooper left to run his own station, CFAX, and hired Terry Spence away to be his news director.

In August, 1975 Hal Davis, now manager, was memoing his staff that Art Finley was returning to the NW family. "He will be working with the Investigators, but will be primarily responsible for an evening slot."

But, two years later, Art left again, this time for good. In a short-lived experiment, NW tried a succession of different evening hosts: David Ingram, Charles MacLean, Keith Spicer . . . even Al Davidson had a kick at the can. Carl Waiz of the NW newsroom served for a time as an Investigator, and a left-wing journalist named Jacques Khouri stepped in briefly.

"There's a bright kid at The Province . . ."

Gary Bannerman was born in Sydney, Nova Scotia in 1947, started his writing career in his Moncton, New Brunswick high school's newspaper. "At 20 I was very experienced politically, knew all the leading political figures. In 1967 I got a summer job at the St. John Telegraph-Journal. I don't think I was there for a month before I knew this was it. A legislative slot opened up, and they sent me to Fredericton to do between-session reporting. When the legislature sat, the senior man came in, but I took over."

No news service had a bureau in New Brunswick, so Bannerman started sending material to them. By the time he was 21, he was writing for TIME, Maclean's, the Globe and Mail, and an agency in Toronto that put him in more than 80 publications. He filed so much copy CNCP installed a teletype in his bedroom! In his last year in New Brunswick Bannerman made $30,000 on stringing. His salary from the Telegraph-Journal was $8,000!

"I love the reporting business. Through my Fredericton base, I met *everyone* who came through, became good friends with people like Dalton Camp and Richard Hatfield." (Bannerman's 1971 wedding to Patricia was delayed because Premier Hatfield, a guest, was late in arriving.) "I met Charles Lynch, the chief of Southam

Some of the methods used to get stories at NW News are . . . unorthodox. Arnold Epp: "There was a strike at the Ministry of Works. "But they wouldn't *confirm* there was a strike, y' know? So I called up mit a thick Cherman aggzent: 'Zo! Am I zupposed to come to verk?' 'No,' they say, 'don't bother! We're on strike!' We went on the air and confirmed the story."

Then there was the time in 1977 when a pilot phoned NW from his plane. He was in the air near the Cranbrook airport. "I think a plane has crashed here." Epp got on the phone to the control tower at Cranbrook Airport.

News. He responded to my energy and enthusiasm, and I wrote him suggesting I would be a perfect choice for one of Southam's international bureaus. He suggested I start in one of the company's domestic offices. 'Pick your Southam newspaper,' he said, and promised to help me get on whichever I picked. I chose Vancouver and The Province.

"In 1970 The Province had lost a lot of staff in a strike, and they needed people. I said it had to be political. Merv Moore was managing editor, he wanted someone at city council. I spent night after night in the Pacific Press Library learning local politics, learning about the people."

When Jack Webster left CKNW the stage was set for a change in Gary's career path. NW newsman Carl Waiz, knowing Hal Davis was looking for people, told him, "There's a bright kid at The Province, a guy named Gary Bannerman."

"I had lunch with Bannerman," Hal says. "I couldn't believe a guy that young could be so bright. His thought processes, his organization . . . he impressed the hell out of me. Initially it was touch-and-go, and I had a hell of a fight to keep him. He was terrible on the air."

He got better.

Earle "The Pearl"

Hal Davis hired Earle "The Pearl" Bradford initially for news. "He'd been working in Hamilton, sent a tape out. I listened for just a few seconds, and said, 'Yeah, we can use him.'"

After Earle died in November, 1987 a warm memorial service tribute to him was read by CKNW's Terry Moore."When 'The Pearl' came to us in 1972," Terry told a gathering of Earle's family, friends and colleagues, "he was already a seasoned veteran . . . of life, and of the industry to which he devoted almost four decades. Born and raised in Vancouver, Earle could reminisce about life in Vancouver when it, and he, were still growing up.

"Earle served with the air force during World War II, seeing action in Europe . . . Then he worked in radio in Victoria, Saskatoon, Regina, Ottawa, Toronto and Hamilton. But his heart was in the west. He 'came home' in 1972 to a position that suited him: the 'evening news authority' on CKNW. But it was his knowledge of Vancouver, its history, its people, its landmarks, that quickly proved his talents were not being utilized to their fullest. Here was a broadcaster who could not only find the story, write it, and present it; he could add his own, personal knowledge to the telling. In a few short months, an outlet for Earle's knowledge and talent was created. It was 'Earle's Court,' where Earle the Pearl reigned for 14 years.

"Earle's Court," Terry continued, "was *the* source of information on the comings and goings in this city he loved, the place on the dial where names were dropped, where gossip was exchanged, where the stories behind the stories were revealed . . . In the end, the pressure of meeting two deadlines a day on CKNW and writing columns for more than 500 issues of TV Week Magazine began to take its toll. But how do you explain the meaning of the word 'retirement' to a man who couldn't grasp the meaning of the phrase 'slow down'? That task was left to the doctors . . . Their insistence that he take a rest gave Earle the new energy and determination to spend a few more days with us, while his private battle went on.

"Ministry of Transport," Epp says crisply, "I understand you have a problem."

"The guy gave me *everything*, so much detail I couldn't use it all. We went with the story, got quoted all over the place. Now, our procedure was not exactly honest, I guess, but . . ." ■

Earle "the Pearl" Bradford holding court.

An indication of the kind of life a program director can lead is given in Denny Boyd's Sun column for September 1, 1979: "(Hal Davis') worst day occurred just a couple of years ago, and it went like this. He was awakened early by a telephone call urging him to listen to Frosty Forst. It was 6:30 a.m. when Davis tuned in to hear Forst announce that he was in love again. Forst's legendary love affairs have inevitably meant joyous highs at the start, trembling uncertainties in the middle, and black depressions at the end, all three levels accompanied by an inability to perform a morning man's functions.

"Fearing the worst, Davis got up and went to the station, arriving in time to hear Al Davidson call someone 'a silly bugger' on the air. Davis called Davidson in and explained that the word is unacceptable as a noun and unthinkable as a verb and has no place in radio. With the beginnings of a slight headache, Davis spent the rest of the day trying to stop the defection of two major commercial accounts,

"That battle is now over in Earle's 63rd year.

"Earle's job was to entertain and inform us. He made us laugh and he shared with us some of the sorrow that is, all too often, a part of the business of news gathering and reporting. We have been entertained and we are better informed because of those things which The Pearl has shared with us."

"We used them for doorstops . . ."

What's the Traffic Department do? Turn on your radio, and you might hear a piece of music followed by a couple of commercials followed by a time check followed by a newscast preceded by the sponsor's commercial and followed by a weather forecast, then a ski report, etc., etc. Keeping track of all that stuff, and making sure the announcer or operator gets it all on at the correct time and in the correct order is called Traffic. All these hundreds and hundreds of bits of information are printed out on a form called the log. And for more than 20 years at NW, the station's "log lady" was Pat McPherson.

"I was working for a car dealership, and George Garrett used to visit. He was in sales at CKNW then — and he was the only radio representative who talked to people other than the managers. He was the most gentlemanly of them all. George found out I was looking for something else, and suggested I talk to Erm Fiorillo. I had a child at home, and didn't like the idea of going into Vancouver to work, so something right in New Westminster looked attractive.

"They put me in 'Traffic.' Traffic meant nothing to me. At first I hated it, just hated it. Hal Davis had developed a manual system, and Vivian Shepherd, who was traffic manager, taught me how to use it. She was so nice, so patient. Then she got pregnant and left, and I was 'elevated' to manager.

"Some fellow from California had developed a complicated traffic management system using punched cards and thin metal rods you fed through the cards, and he persuaded Mel Cooper, the manager, to buy it. Well, it drove us crazy. We struggled with it for a couple of months, then Hal killed it and we went back to his manual system, which was much better. We had a party, with balloons and banners, to celebrate the death of the metal-rod system, and then we wrapped elastic bands around the rods and used them for doorstops."

Hal Davis, who describes Pat as "one of the most loyal and hard-working people CKNW ever had," recalls an early conversation with her about computers. Hal knew that working with these new-fangled devices was not enjoyed by all, diffidently mentioned that to Pat. "She said, 'I like the job, I want the job, and if that's what it takes to keep the job, I'll do it.' She saved our ass."

"I thought traffic was the worst job in radio," Anne Bolton says. Anne worked in the department starting in 1952, was there for nine years. "In accounting, for example, you can put stuff off. But Traffic? No. It had to be right there, every day."

"Traffic is almost kindergartenish in its simplicity," Pat MacPherson says, "but it all has to be done correctly. Drop one step in the process, and the whole thing comes tumbling down."

"He'd phoned the wrong guy!"

Paul Preston, CKNW's production director, was born in Three Hills, Alberta in June, 1942. "I left for Edmonton after graduating. A fellow named Bill London at CFRN was a friend of the family, and he needed an operator for his Sunday show, Music for

Listeners. I got $1 an hour, and my first day was July 1, 1961. I'd just turned 19. I had a day job selling shoes. Around Christmas CFRN's all-night man, Reg Madison, left, and I took over his show. Reg came originally from Two Hills, and I was from Three Hills. It seemed a natural progression." In quick progression, he worked in Drumheller, Lethbridge and Calgary, and was at CFAX in Victoria late in 1968 when he got a call from CFUN's Al Jordan.

"He'd phoned the wrong guy! Al was looking for an early-morning jock to fill the spot vacated by Douglas Miller, and he'd heard this guy on CFAX he liked. He'd been listening to Barry Bowman, but I guess he hadn't caught his name. After Al met me, it was too late and I got the job. To this day Al says it's probably one of the best mistakes he ever made!"

Paul moved from CFUN to NW, and in his very first week filled in for Frosty Forst, then doing the afternoon drive show.

Wayne Cox, here in studio, was thrilled to be working with the big names at CKNW.

Just For Fun was still on the air, and Paul recalls getting Hal Davis, Warren Barker, Wally Garrett and Bob Hughes together in one studio to record it. He worked with Al Davidson. "Al was in his prime then; he could read a great spot. He could read a telephone book and make it sound great: his timing and inflection were impeccable."

Paul filled in for production head Dick Abbott when Dick was away. He'd do dubs, some voicing, and operate "Fat Albert," the automated cartridge-machine then in use at CFMI. "I continued as Dick's second-in-command to '76 when he left for Little Mountain Sound. Brian Antonson took over. Then Brian left for BCIT, and Kenny Harris succeeded him. I took over production in 1982. We have three production studios and a satellite dub centre, and we get a lot of stuff done. There was a time when only 30 per cent of our spots were pre-recorded, now it's 99 per cent. And, no! We don't record them at a louder level to annoy you!"

"That's a number one feeling . . ."

"I had an early contact with NW while I was at CKCQ in Quesnel," says Wayne Cox, "and it was an indication of what kind of a place it was and what kind of a news director Warren Barker was. I was doing the morning show, and Warren called. He introduced himself, and said 'I understand there's a fire at a hotel in Williams Lake.' And I said, 'There *is?*' He was right, too!"

which he was unable to do.

"That night, he did not go home. He went out and tried to revive himself with a good dinner. It was after 10 p.m. when he got into his car, feeling weary but whole, shot at but missed. He turned on his car radio and heard Jack Cullen's voice, singing 'They called her frivilush Shal, a peeculier short of a gal . . .'

"That was the end of Hal Davis' worst day in radio." ∎

Wayne had been advised: stay no longer than a year at your first station. Otherwise, you'll be there for life. So: "CHNL in Kamloops was opening, so, 13 months after I'd started at CKCQ, I drove to Kamloops and got a job. It was spring, 1970. And I was at CHNL for about a year-and-a-half, doing middle-of-the-road music. It was an NW kind of thing.

"I vowed if I ever got a chance to get back to Vancouver I would only work at NW. It was stable, solid, no revolving door. Well, as it happened, Mel Cooper, who was manager, had a brother, Wayne, who ran a grocery store in Kamloops. Wayne was having dinner with Mel in Vancouver, and gave me a plug. Hal Davis drove up to Kamloops, got a motel room and sat there and listened to me! Then he called me. 'Hi! My name's Hal Davis. How'd you like to work for CKNW?' I flipped. I knew who he was right away.

"I came down to NW at the same time they were talking to Dave McCormick. So Dave and I shared a weird combination of jobs and shifts: operating talk shows, doing traffic reports, bits and pieces of all sorts of things. But you might as well have handed me heaven.

"Around 1973 I was called into Mel Cooper's office. There's Mel, and there's Hal. They tell me they have an exciting prospect for me: the noon to 3 show. My first reaction was: what about Jack Kyle? They said, don't worry, we're arranging that. So that's how Wayne Cox and Friends started. There was music, and I'd talk to some regular guests. Clary Crowell was an NW salesman, but he was really into horoscopes, so we did those; Dolores Hale was a psychic; and there was a guy named Earle Bradford in the newsroom who was grousing about his assignments. I said, 'Earle, come on my show.' That's how he came out of news and started doing features, and that developed into Earle's Court, with Earle being a man-about-town and doing items.

"Wayne Cox and Friends lasted five years, then NW went to talk. When I'd started the show, I beat out Barrie Clark doing talk on CKWX. And when they replaced me, it was with Barrie Clark! I got into sports a little bit, did some sideline reports during Lions games, but it wasn't really my calling. I worked daily with Al Davidson and others, watching them throw it against the fan daily. That wasn't my style. I left in '78.

"But I have to say what a thrill it was for a kid in his 20s to be working as a headliner alongside people like Bob Hutton, Jack Kyle, Jack Cullen, Frosty Forst, Jack Webster and Rick Honey, at the number one station in western Canada. That's a number one feeling that never leaves you."

"Am I still in Canada . . .?"

Ted Smith, who was at CKNW from 1973 to 1985, and who would give a dramatic kick-start to CKNW's revenues, was born in 1943 in Toronto, grew up in Orangeville. "My dad's health was not good. He never made much money, and I always had to work and help out. When I was 14 and going to school I had three jobs: after school I'd go to the hospital and rent TV sets to patients, then I'd go home, eat quickly, and ride my bike to the local bowling alley where I'd set up pins from 7 to 11 every weeknight. I'd do my homework there. On weekends, I worked as a grocery clerk at the local IGA.

"I learned the work ethic at a young age.

"I trained as an RCAF pilot, and after leaving the air force started to pursue a career as an airline pilot. I discussed it with the airlines, and was to go see Air Canada in six months."

Instead, following a conversation with Steve French of CJOB, Ted ended up in radio sales. Within 19 months he was CJOB's top salesman. And one day Ted was called into general manager Rory MacLennan's office. "Rory calls me in, he was a great pipe smoker, he says, 'My son (puff, puff), you've been doing a great job (puff, puff). How would you like to be our national sales manager?' 'Gee, Mr. MacLennan, I don't even know what a national sales manager does.' '(Puff, puff) You'll learn.'"

One year later, Ted was promoted to general sales manager of CJOB, both AM and FM.

"In this business," Ted says, "credibility is like virginity. Once you lose it, you never get it back. I've always been straight with my clients, and have asked everyone I've hired to be the same.

"I spent a little over 10 years at CJOB. Around 1973 Bill Hughes came to Winnipeg to see me. Bill was executive vice president of Western Broadcasting, which owned CJOB and CKNW. Bill says, 'We've got problems in our sales division in Vancouver. We'd like you to be our director of sales, and in a couple of years take over as general manager of our Vancouver stations.' My initial response to him was Thanks, but No. 'I've heard your management style is quite dictatorial. I'm a believer in a more democratic style.' A month later Hal Davis came to see me. Hal says, 'Bill Hughes is moving downtown. I'm going to be running the station. I need you to handle sales.' I felt I could work with Hal, so I went out to have a look. It was the first time I'd been in Vancouver since my RCAF days. I had just come from Winnipeg, and 40 below! I looked around at this place, and said, 'Am I still in Canada, or have I made a navigational error?'"

There was no error. As Ted would soon discover, he was in exactly the right place at exactly the right time.

"Yeah, but they're all so OLD . . ."

Brian "Frosty" Forst is part of the well-known Forst family, whose furniture and appliances stores were Lower Mainland landmarks for decades. Forst's Stores sponsored the noon news on CKNW for many years.

You could probably trace Frosty's radio career back to the day his dad brought home an old Seabreeze tape recorder. "My friend Bob Hicks and I played 'disc jockey' on that thing." For Frosty, going from pretending to doing the real thing was a natural progression: he took a course in broadcasting run by CKWX program director John Ansell. "I told myself I'm going to work at the top station, on the best shift."

Brian "Frosty" Forst.

Ansell was impressed by the young Forst's skill at reading commercials. Ansell spoke to CKWX manager Tiny Elphicke . . . whose brother Cecil was manager of CKPG, Prince George. Brian, 18, went north. He got to Prince George the same year (1956) the PGE got there.

He wasn't there long. Red Robinson, very successful at CJOR, had been lured away by CKWX. "CJOR held a teenage disc jockey contest to find a replacement," says Frosty, "but none of them was any good. I was the right age. They phoned me.

Bob Mutis: "One of the ongoing Orphans' Fund events is the Ladies Bowling League. We usually took the ladies to the Food Building at the PNE and wined and dined them. There were celebrity dealers and prizes.

"We had a Honda Civic for a prize in a random draw at the end of the day. There were 300 ladies there. By the end of the day we have a huge room full of pleasantly sozzled ladies. Bob Hutton, the MC, makes the draw and announces the winner's name. It was Val White, and she bowled at lanes somewhere in Burnaby. Well, wouldn't you know it: There were *two* Val Whites, and they both bowled at the same alley! What a disaster!" The correct Val White was eventually selected — and NW, realizing what a crushing disappointment it must have been to the other lady after hearing her name called out, sent her and her family to Hawaii." ∎

Along about 1980 manager Ted

Smith told Rick Honey the station

hadn't been getting what it want-

ed out of promotion ever since

the departure of John Plul. Would

Rick help? Yes.

Still holding down his drive-

show shift, Rick mapped out a

year's worth of promotion ideas.

One of them still pays dividends

to the CKNW Orphans' Fund:

Pledge Days. Following a visit to a

New York City convention of

broadcast promotion people, Rick

saw the advantage for an event

like Pledge Day of VISIBLE radio.

"When we put Pledge Day into

the Bayshore, I wanted it to look

like a TV set. We did a three-hour

drive on Bannerman's show, with

Shirley Stocker producing, and it

went very well. We had no prob-

lem getting cooperation from

stars; I've sat beside Ella Fitzger-

ald and Ginger Rogers, Milton

Berle, Mitzi Gaynor, the Irish

Rovers, Bill Kenny, the Beach

Boys, BTO, Lily Tomlin, Anne Mur-

ray, etc., etc., and etc." ∎

'We're holding a teenage DJ contest, and you're gonna win.'" He did, too.

Now, this may be hard to believe, but Frosty Forst is not an extrovert. All the things that Red Robinson had done so eagerly at CJOR — hosting the Kitsilano Show-boat, doing interviews with musical stars, hosting live programs — were impossible for painfully shy Brian Forst! "Bruno Cimolai was my co-host, he did all that stuff."

That's likely one of the reasons his experience as a CJOR disc jockey was brief. They fired him. "That was my first firing at OR. The second one came after I did news for them for a while."

Brian Forst, future radio powerhouse, found himself working in the stockroom of a company distributing ladies' foundation garments. Then he worked briefly in Woodward's parking garage.

But you can't keep a fiercely ambitious man down, especially if he's good. In quick succession, Brian worked at CJOR, then CKLG, and then at CFUN.

"The 'Frosty' thing started there. We all had nicknames. Dave McCormick was Big Daddy, Jerry Landa was Jerry Lee Landa, there was Happy Pappy Al Jordan. Red Robinson was there, but he went to WX later. J.B. Shayne and Jolly John Tanner were there. Roy Jacques was news director, and he had guys like Cameron Bell and Jim Nielsen."

At the same time Frosty was offered a job at KPOY in Honolulu, Hal Davis of CKNW came calling. "Hal offered me a job. My dad was saying, 'Go to NW, go to NW,' and I was saying 'Yeah, but they're all so OLD — Wally Garrett, Bob Hutton. And they were *folksy,* playing Lester Lanin all afternoon. After I began at NW I start-ed suggesting to Hal Davis we drop stuff like garden reports!"

Brian "Frosty" Forst had come to CKNW, and the folksy old station would never be the same.

"They were content driving cheap cars . . ."

Ted Smith started as NW's sales manager in December of 1973. "CKNW had problems. Their revenues had been flat — around $3 million a year for three years. They had 11 people in two separate sales departments, one for CKNW and one for CFMI. In my opinion, this was stupid. The first thing I did was combine the departments. You want your best people selling both stations. There was one standout in the sales staff: Jack Braverman, the best retail salesman I've ever seen.

"The rest had reached their comfort level. They were content driving cheap cars and wearing polyester suits. So we had Braverman and the 'B Team.' Over the next 14 months I didn't 'fire' any-body, but I persuaded 10 of the 11 they didn't have a future at NW, and it might be cosier for them to find a job while they still had one. The 10 left, I replaced them with five people who had something to prove, and a desire to get ahead.

Ted Smith (left) came on board in 1973.

"When I came in '73 I made a lot of changes, and sales increased by more than $1 million a year for the next 10 years. After I'd been there two years as director of sales a decision was made in the head office in Vancouver to move

NW's general manager Hal Davis out of the GM's job, and into Western International Communications as director of research and development. I was made general manager, and a year later added the title of president. In all, I was 12 years at the station, almost 10 of them as general manager and president.

"In 1985 I was at a hockey game with Frank Griffiths, Sr., our chairman. Play stopped for a moment, and Frank leaned over. 'Do you think you could run our group *as well* as NW?' I said, 'No.' 'Do you have someone who could run NW?' 'Yes. Ron Bremner.'

"I had made Ron my sales manager around '76, '77, and groomed him."

In early 1986 Bremner moved up from sales manager at CKNW to general manager, and Ted Smith became president of the Westcom Radio Group, a Western International Communications subsidiary.

Rick Honey came to CKNW in 1973 as part of the 'youth movement.'

"We have eleven stations in Canada. The difference between the two jobs? When I ran NW it was like standing on the bridge steering the ships . . . now I feel more like I'm standing on shore, shouting directions."

"I don't want to wait a week . . ."

"When I was 12," Rick Honey remembers, "my father, who was a policeman, took me to a different business every week to see what my career would be."

One of those places in Winnipeg must have been a radio station, because not long after that, he started working as an operator and music librarian at the FM side of CJOB. "FM was brand new at the time. I think there were two sets in the whole city, and my mother had one of them."

Rick had left school after Grade 10, "just sort of wandered out." Two years later he was invited back to the old school to give a talk on radio.

Rick moved around in radio and TV, to Kenora, then Port Arthur, and ended up in the Maritimes. In 1969, on a recommendation from Robert Wood of Toronto's CHUM, he got a call from Frank Callaghan at Vancouver's CKLG.

"I looked around Vancouver, and knew we'd be here forever. Three weeks after I started at LG I got a call from CHUM! Would I be interested . . . but I wasn't by then. I went on LG from noon to 3, replacing Terry David Mulligan. Other people there? Roy Hennessey, Jim Hault, Daryl B, John Tanner, Tim Burge, J.B. Shayne, Bill Reiter was doing the all-night show . . .

"I did a lot of MC work, too. I remember I emceed a B.C. Lions event, and made them laugh. Hey, that felt *good*.

"I was at LG from '69 to '73. We'd listen to NW, and I'd think: that's where I want to be. I could talk to people, interview, be me. Well, Hal Davis called me one day. My heart stopped. Frosty had asked me years before if I'd be interested in just being around NW, and Hal's call was part of that. Frosty had recommended me. So we had the usual clandestine meeting; we got together in the Doric Howe Hotel at 10 o'clock Tuesday morning. I had hair down to my shoulders, but I wore my suit."

In 1955 Bill Rea, on business in the States, sent engineer Jack Gordon a photograph of a glass-walled mobile studio. "Can we do this?" he asked. Gordon had it designed and released for duty by 1957. "The theme of that studio," he said, "was people moving out to meet people." So he shaped it with that in mind, then commissioned well-known artist B.C. Binning to devise a color scheme. Wearing its First Prize ribbon, it rolled along in the PNE Parade to begin its long broadcasting life at the Exhibition Grounds. Today, it serves another owner as a food concession!

NW's staff is happy with its replacement: Today's Crystal Palace has air conditioning! ∎

When morningman Brian "Frosty" Forst came to CKNW the folksy old station would never be the same.

Philip Till began freelancing in 1974, which led to a curious connection with the National Enquirer. Based in Europe, Till had never heard of this sensational story-concocting weekly. He jumped at their request for a story on a new phenomenon in Europe: abortion clinics. "They offered me $350, about twice what I made weekly at UPI. I duly delivered 3,000 words. I found out later the article was reduced to 50 words, and carried the headline I ATE MY BABY!" ∎

CKNW was shaping a 'youth movement'; talking to Rick and Wayne Cox and people of that age was part of the plan. Morning man Bob Hutton's audience was getting older, and, says Rick, "it was getting harder to sell fridges to them. Hal asked, 'If we — CKNW — wanted to do such and such on the air, who should do that?' And I started listing names: Red Robinson, Fred Latremouille, Roy Hennessey, Jim Hault . . . and me. And, I said, I'm at the top of that list. Hal called Mel Cooper, the manager, from the hotel room and we arranged to meet the next week at the same time at CKNW. Before the week was up, I called Hal. 'I don't want to wait a week. I want to talk to you sooner.' Hal was thrilled I'd called, that I was excited about coming to work for NW. 'You come in tomorrow morning at 11.' Not ten minutes after that meeting I got a call from Jack Wasserman. 'What's this I hear about you moving to CKNW?'

"John Fox, the sales manager, met me the next day. He took me around, introduced me to people. Now, I was used to working in a pretty flaky place. But here? No T-shirts, no half-clad babes, the place looked like a hospital."

Rick just watched for a month, with Bob Hutton showing him the ropes. On April 3, 1973, when he started on air (in a suit and tie, his hair properly cut and combed), it took a bit of adjusting. "I didn't feel totally comfortable. The salesmen said I was screaming on air."

The first thing he said on the air: "How do you like me so far?"

In April of 1993 Rick Honey celebrated 20 uninterrupted years as afternoon drive-time host on CKNW!

"A seagull dropped a load . . ."

One of the fastest-rising of CKNW's people started out with ambitions to be a teacher. Even when he graduated from high school in his native Hamilton, Ontario, and joined an advertising agency, 18-year-old Ron Bremner had that idea. He was at Russell T. Kelly Advertising a year-and-a-half.

"I remembered something Tommy Darling, an old family friend, had once said to me. 'If you're ever interested in radio, call me.' Tommy was the president of CHML, by then part of the Western Group. I called him. 'Remember, five years ago, you said "If you're ever interested . . . " Well, I'm calling.' He said, 'Be in my office in 20 minutes.'

"Tommy set up an interview for me with Arnold Stinson, the general manager of Standard Broadcast Sales. Standard represented virtually every major station in Canada. He hired me in September of 1972. I got the 'left-over' accounts. They were small, but it was the best training I could have. As a sales person there, you were more afraid of coming back without a sale than of facing CEOs. Stinson encouraged bypassing ad agencies, and going to the client directly. He was always proudest of you when an agency complained you had called on their account and made a deal."

Ron got a call one day from Ted Smith, general sales manager at CKNW. "Ted said, 'What are you doing this weekend?' It was Easter weekend, 1974. My wife and I flew out to Vancouver, talked with Ted during CKNW's Easter Egg hunt at the PNE. The weather was beautiful. It was a *great* day to interview a guy from Toronto! A little later, back in Toronto, Ted called and offered me a job. We came out in May of 1974, and I started as a salesman for CKNW and CFMI. I took over the list of a departing salesman — half the accounts he'd told management he had, he didn't have. I think I was the first person Ted hired at CKNW — he wanted to revamp the sales department, wanted a new kind of thinking there. He was very focused and determined."

In fact, Ted Smith would go on to clear the sales department of all but one of the people there when he arrived: the formidable Jack Braverman.

"I remember my first day in Vancouver," Ron continues. "Ted took me out, we made our first call together to a Gastown client. We're crossing the street and a seagull dropped a load on my brand-new suit. Ted was in hysterics. I told him my mother used to say that was good luck.

"Ted used to say I made more cold calls than anyone. I stood once at the south foot of Lonsdale in North Vancouver and walked up one side of the street to McDonald's, and back down the other side, and went into *every* store trying my pitch. And I made sales.

"I'd try things. I said to Ron Bezeau of Ace Carpets in Maillardville, 'How'd you like to own a radio station for a weekend?' He'd get 10 spots on Saturday, 10 on Sunday at $9 each.

"I'd come home, my wife would have a stack of business cards on the table, potential new business. 'You'd better hurry,' she'd say, 'Jack Braverman is probably on his way over to these places right now!'"

". . . you rely on each other . . ."

Former NW news beater Marlaina Gayle had one of the most exotic ethnic backgrounds at the station: half-Argentinian, half-Ukrainian in descent. And her entry into the world was off-beat, too: "My mother was at the Stanley Theatre in Vancouver

Bill Hughes' interest in world travel was spurred by the 1950s program Gangway. He was national sales manager at the time, but also hosted this regular portside program, in which he took a "portable" unit (in two suitcases weighing 40 pounds each) and went aboard ships anchored in New Westminster harbor to interview the crews. New Westminster was a deep-sea port then, and sailors from all over the world could be found there.

Bob Giles took the program over when it returned in 1956, after a brief hiatus. Eventually, it was phased out. ∎

After two decades dominating the mornings, Bob Hutton retired.

Jim Cox's beginnings in football were not smooth. Hal Davis recalls when he and Bill Surphlis, who was involved in junior football, sat in with Jim the first time he would do football play-by-play. "We were at Brockton Oval," Hal says, "and about to carry a junior game, but Jim had forgotten to tell us he had never seen a football game before. We had to tell him they needed to make 10 yards in three downs. He ended up being the dean of football broadcasters in Canada, did a great job." In fact, Jim came to enjoy football immensely. "It's more sophisticated than hockey. The game is based more on deception. I think of it as chess played with live men . . ." He would call play-by-play on B.C. Lions' games for more than 25 years. ∎

watching a Jerry Lewis movie an hour before I was born." That was December 28, 1957. Today, Marlaina is consumer reporter at The Province, writes one of the most widely-read columns in that paper.

"Warren Barker had started hiring women in the mid-70s; when I started Doriana Temolo was there, Belle Puri, Yvonne Eamor, Barbi Whiting. Al Davidson called me Mary Tyler Moore. 'Oh, Maiiiirrr . . .'"

Still raw and untested, Marlaina found the pace too fast, transferred to the slower rhythm of CFMI, and "started learning a lot by osmosis." The two stations' coverage of the horrific 1977 air crash at Tenerife alerted her to the fact that, for CKNW/CFMI, news was not a fly-by-night thing. "They wanted to *know* and they wanted to know *first*."

Marlaina graduated from BCIT, and Warren Barker told her she could probably get a job in the newsroom, and spend the rest of her life there and make no money. He suggested she get out and get some seasoning.

She did, at CKPG, Prince George; at a Calgary rock station, at CFAX, at CKNW again, CBC-TV News, NW for a third time . . . and now The Province.

Marlaina's memories of NW are good. "The news system is so fixed it was as if I'd never been away. You just get plugged in and away you go. Leaving NW was like leaving home. You end up being part of a family, you rely on each other, you know everything about each other."

". . . orange crates full of documents . . ."

Gary Bannerman: "When Jack Webster left to go to CJOR, it dealt a blow to NW. Ed Murphy at WX was a strong number two. Hal Davis and Mel Cooper got Murphy away from WX, then they got Art Finley. But how do they go about battling Webster? Cooper's idea was to *bolster* Murphy and Finley with reporting from the field, an emphasis on the concept rather than on personalities. Terry Spence was the best man in NW's newsroom, and he wanted to be an investigative reporter. The Investigators started. On Day One, they had Ed Murphy, Terry Spence and Art Finley. The station could afford one more person. Maybe, they thought, someone with a newspaper background would be a good resource. Carl Waiz from NW and I worked together at city hall, and Carl suggested me to Hal Davis. Hal phoned me out of the blue, and we met."

Bannerman started at NW August 21, 1972.

He didn't take long to make an impression. In February of 1973 his commentary on Vancouver police department policies resulted in more than 700 irate phone calls to CKNW, the most the station had ever got on any issue.

Jack Wasserman wrote that Bannerman's 90-minute study of the local heroin problem had shed more light on the subject than the LeDain Commission. And it was Wasserman who announced in June that Ed Murphy, "anchorman of CKNW's Investigators," was leaving NW to go to CJOR.

With Murphy's departure, Hal Davis was again in need of a spark, a strong open-line host. Art Finley didn't like doing the hard stories, and was talking about returning to the U.S. The Investigators name continued, but the concept altered: in effect, NW went back to the star system, and the star was Gary Bannerman. "I tried to temper NW's voracious appetite for BIG stories. Hal and Mel thought we'd be getting major breaks every hour. It can't be done. These things can take weeks, sometimes months, of research.

"B.C. had no ombudsman at the time, and we'd be getting people coming in with three orange crates full of documents. Seventy per cent of them were frightful malingerers. We did exposés of crooked spas, crooked car dealers . . . everyone of us on the Investigators can list big stories."

By December of 1973 CKNW's Investigators were outrating CJOR's Webster and CKWX's Barrie Clark. In March of '74 CKWX threw in the towel, dropped its talk shows, and switched to a country-music format.

Also in '74 Shirley Stocker joined NW. She became Gary's producer, occasional co-host and fill-in. They developed a strong professional rapport, and he came to count on her solid support. Cracked Ted Smith, "It took Shirley four years to get Bannerman to say 'incredible' instead of 'bullshit.' "

His writing background made Bannerman quotable. He made the papers in July, 1975 with his comments on the beginning of sex education in B.C.'s schools: "Our schools teach the kids reading and writing, and they can't spell. They teach them arithmetic, and they can't add. Now they're teaching sex education. I guess that ends the worry about the population explosion."

Bannerman has had more than 150 libel actions brought against him, has never lost one. Two were settled out of court. One of those occurred in 1978 when Bannerman and CKNW were sued by former Surrey mayor Ed McKitka for alleged defamatory remarks.

The May, 1978 ratings showed Bannerman beating Webster in local ratings, within a whisker of him in total audience. That news made manager Ted Smith so happy he sent a radiogram to inform Gary, who was cruising aboard the Island Princess. 1978 had more good news in store. Grace McCarthy, then B.C.'s minister of tourism, was in London having lunch with Patrick Reid, the president of the International Bureau of Expositions. Out of the McCarthy-Reid conversation came Vancouver's Expo 86. Bannerman would be more and more heavily involved as Expo approached.

In 1979 open-liner Barrie Clark came over to CKNW. Clark's background was impressive: he had been a broadcaster for 16 years, a Liberal MLA, the province's Rentalsman, and had preceded his NW arrival with four years' service as B.C.'s ombudsman. There was immediate friction between Clark and Bannerman. Years later Clark told reporter Richard Skelly, "I found Gary to be the most difficult man to work with I had ever encountered in a lifetime of broadcasting." Clark demanded, and got, a wall erected between his work area and Bannerman's in the Holiday Inn studios. The two men entered and exited by different doors. Clark would eventually leave NW, works today as an open-line host for CKOV, Kelowna.

In 1982 Bannerman won Vancouver Rotary's annual award for "service above self," followed the next year by the British Columbia Association of Broadcasters' Annual Community Service Award.

"I get into everything around here . . ."

The morning of her interview for this book Shirley Stocker, CKNW's executive producer for public affairs programming, had to push the time back an hour because Rafe Mair had a bad case of laryngitis . . . and Shirley had to jump in to replace him.

Gary Bannerman, on his April 3, 1985 show, had conveyed an opinion on the ability of Canada's Native people to govern themselves. His remarks were unthinking and intemperate, and created a firestorm of negative publicity. He eventually apologized: "Every once in a while," he told his listeners, "you run into a truck. In the worst cases, you find the truck is yourself. Some of my remarks are indefensible and I make no defence, none." He then opened up his telephone lines to let his critics at him. "I still respect Bannerman as a broadcaster," the Sun's Denny Boyd wrote the next day. "But I hope in future he takes a deep breath, counts five and checks his ammo before he fires from the hip. There's no room in radio for Rambo." ∎

Gary came to count on Shirley Stocker for support.

For more than 20 years every NW hourly newscast ended with: "Are You Listening! Before the next half-hourly newscast we will phone you. If you have the answer to this question, you will, win (whatever the jackpot was at the time).

"Here is the question . . ."

The feature started on the 8 a.m. news and went to 9 p.m. If the answer wasn't forthcoming, the jackpot grew until someone came up with the right answer. The questions could vary from "On what street does the Second Street bus run?" (an actual example!) to something pertaining to the newscast itself. Names were selected at random from the telephone book. After his newscast, the news reader made the phone call, and the result was reported on the half hour.

After more than two decades the feature was dropped in 1973, as an economy measure. There was hardly a ripple of comment from the loyal listeners.

So much for indispensable features. ∎

Being on air herself was no novelty, as NW listeners know. Stocker has been a regular presence on the station for 20 years.

She was born and grew up in Ottawa, started in the accounting department at CBC there. Shirley was Miss CBC Ottawa in 1967. She moved from accounting to a research position as liaison between the CBC and several federal government ministries, a job that occasionally got her on the air. Consumerism was beginning to rivet public attention, and Shirley would occasionally interview consumer affairs minister Ron Basford for CBC. Then she began doing regular two- and three-minute reports on consumerism, one of them national.

On a two-month sabbatical, divorced and with three children, Stocker came west to Vancouver. She had no prospects, but tried at the CBC's Vancouver office and was hired. "I started doing investigative consumer reporting, and people started noticing. Allan Fotheringham wrote about me, Jack Wasserman wrote about me, Earle Bradford commented on my work on his NW show . . . and then I got a call from Hal Davis. He said, 'I don't know your work, but there's certainly *something* going on. Do you want to come talk to me?'"

NW was looking for a female reporter for the show Gary Bannerman and The Investigators. "I came down and talked to Hal and Bannerman. Gary asked, 'What kind of stuff can you do?' and I said I could, for example, probably report on vaginal sprays with more authority than he could. They said they'd give me six months, see if I liked it. Things started going really well. But it was disorganized. Everyone vied for the same guests, schedules were mixed up, it wasn't coordinated . . . Gary was getting frustrated. He asked me if I would organize things. I still did a fair amount of on-air work with Gary, but after a couple of dozen fights among the staff, I was put in charge of coordinating the talk shows. And that's when my organizational skills came through."

And she kept her reporting skills honed. "I did a show once on asbestos in kettles. We got an advisory from Consumer Affairs that some manufacturers were putting asbestos in their electric kettles. I made a few calls, then went on the air and broke the story. It was a hot report. The guest on the air at the time was furniture and appliance dealer Ben Wosk!"

Stocker's plate is full: in her stable of talkers are Rafe Mair, Bill Good, Philip Till, Gary Bannerman, Lee Powell, and CFMI's Dan Russell. She's particularly proud of her association with Till: "He was my find."

By the way, a snoopy interviewer can't help noticing Shirley also handles the talk-show studio petty cash, and fixes the typewriters! "Oh, yeah, I get into everything around here.

"A real career highlight for me," says Shirley, "is the CKNW Orphans' Fund Pledge Day. I organized the first one, and it went well. And now I'm involved in Pledge Day every year: in 1992 our one-day program brought in more than $500,000 for the Fund."

"I used NW's system against them . . ."

How many newsmen do you know who can get stories by pretending to be German laborers? (See page 96, sidebar.)

CKNW newsman Arnold Epp was born in Vancouver in 1941. "I came from a family of strict Mennonites; my dad was a co-founder of the first United Mennonite Church in South Vancouver.

"When I was seven or eight I used to pretend I was broadcasting hockey games, but I didn't get into broadcasting until relatively late: I was 26. Frank Callaghan was running a broadcast school. I went there, and what I got out of it was that there was damn little glamor and a lot of hard work. I got a job at CJDC in Dawson Creek, radio and TV. I was a deejay, did news, sports. I was there four months, then went to CKPG in Prince George."

Arnie next moved to CJOR, then to CKVN, then back to OR where Erwin Swangard was now news director. "When I got there, I started using NW's system against them. I'd come in with my briefcase stuffed with stories I'd written already — labor checks, the cop shop, and so on. I did labor stories a lot when I was at OR; labor's easy to do: the people are accessible. Finally, I'd had enough of OR. Swangard, for all his news sense, was features oriented. And NW was the only one spending money.

"On June 1st, 1976 I started with NW News. I'd done beat at OR, but I hate sitting at meetings. I miss the story and fall asleep. I came here with the understanding I wouldn't go outside. It works for me: I have a knack about whether a fire story is worth it, a knack for police stories. I come in about 9:20 a.m., leave about 4:45, sometimes longer, never shorter.

"It's exciting working here. With Gord Macdonald in now as news director, the system's almost the same. Gord is Warren Barker incarnate. He's the only one with the energy level to run this place, and he's got the education. He's fine-tuning the system, so we're bound to see changes. I think the station's reliance on star names reading the news is overplayed. It's the *news* that matters, and getting it first."

Getting it first is second nature in this ferociously curious newsroom. Arnold recalls the time prison inmate Andy Bruce called CKNW to announce he was holding hostages, one of them a guard, in the B.C. Pen's public holding area. Epp called the prison for details . . . "and they didn't even know there was a situation!"

"I'm a 24-hour-a-day guy . . ."

Jack Cullen opened a record shop in Brentwood Mall June 12, 1971. To celebrate, NW brought its personalities in to do an all-day remote from the store. Jack's studio had been installed behind glass at the back of the store. He expanded his retail empire too quickly, opened stores in Guildford and Kingsgate. They closed, and he eventually sold the Brentwood store to a chain.

And during this time he got an attractive offer to come over to CJOR. By now, NW didn't want to lose this audience-pleaser, so Jack Stewart — NW's program director at the time — came up with a neat solution: they raised Cullen's salary handsomely and bought his collection. Jack would continue to have exclusive access to it until he decided to retire or died. NW paid Jack $100,000, and gives him a monthly stipend to keep it updated.

Jack's hoarding ways go beyond music and vintage radio programs. He has more than 15,000 movies in his personal collection. "I'm a 24-hour-a-day guy," he says, "Everything I do is related to my work/hobby. I don't have a pension plan with NW, I'm not a staffer. That's why I'm still working."

In March, 1993 John Francis Cullen, self-described "boy disc jockey," was awarded the Canada 125 Medal.

Jack Cullen added to his vast collection of recorded material in ways that were sometimes . . . mischievous. This famous tale bears retelling: Frank Sinatra was appearing at the PNE Forum. Cullen got there an hour before the show, and, in Sun columnist Jack Wasserman's words, "spread some liquid sunshine among the attendants and hid the pre-set tape recorder under the stage. He wired it into the Forum sound system and arranged for someone to plug in the AC when the show started. The only dicey moment came half-way through the show when Cullen had to leave his seat, get under the stage and change the tape." Luckily, Sinatra was singing a ballad and the lights were low. ∎

Self-described "boy disc jockey" Jack Cullen.

A little of everything . . .

Announcer/operator Leigh Mackay started working at CKNW September 1, 1976. His voice is heard more often than his name . . . although Joy Metcalfe is often heard to thank him when he introduces Joy's Journal. Leigh, by the way, named Joy's show — just as he'd named its predecessor, Earle's Court.

Ten days after starting at NW Leigh went solo with a remote from Wosk's on SW Marine Drive, and the day after, began doing the Sunday Road Show from 5:30 to 8 p.m. Soon he was doing the weekday road shows, filling in for Rick Honey, then the weekend morning shows. He has subbed for Frosty Forst when the Frostmeister is ill, even did the Owl Prowl for vacationing Jack Cullen.

Leigh's done a little of everything, actually. One thing he did, for which a CKNW historian is hugely grateful, was to compile in his own computer a chronology of station events. Much of the research on this book was considerably smoothed thanks to that detailed chronology. (We learn from it that Arthur Griffiths, son of owner Frank Griffiths, spent the summer of 1978 working in CKNW's promotion department . . . and assigned himself the task of washing the Crystal Palace.)

In September, 1981 Leigh became supervising operator for both AM and FM.

"How'd you like Jack Webster . . .?"

The problem of the pesky Jack Webster, hurting CKNW with his ratings at old rival CJOR, was ended in 1978 when the feisty Scot was lured away by television. That "luring" had taken some doing, and it is possible Webster himself does not know the full story. It's a fascinating look at the behind-the-scenes manoeuvering that makes broadcasting such a volatile profession. In his autobiography, Webster says Bill Elliott gave him an offer to join BCTV. There was more to that offer than Jack knew.

This is the first time this story has been told in print.

Ted Smith's natural instincts, when he realized Webster's CJOR broadcasts were eroding CKNW's dominance, were to make Webster an irresistible financial offer to tempt him away from OR. It had worked before. Smith met with Webster to discuss the possibilities. Webster said he missed many of the NW people, but there was a major obstacle: his contract specifically forbade him to work for any other local radio station for two years in the event he left CJOR's employ.

Smith asked Webster if he'd ever considered a career in TV, and did his contract prevent it. The answer: no to both questions.

Later, and without Webster's knowledge, Smith picked up the phone and called Ray Peters, president of BCTV, Vancouver's CTV affiliate. "Ray," he said, "how'd you like to have Jack Webster do a talk show for you?"

"I'd like it fine," Peters replied, "but do you know what he makes? We can't afford him."

"How'd you like him for nothing?" Smith asked. "We'll pay his contract for the first two years."

Silence.

"Oh," Peters said. There was more silence for a moment. Then: "O.K." He agreed to keep the arrangement confidential.

Not long after, BCTV made their generous offer to Webster to come do a talk show for them. Webster accepted, and left CJOR.

End of problem.

"It worked like a dream . . ."

A breakthrough by CKNW's engineering staff, which faced a technical challenge in the planning of CFMI, had consequences for NW, too . . . so the story of the creation of the Aristocart has a place here.

Radio stations like tape cartridges. They're plastic holders for short loops of tape typically holding one piece of music or a few commercials. Inaudible cues on the tape stop it when it comes to the end of the song or announcement. They're flexible: it's easier to slap a cartridge in than find a specific cut on a long-playing record or a reel-to-reel tape.

Today, with CDs and other technological advances, the use of "carts" is diminishing. But for a few decades they were *it*. And the Aristocart marked a technical advance that quickly made it an industry benchmark.

When CFMI started, a decision was made to have the station automated. That meant only the news would be live. It was a low-cost way to run a station. The snag came with the simultaneous decision to go *stereo*. The greater clarity of FM, and a growing public desire for it, made stereo broadcasting essential.

There wasn't a cartridge available that would accurately play stereo.

"The problem," says former NW engineer Don Kalmakoff, "was maintaining the phase relationship between the left and right channels. If you're listening to stereo, no problem. But most people back then were listening in mono. And if you didn't constantly maintain that phase relationship, the mono sound was muggy, wishy-washy.

"Then one night it suddenly dawned on me what we were doing wrong. I phoned Dave Glasstetter and Dick DiPalma. 'I've got it, guys!' They say, 'Sure, sure.' I say, 'Meet me at the station.' We all gather at NW. It's midnight. I explain the concept, and we get to work on the lathe in the shop. By 4 a.m. we had our prototype. Dick DiPalma still has it. We put it in, we played it, it worked like a dream. We were ecstatic."

Don Kalmakoff made a years-long career of selling the Aristocart. Dave Glasstetter and Dick DiPalma both got

Jack Gordon and Aristocart inventor Don Kalmakoff in studio.

$750 for their part in its development, and had the satisfaction of seeing it in use in booths at broadcasting conventions. But there was another reward, as Dave explains: "Mel Cooper called us in one day, very stern and serious looking, says there are real concerns with the Aristocart. We're worried, wondering what's wrong. Then he grins and opens a door, and there's a big party for us: champagne, cake, the works. We had just won the Keith S. Rogers Memorial Trophy for the Aristocart's development." ■

Adding to the Aristocart's innovations was an improvement in the system of moving the tape through the cartridge and past the tape heads.

That was Dave Glasstetter's brainchild. "Pressure pads in cartridges," he says, "have to be made of very soft material. They hold the tape firmly in contact with the head, but there has to be negligible resistance to the passage of the tape. The pickup head is slightly rounded, and pushes up against the tape.

"I thought of using plumber's tape. This is white stuff, very soft and thin, plumbers use it to join two pieces of threaded pipe. It forms a seal. I sandwiched this stuff with adhesives and bonded it to the foam rubber pressure pads. Then I put together a machine that fed it out in strips. We 'cured' it for two weeks, it bonded, then we punch-pressed chunks of it out to put into the Aristocarts. It worked." ■

*Rick Hansen on his
"Man in Motion" World Tour.*

"The Line-up Now Was Utterly Different . . ."

THE EIGHTIES BEGAN WITH A MOMENTOUS EVENT, AS PRIME Minister Trudeau announced his intention to entrench a Canadian constitution. CKNW reported on the emergence of a genuine Canadian hero, Terry Fox. In 1985, inspired by Fox, one-legged Steve Fonyo would complete a cross-country run and raise further millions. The Vancouver Canucks made a tantalizingly close encounter with the Stanley Cup in 1982.

B.C. Place Stadium opened in Vancouver. Prime Minister Trudeau went for his famous walk in the snow; North Vancouver's Bryan Adams began a climb toward musical fame; Pope John Paul II visited British Columbia in September of 1984, attracting huge crowds (and CKNW).

On the international scene, the Soviet Union selected a new leader named Mikhail Gorbachev. Back home, Premier Bill Bennett stepped down and was succeeded by Bill Vander Zalm; Expo 86 opened and brought the world to British Columbia — and gave opening-day crowds a close look at a fairy-tale couple, Prince Charles and Diana, The Princess of Wales. The $1 "loonie" made its debut; Wayne Gretzky went to Los Angeles and Canada went into shock, and Ben Johnson lost his 1988 Olympic medal when tests showed he'd been taking steroids; the Skydome opened in Toronto in 1989, and that year ended with Audrey McLaughlin being elected leader of the NDP, the first woman to lead a national party in Canada.

At CKNW the pace of the Eighties was every bit as rapid. NW became the first AM outlet in Greater Vancouver to go stereo, and in 1980 Dave Glasstetter of the engineering staff developed the "Phone Box," a device that became an industry standard — it allows the host to have a speaker phone beside him when he's on the air, without squealing feedback being generated.

Terry Moore, a boisterous and affable talk-show host, joined CKNW in 1980. Another familiar name that popped up that year: Bob Robertson. Bob, whose skill at voices was frequently put to use at NW, is co-host with Linda Cullen, another CKNW graduate, of the popular CBC series Double Exposure. An era ended when Bob Hutton finally cut the last tie that bound him to CKNW, and went into retirement.

A new CKNW Crystal Palace made its debut at the 1981 Abbotsford Air Show. The on-air staff really liked the new model: it had air conditioning!

Jack Cullen's Owl Prowl, which had been shrinking and growing and shifting around on the late-night schedule like a musical amoeba, finally settled into the 9 p.m. to midnight slot it occupies to this day.

Do a daily program long enough and things like this happen: in October, 1983 Bill Hughes, with wife Dorothy by his side, was on the Great Wall of China interviewing people on tape for his Roving Mike show. Asked one amiable tourist, "Are you Bill Hughes?" It turns out the fellow, an Australian, had been interviewed by Bill in Vancouver on a vacation nine years earlier! And more than once Fraser Valley listeners have stopped prairie-bound buses because they've heard old friends being interviewed on Roving Mike and want to see them once again! ∎

Hal Davis: "Frank Wade wrote a series of 45-second vignettes for CKNW called This is Christmas, and we still run them more than 40 years later. We sell them to other stations, too."

Speaking of Christmas, one tradition Hal began as program director was a 12-hour (you read that right) program of music and memorabilia for Christmas Day. "It's always a problem getting people to work on Christmas. So I started a plan in which every dee-jay recorded a series of 15-minute bits. This led to the production of 'Christmas Is,' the first major undertaking of Western Produc-tions. Dick Abbott and David Hoole turned the idea into a 12-hour package of everything that

Ron Bremner's rise in the station's hierarchy continued as he became vice pres-ident and director of sales. Rod Gunn returned to the corporate fold as general man-ager of CHQR, Calgary, another station in the growing Western Broadcast chain. Paul Preston had his considerable production talents put to use in 1982 when he was appointed production director. And after 30 years with CKNW, one of the sta-tion's most highly regarded people, Erm Fiorillo, retired. The aggressively inven-tive John Plul returned as promotion director, and was named vice president, marketing a year later.

In 1983 station pioneers were shocked and saddened to hear of the death in Santa Barbara of station founder Bill Rea.

Doug Rutherford, who would go on to become NW's program director, joined the station in 1983, would take over the reins of WIN, the Western Information Network. WIN began to transmit on satellite in 1984, first radio news service in Canada to use that technology. And that satellite was also put to use in transmit-ting province-wide, to any station requesting it, NW's all-night record show. First host was Jack Kyle.

A major new name appeared in 1984 when former cabinet minister Rafe Mair joined CKNW. Rafe — with wife Patti as an effective producer and guest digger-upper — would make a big impact on the city's talk-show scene. In 1987, when Bar-rie Clark left, Rafe moved into the 12:30 to 3 slot, moved again the next year to the 9 to noon slot where he dominates.

There was an alarming note at CKNW in 1985 when two boats owned by mega-controversial sports director Al Davidson burned under mysterious circumstances. Davidson was cleared of arson charges over the fires, but they were merely a harbin-ger of worse to come for the pugnacious Big Al. Some threatening remarks aimed at colleague Neil Macrae led to Davidson's removal from the air and, eventually, his departure from the station.

Pioneer Jim Cox retired — sort of — in 1985. Ted Smith capped his speedy rise through CKNW's ranks in 1986 when he left to join the executive team at WIC. Today, Ted is president and CEO of Westcom Radio Group Ltd., the umbrella com-pany under which CKNW and its 10 sister stations are grouped. Smith appointed his protege, Ron Bremner, to succeed him as president and general manager of CKNW. Ron continued NW's amazing financial growth until his own departure to head BCTV.

One of the stellar personalities in the station's history, Jack Kyle, retired in 1987, some 32 years after he'd first come to NW. Some of those 32 years had been spent elsewhere, but for thousands of listeners Kyle had been the quintessential CKNW on-air star: bright, amiable, community-minded, informed and totally profes-sional. There was sadness in 1987 when omnipresent items broadcaster Earle "The Pearl" Bradford died after a lengthy illness. Earle had been succeeded weeks earli-er, when illness forced him off the air, by an effusive and alarmingly energetic newspaper columnist named Joy Metcalfe. Rod Gunn, who may hold the record for departures from and returns to CKNW, came back in 1990 when the station made him general manager.

Gary Bannerman left under unhappy circumstances in 1988, but would return; and Rafe Mair moved into the vacant morning talk-show slot. Replacing Rafe in his 12:30 to 3 slot was Bill Good. Good had been spotted hosting a lively TV panel discussion by NW manager Ron Bremner, who quickly realized he'd found an ideal talk-show host: Good was quick, brainy, tough, a good listener and a strong personality. He came from good stock, too: his father, Bill Good, Sr., was a veteran sportscaster who needs no introduction to the country's sports fans. The elder Good had himself been a CKNW broadcaster.

In 1989 savvy J. Paul McConnell, a familiar voice to Lions fans, came to NW and went on to become sports director.

Dr. Art Hister debuted on CKNW that same year with knowledgeable, and often pun-filled and funny, regular commentaries on health matters. And it was houses, not bodies, that were the focus of Shell Busey's hugely popular features on home repair and renovation. A broadcaster with a striking resumé, Philip Till began The World Tonight at NW in early 1989. Till's experience is astonishingly varied and distinguished, and it's taken him to hot spots all over the world. Hal Davis retired from his administrative post, but continued to read the 8 a.m. news, highest-rated on the day's schedule.

CKNW's program line-up now was utterly different from that of its earliest days. And so was its balance sheet: as the Eighties drew to a close, NW was trembling on the brink of grossing $10 million in one year. And in 1991 it would reach that level. In a day when other stations were faltering, even dying, CKNW was setting new records, in ratings, in revenue, in influence.

Bill Rea, if you could see us now!

CKNW and others reported on Terry Fox, a genuine Canadian hero.

"You gotta be ready!"

Terry Moore, who appears regularly on CKNW and on CHQR in Calgary, might have been an opera singer. He can still belt out an impressive aria, but radio and acting won the day. Terry was born in Winnipeg in January, 1936.

He got to Vancouver by mistake! "I'd just been divorced, my five-year-old son, Patrick, was living in El Paso with my sister, and I went to visit him. I thought he was there. Turns out he was visiting his grandmother, my mother, in Vancouver. I'd never been to Vancouver. When I saw him and saw Vancouver, I flipped. I went back to New York, quit WTFM and came back and started knocking on doors."

"I started at NW June 30, 1980. The first thing I did was three weeks of vacation relief for Gary Bannerman. My official job is replacement host for all the talk shows. Sometimes, if someone's ill or stuck in traffic, I'll get 15 minutes notice. The shortest notice I ever got was five minutes. You gotta be ready! I've done Barrie Clark, Gary Bannerman, Rafe Mair when he was on in the evenings . . . I was sitting in for Philip Till when the San Francisco earthquake struck. Shirley Stocker and the producers leaped in, and we started getting reports, ham radio people talking to us, it was an incredible day."

You hear Terry do the weather on Frosty Forst's morning show, too. He's there regularly at 6:15, and adds Norm Grohmann's weather bits when Norm's on holiday.

is Christmas — classic Yuletide music, memories, humor — some original, some traditional. It has been syndicated and some Canadian stations, CKNW included, have played it every year for the past two decades." ∎

And he hasn't forgotten how to act. Terry got good notices as a bumptious American in Sandy Wilson's 1985 hit, My American Cousin, and its sequel, American Boyfriends. He did a Wise Guy, has been in other movies and TV shows. "But it's difficult to make a living as an actor."

Terry's also a best-selling author! His collection of household hints, Toothpaste and Peanut Butter, has sold an astonishing 65,000 copies in Canada.

In 1992 WIC (Western International Communications, CKNW's parent company) asked Terry to go to CHQR, in Calgary, which was changing its format to talk. "I was reluctant at first, but finally said okay. I wanted to show I could do more than fill in. So the Terry Moore Show is on from nine to noon in a time slot that used to rate number 8. Now it's number 3 in the market, and we're nibbling at number 2. It's like Rafe's show: news, politics, lifestyle."

"The boats have blown up . . ."

"Our social life after we came to CKNW," Al Davidson's widow Pat laughs, "was a post-game dinner at the Admiral Hotel. If we went to a movie, he'd stop at the police station to check the blue sheets. He never shut off his work at home.

"Al didn't *like* knocking the teams he covered. Most teams want pats on the back, but that's not the way life works. Al never sought plaudits for himself, and he felt they should behave the same way. Interviewing the Lions after a losing game was agony to him. Often he would hold back what he thought: 'They're down,' he'd say, 'why kick them when they're down?'

"He would sound vitriolic on the air, but when he said 'Nothing personal,' he really meant it. He was too busy to hold a grudge."

The subject of Al's boats has to be mentioned. "I got a call from a friend, Barbara Ann Beale. They had a boat near Al's, and they helped in his charter business. She said, 'The boats have blown up. Al was on the boats.' Then she wasn't sure he *was* on the boats. She'd heard it on the news. Ron Bremner (CKNW manager then) phoned. 'Where's Al?' he asks. 'If he needs a lawyer, call me.' Then Al called. He sounded totally out of it. He was in a coffee shop, he had driven there. He sounded in shock. I wanted to come and get him, told him he couldn't drive in his condition, but he refused to let me come and get him. He drove home. He was white-faced. I gave him some Tylenol, and sent him to bed.

"The police came, I wouldn't let them wake him. 'He's in shock.'

"He loved that old boat, the Seawatch. He couldn't part with it; he called it the 'old girl.' The lawyer Bremner got told Al not to talk. Al wanted to. 'I've got nothing to hide,' he said.

"You talk about the troubles of Job. My mother was terminally ill that year. I went to Saskatchewan to be with her. Al phoned me there, and told me he'd been charged with arson.

"He was deeply affected when people joked about it — he thought there was a cloud over him. Al asked Bill Berardino to handle his defense, and Bill did a fabulous job. He'd phone me in a crisis.'

"The irony was, we had big plans for the boats. Expo was coming up, we'd had brochures printed. I had to pick them up after the fire. Then we got into a legal hassle with a cousin of mine, who was a partner in the charter business. We had one boat left. We did some charters, but we couldn't make a go of it.

"Al Davidson's life was . . . *untidy*. His focus was on his job. His family was important to him, but I remember his telling me — he warned me — before we were married that his work was 100 per cent for him. I could have married a shoe salesman. I couldn't have stood it."

". . . like coming into the Superbowl . . ."

Ron Bremner joined CKNW's sales department in 1974, hit the ground running. His success did not go unnoticed: "In '79 Al Anaka left NW and went to the Courier as part owner; Ted Smith, the general manager, made me acting general sales manager. This was my first exposure to management. Now I'd be working with reps in Toronto, but I'd had experience there, so that worked for me." Three months later Ron was confirmed in the GSM's title.

Ron thinks sales is an "ideal" way to come up through the station hierarchy. "You work with every department: programming, accounting, traffic, promotion. You don't have tunnel vision."

He was named vice president and director of sales in 1982. "It was the same job," he laughs, "but I think Ted gave me the title instead of a raise." When Ted Smith, in his turn, left the GM's job in 1986 to head the Westcom Radio Group, Ron moved into his office as vice president and general manager.

Ron Bremner joined CKNW in 1974.

Al Davidson gave Bremner an immediate opportunity to handle a crisis: 1986 was the year Davidson's boats burned. (And the Al Davidson-Neil Macrae face-off occurred less than a year later.) Expo 86 was a huge challenge, too, one that led Ron to describe John Ashbridge's logistics plan for covering the exposition's opening as comparable to the invasion of Normandy.

1986 was confirmation that talk radio was in solid at NW: the Expo studios were built expressly for the station's open-line hosts. What *is* this fascination with talk radio in Vancouver? "It's the nature of the market," says Bremner. "It's an outspoken market, a west coast syndrome. For many years, B.C. was a hotbed of socialism. And there have been a lot of colorful characters: Webster, Murphy, Burns. There was the competition between NW and OR. It's 'involved' radio.

"The beauty of NW," Ron says, "is the strength of the team: strong producers, strong people on the board, strong in news, strong researchers, strong administrators, strong in sales . . . Coming into it was like coming into the Superbowl! Bill Rea would like CKNW today.

"And the station's a family. It really is, with staff down at the docks at 6 a.m. selling herring for the Orphans' Fund."

Bremner was promoted to president of CKNW/CFMI in 1989, then made another move in the corporate structure to become president of BCTV in September of 1990. On being asked the difference between managing a radio station and a TV station, Bremner laughs. "I tell people I wasn't in radio, I was in psychiatry. And I'm not in TV, I've just moved to a bigger ward."

"The staff would come to me with things . . ."

The job of comptroller puts its occupant in touch with every department of the station. The comptroller, with hands on the pursestrings, knows what EVERYONE is doing. "You get to know the workings of all the departments," says Erm Fiorillo, who held the job for more than 30 years, "you know the payroll, you know all about the station's expenses, you're responsible for budgets, financial statements, staff benefits, and you keep informed on sales.

An NW listener was looking out his office window on the afternoon of June 17, 1958 and saw the Second Narrows Bridge, then under construction, collapse. He couldn't believe his eyes, but got on the phone to the station. "I think the Second Narrows Bridge has fallen. *Something* has happened there." Hal Davis rushed into the news room, and told desker Bill Fox. Fox confirmed the report in seconds, and went on air with a bulletin. CKNW was the first to break the story . . . and it was horrific: 18 men had died in the tragedy. Another man was to die later in the search for bodies. Jack Webster was in his car, heard of the bridge's collapse on NW, and dashed to the scene to send the station a live report. ∎

"For me, the accounting job at CKNW was really secondary. The most fascinating experience for me was having creative areas opened up: promotion, marketing, writing, sales . . . and the people-meeting. These were the fields I was really interested in.

"I've always been a good listener. I've had my own share of problems, but I've always been interested in other people's problems. The staff would come to me with things; after the breakup of his first marriage, one of our on-air people came to talk to me; he stayed at our place for a while . . . I was always there for Al Davidson . . . I'd advise people on personal financial problems . . . It was my nature."

A memo dated February 17, 1951 informs the staff that Erm Fiorillo has been appointed to "check with Dun & Bradstreet regarding new clients."

Erm immediately made his mark: "I called my opposite numbers at the other radio stations, and shared information with them. Things like deadbeat accounts, who to avoid . . . Well, this was unheard of, but it was useful. Later I became the office manager."

Erm continued in the capacity of credit/office manager and finance director from 1956 (adding the title of assistant general manager in 1978) right up until his "retirement" in 1982. That retirement didn't quite take: he continued on a part-time basis to October, 1991 and then retired officially. From 1982 to 1991 he continued to serve as treasurer and administrator of the Orphans' Fund, completing more than 20 years in that capacity. And he is still a director of the Orphans' Fund.

"God, the mail was smelly . . ."

"My first job at CKNW," says John Plul (now vice president, marketing and head of promotion) "was administering the Orphans' Fund. In 1965 it was separate from promotion. The job was coordinating the fund-raising projects, getting them on the air, administering the spending of the money. After a couple of years in that job, the Orphans' Fund wasn't enough; I was looking for more work. I've always enjoyed organizing events. So I added some executive assistant duties at NW, and was involved in the physical move to the new location on McBride Plaza. This office we're in is where the meat locker was. The vault in accounting is the original store vault.

"I went to Bill Hughes one day and said, 'The Orphans' Fund is our biggest promotion. But it's outside the promotion department. We should combine them.' So they did. Gary McCartie, who had headed promotion, had left to start Creative House and I succeeded him.

"I'm also head of marketing. What's the difference between the two? Promotion is getting our call letters out to the public, getting the public to know there is a radio station called CKNW. Marketing is planning a concept, an idea, usually a *project*. It usually has a sponsor.

"We started doing a lot of program-related promotion, involving on-air personalities. Norm Grohmann hosted a B.C. Tree Fruits contest, for example, looking for the world's longest apple peel. God, the mail was smelly! Lougheed Mall was just opening, so we took a car, and took photos of the parts. We had the car crunched, and people had to guess the year and make of the car."

In 1975 John's life changed. "Grace McCarthy had been asked by Bill Bennett to reorganize the Social Credit party. Grace became the president of the party, and asked me to help her. We worked well together . . . and for three years, I met and worked with her virtually every day. When Social Credit got back in, Grace became deputy premier and minister of tourism. She called Ted Smith and asked if she could have John Plul for a year. Ted okayed it, and Linda Lee came in to replace me as head of promotion.

"Then Grace left the tourism portfolio, and Don Phillips came in, to be followed by Elwood Veitch, who was followed by Pat Jordan, who was followed by Claude Richmond . . . I came back to CKNW in 1982."

On December 14, 1983 John was named vice president of marketing.

Plul examines everything NW does for its promotional potential. Sometimes even non-CKNW events can be used. "I'm not quite sure how he did it," program director Doug Rutherford laughs, "but Plul managed to turn the Pope's visit into a CKNW promotion."

"I grew up listening to Jim Robson . . ."

CKNW sports reporter Neil Macrae was born in Vancouver in 1951. "I went to Point Grey High until I was kicked out for spending too much time in the pool hall. I took Grade 12 at Churchill. At 18 I wound up in radio at CJVI in Victoria. I was there for a year, did the all-night show. I came in on my days off and did the noon sports for free.

"I always wanted to be in radio, and in sports in radio. I grew up listening to Jim Robson re-creating baseball on WX. I went to CHWK in Chilliwack next, doing a mixed bag of things. I refused to live in Chilliwack, partly because I was dating a girl in Kits, so I commuted. Every day.

"Then Neil Soper hired me at CJOR to operate for Ed Murphy and Pat Burns. I remember one show not long after I got there, a caller swore while talking to Burns. There's a seven-second delay, so I jam my thumb down on what I thought was the kill button. All that happens is the front door buzzes."

It's around 1972, Jim Pattison (who owned CJOR) had just bought the Blazers. Neil got on air at OR with a late sports report and a feature called Blazer Report. "J. Paul McConnell, who was the one-man sports department at CKWX, heard me and called one day. 'Interested?' Sure. So I had a beer with J. Paul, and started working at CKWX. I was there five years, doing sport, then they had a format change. Then CJOR called me; this is about 1978.

"Well, Jack Lee liked my style. When he went over to WX, he hired me back. I did exactly the same thing at WX that I'd been doing at OR: a one-hour sports talk show. I did that for three years. During the last year on WX I started doing White-caps color; Ian Michaud did the play-by-play. One day I came back from a game in Tulsa to discover I'd been fired.

"I called Ted Smith at CKNW. Ted says, 'Come and see me.' I did, and Ted *told* Al Davidson to hire me. I started doing week-end sports. It was 1983."

"His voice never went . . ."

When Bill Rea and his family left Canada, they wasted no time. Rosalind Gies says her father went directly from Ottawa to Santa Barbara, California, the rest of the family coming later. "Mother sold the house and they left everything, just walked away from it. The contents were auctioned off."

Erm Fiorillo: "Bill Rea really wanted that TV licence. When he didn't get it, it seemed to take the fight right out of him.

John Plul, head of NW's promotion department: "We work a lot with the sales people. Here's an example. Pepsi was telling us NW was too 'old' for Pepsi drinkers. I got together with the sales manager, Ted Smith, and Jack Braverman, account executive, and we talked about this. Pepsi's slogan at the time was 'Pepsi's got a LOT to give.' That gave us the idea. We went up to the 108 Ranch to sell them the idea of giving a building lot to CKNW. They bought it. NW listeners were told they had a chance at the PNE to win the lot by bringing in their Pepsi bottle tops. The idea of recreational properties was new then. 108 Ranch got exposure for the contest in Safeway Stores, and in Pepsi liners, and at the PNE."

And Pepsi sold a lot of Pepsi! ∎

John Plul (right) joins in at an Orphans' Fund picnic.

Bill and Marjorie Rea with their three daughters poolside at home in Santa Barbara, California, 1957.

It seemed he had even lost his love for radio. I believe his family had a great deal to do with his decision to finally sell to the Griffiths/Ballard group."

Their nearest neighbor was a mile away, so youngest daughter Erin (Catherine) had no playmates. "Dad took me *everywhere* in Santa Barbara on his shoulders." She remembers, too, sitting in her high chair watching the family eat. "They were all so *fast*, Dad was so *involved*."

Her father became, in Erin's words, a "golf nut." He was out on the course all the time. In his library at home were more than 500 books on golf. He began collecting golf clubs, had nearly 300 putters. He built his Ventura radio station right on a golf course. "It was the height of the Cold War," Erin says, "and he built the station half underground so it would be more protected if a bomb hit. 'Babe,' he told me, 'we're the only station between San Francisco and Los Angeles that could survive a nuclear attack.'"

Bob Hutton visited KUDU (ex-KBBQ) in Ventura once. "Bill copied everything he'd done at CKNW: he called KUDU Top Dog, he started an Orphans' Fund, he started Are You Listening . . ." Bob Hughes actually worked briefly at KUDU as a salesman, and did a weekend deejay show.

In March, 1983 Rea phoned Jack Cullen. He said he wanted to come up and throw a party, and extracted a promise from Jack to organize it. The party never happened.

A week after that call, April 5, 1983, Bill Rea died. Cancer of the pancreas had taken him from 200 pounds to 150 pounds in a matter of months. "But," says Erin, "his voice never went. It was there to the end." He was 74. His sister, Margaret, living today in West Vancouver, remembers Bill holding her hand near the end and saying, "I've had a good life, Marg."

He had not been forgotten. One week before he died, and more than 25 years after he had left CKNW, someone approached Bill Hughes and asked, "How is Bill Rea?" His ebullient and optimistic personality ensured he would be remembered for many years.

Bill Rea was posthumously inducted into the Canadian Association of Broadcasters' Hall of Fame. His daughter Rosalind traveled up from California to accept on his behalf. The presenter was Bill's old friend and rival, Tiny Elphicke.

"You may have the guy right under your nose . . ."

Doug Rutherford, CKNW's program director, wanted to be a cop. (Come to think of it, one important aspect of his current job is analogous to a cop being called in to handle domestic disputes.) Doug was born in 1954 in Edmonton. "My dad, Walt, was news director and a talk-show host at CJCA. In 1970 he got the job as news director of CKWX, so we all moved to Vancouver. It wasn't until I was taking law courses at Douglas College that I started hanging around the CKWX newsroom. Then my dad kicked me out and got me an interview with Bill Coombes, program director at CHWK in Chilliwack. Coombes hired me and I started in the newsroom in the fall of 1972.

"Then I accepted an offer from CKIQ in Kelowna. My brother Dave worked in the newsroom there during the day, I had a night shift. I was at CKIQ for eight years, the last six as news director.

"On my 29th birthday, January 18, 1983, I accepted a job in the CKNW newsroom. My brother Dave was already working in the NW newsroom by then, but he eventually left to take the job of news director at our sister station in Calgary. Then Barrie McMaster left NW, and Ted Smith, the GM, ran an ad for a program director. They flew a bunch of people out, interviewed them. Ted, and Warren Barker, Ron Bremner, Erm Fiorillo and Hal Davis were sitting around looking at this list of people, and none seemed to click. Then Hal Davis said, 'You may have the guy right under your nose.'

"They made me acting program director in September of '84, and the next day I was on my own. I learned later Ted had listed NW's on-air people and was very candid about them to all the candidates. We had some on-air people who stood out as being hard to handle . . . 'This will be the toughest part of your job,' Ted told them, 'Think of it as Excedrin Headache 980.'

"My first crisis was Gary Bannerman and the Indians." (Bannerman had made some unwise comments on Native abilities.) Doug's handling of it was part of the reason he was confirmed as program director January 1, 1986.

Doug believes in pretty much letting his on-air people alone. "These guys are thoroughbreds; once they're out of the gate, they run their race. I don't do post-mortems."

A lot of what a program director does is put out fires and smoothe ruffled feathers. "When Barrie Clark and Gary Bannerman worked at the same time down in the Holiday Inn studios, there was a lot of animosity. We built a wall between them."

'the musicians' union is real tough. They're just dead set against it and they're real tough.' So the bystander said, 'When you get around to playing it, give me a call.' The deejay said, 'I'll be glad to,' as he took the bystander's business card and shoved it in his pocket without looking at it.

"When he does look he'll see that the 'innocent' bystander was Ray Tyldsley, new secretary of the 'tough' musicians' union." ∎

Then Gary was gone. "Bannerman had become old-fashioned: three guests, one hour each. Health concerns were part of the decision to drop him, but the numbers were bad: 40,000, 45,000. Webster was on TV, and whatever CJOR was doing at the time was having an impact. Gary's back now because he got his health in order, and he seemed vastly more amenable to change."

Doug handled a major crisis in 1987 when he took Al Davidson off the air, following the Neil Macrae incident — described in more detail elsewhere in this book.

"I wanted to hire Philip Till to replace Dave Abbott. Abbott couldn't figure out the problem of doing a TV talk show in the morning and NW in the evening. Shirley Stocker had met Philip Till; I had a gut feeling we could create good evening programming using his experience and talents. We can't afford to write off the evening. NW is personality-based; we have to give people a *reason* to listen. Cullen and Till are distinctly different. Other stations throw everything at breakfast, and let the product carry the rest. We won't do that. So Philip Till was a risk. It's turned out very well."

"Eight stories stacked on your tape . . ."

CKNW's room in the lower depths of the legislative building is a small, drab and featureless cubicle, its walls lined with dozens of political cartoons and aging memos. There are no windows, and nothing to see beyond if there were. There's a rack of tape recorders, the TV monitor, and telephones crammed in here. It's no place for anyone with claustrophobia. Come to think of it, it must be particularly close for NW reporter Kim Emerson: he's 6'4".

As we talk, Kim keeps his eye on a television monitor showing debate in the legislative chamber. He'll file at least three reports during our conversation, and grabbing a tape recorder runs out at one point to interview a cabinet minister. He returns, feeds the interview to the newsroom in New Westminster, then settles back again . . . and reflects on his beginnings in the NW newsroom.

"It was a lot noisier and a lot busier there. You always think you're working hard wherever your are — but at NW you KNEW you were working hard. A year-and-a-half goes by, and then Ian Jessup left his NW job in the Legislature. Warren told me a long list of people had applied for the position; was I interested? Absolutely! Well, there were a couple of events happening: a cabinet retreat in Kamloops, and some other cabinet business in Nanaimo. I'd cover those, and we'd see how things worked out.

"There would also be a week in the legislature. When I got here, I didn't know how the equipment worked, didn't know how the legislature worked. But people here were really helpful. And Bill Vander Zalm was premier, so there was no shortage of news. Every morning when he drove up here, he'd have *something.*

"So now I'm here. I'm the only one here. It's busy whether the legislature's in session or not, and I'm here at least from 8:30 a.m. to 6. When cabinet meets, and they meet every Wednesday, the day starts at 7:30."

And the legislature can be tricky to cover. "You can have eight stories stacked up on your tape," Kim says, "but you can't get back down here to feed stuff because you need more detail. It's better being down here than in the Press Gallery; the Gallery isn't designed for radio in any way.

"It took me a while to get used to the power and influence CKNW has here. Almost every other news outlet here listens to NW. But everyone's here, so if you get a scoop, it'll last an hour at most. In Vancouver, you might have it for half a day."

There are occasional slapstick episodes on the best-run shows: two minutes before one Gary Bannerman program was due to begin, Bannerman's guest hadn't shown up. The door opened and a fellow walked in and Shirley grabbed him and hustled him into the studio and into the chair facing Gary. The mike went on and Gary asked his first question. "But I'm not Mr. So-and-so," the hapless fellow replied, "I'm from the telephone company." He'd come in to repair one of the studio phones. Luckily, the real guest was now on hand. ∎

Covering stuff from the legislature, Kim says, is different on radio. "If you talk politely to Moe Sihota, for example, he responds quietly and politely. That's no good for radio. Say something provocative, and he'll respond with some fire. That's good stuff. Anita Hagen will walk away from rude questioning. The Lieutenant-Governor, David Lam, speaks so slowly we've actually used varispeed on the tape machines to speed him up. Everyone's different."

"I don't even want to talk to him . . ."

"When Patti and I joined CKNW in November, 1984 we were literally delirious with joy." That's Rafe Mair speaking. He should be even more delirious now: his show has the highest average quarter-hour ratings on CKNW. The reason: Mair's damned good at what he does, and he has an excellent producer: his wife, Patti.

They met when Rafe was a cabinet minister in the Bill Bennett era: Patti was working for consumer minister Phyllis Young. When Rafe took over that portfolio, Patti continued to work for him. She married the boss, right? "Ha!" Patti says, "*He* married the boss!" Rafe's experience in a number of portfolios (consumer services, consumer and corporate affairs, environment, health) would prove to be invaluable in his later career as a talk-show host: when Mair talks about government, he's on familiar ground.

"Jack Webster got me into radio," Rafe says. "I was minister of health at the time, and having lunch with Jack. He asked me if I'd thought of getting into radio. I said no. He put me in touch with Mel Cooper in Victoria."

Cooper first called CKNW's Ted Smith. "Mair had everything," Cooper says, "voice, brains, personality, bluster . . . but Ted wasn't interested. 'I don't even want to talk to him.' So I called Jimmy Pattison next."

"Before long," Mair says, "I was chatting with Al Anaka and Frank Callaghan at CJOR, Pattison's station. They asked me what salary I was thinking of, so I thought I'd be outrageous. 'I want $100,000.'

He got it. "And a year later I got $130,000, and $165,000 the year after that. Then manager Harvey Gold fired me, and knocked me on the air. I sued for slander, collected $50,000 or so. I left OR in April of 1984, and by October was at CKNW."

Ted Smith, general manager at the time, recalls Rafe wasn't getting along with OR's management. "He came out to see me at NW. I told him that all I could offer at the time was the creation of a talk show after midnight. And it wouldn't pay much. I asked him to think about it. Rafe went into my john, he was in there two or three minutes. I hear a flush, then he comes out. 'I've thought about it,' he said, 'I want it.'"

So Rafe, with Patti as producer, began a midnight to 2 a.m. talk show. "We took a salary cut when we came to NW. And how!" Back then, the station's talk shows were done from the top floor of the Holiday Inn on West Hastings, and they wondered if they'd end up talking on the phone to a bunch of drunks with nothing better to do. Happily, callers were sober, even though many of the topics were the kind that couldn't be covered in daytime.

"Rafe turned up a brand-new audience for us," program director Doug Rutherford says, "They were intelligent, articulate. It was a real surprise."

"At first," Ted Smith says, "Rafe was *too* political. It was like pulling hen's teeth to get him to do non-political stuff, like life style. I give a lot of credit to Doug Rutherford for Rafe's success."

Roving Mike had a sister program in the '40s. Called Roving Telephone, it was a kind of night-time version of the more well-known show. It was handled during most of its life by Hal Davis. He'd call people at home and ask their opinions on issues of the day. No one's quite sure how long the show lasted, but a tape exists of Jim Cox introducing the 1,449th edition. Bill Rea hosted. During that particular show, he voiced an ad for Phillips Radio and Furniture. Buy one of their ice boxes, Rea said, and you would get "150 pounds of ice, absolutely free." And, just to show some things don't change, the same tape has a listener asking if he should turn down his radio while he talks. "You'd better," Rea cautioned him, "or it'll whistle on the air." ∎

Naturally, not every Rafe Mair subject is as serious as the constitution. The Mairs like to let their hair down frequently, change the pace. "We don't screen calls at all," Patti says. "If the crazy anti-Catholic lady calls, she gets on. She may not be on as *long* as she likes . . . We try to limit regular callers to one a week, and we tell them that. You're not there to pander to the callers. We have more than 100,000 listeners; the callers are a very, very small proportion of that audience."

"I like the open-line any-topic time the best," Rafe says. "You never know what's coming up. That's fun. What's my least favorite guest? Psychics, I guess. I find my mind wandering." Patti chimes in, with a wry smile. "I put on guests according to audience needs, not Mr. Mair's." ∎

Rafe Mair turned up a brand new audience.

Rafe held down the midnight shift for a year, then moved for another year to the 6 to 9 p.m. slot. In 1986 Barrie Clark, who'd been doing afternoon talk for NW, left and Rafe moved into that time period. As he moved up in the day's schedule, he also honed his skills. By the time the morning slot became available Rafe was ready. It was September 1, 1988. "I felt almost as nervous that first morning as I did when I first went on air. But we got through it."

And how.

"Why don't you come back?"

Grace McCarthy was excited about her proposal to have B.C. host Expo 86, but Premier Bill Bennett was less than warmly supportive. McCarthy went on Gary Bannerman's show to lobby for the exposition. That started a solid Expo-Bannerman connection: virtually every key Expo executive appeared first on the Bannerman show. And during Expo itself, Bannerman was right there on the site.

In 1988 Gary and CKNW came to a parting of the ways. "In hindsight," Gary says, "it was long overdue. Ron Bremner never quite understood what we wanted to do to the show."

(Ron Bremner: "Bannerman was number one in his time period, but I didn't renew his contract. There started to be a sameness to the programs.")

"Some say it was my drinking. There was nothing ever obsessive about my drinking — days would go by without a drink, or there'd be one of an evening. In the spring of '88 a new contract had just been negotiated, and it was a good one. Bremner and I were getting along great. Then I discovered I had a serious liver problem, and was near death. It wasn't cirrhosis. For a period of several months, I stopped drinking, ate better foods, exercised . . . and three days before my attack my liver showed fine. Then, I had an attack. The liver is very regenerative. I had a 100 per cent recovery. My old contract was due to terminate August 31st. I had a long list of things I wanted before I'd return. Ron Bremner said no. It was probably a blessing. I started golfing every day, while recuperating."

Ironically, in that same year Bannerman won the TV Week Viewers' Choice Award as the "best radio talk show host." He started getting offers from elsewhere. Most persistent of the pursuers was a fellow named Ron Vanderberg, looking to buy CHQM's AM station. The CHUM group owned both QM outlets, but wanted only the FM arm . . . and already owned a Vancouver AM station, CFUN.

"Ron had people with money, I knew people with money. But the equity partners would have 80 per cent, and Ron and I would have just 10 per cent each . . . and no control. At about this time Rod Gunn came back from Calgary to manage NW, and Ted Smith and I bumped into each other at the yacht club. Ted said, 'Why don't you come back?' Ted and Rod and I had lunch, and I told them it was a nice idea, but I was involved in the purchase of a radio station. Well, CHQM accepted my offer, but in the end I couldn't raise enough money."

On April 22, 1991 Gary was back. He voices a daily editorial and fills in on the station's talk shows. He has a thriving consulting business as an outside interest.

"Everyone should be able to do it all . . ."

Chris Olsen is NW's assistant news director, and "beat captain." He's been in radio 20 years, starting at CITR on the UBC campus in late 1974.

"I'd applied several times to CKNW, and in 1983 Barrie McMaster, who was program director then, called. He had a part-time job available, doing afternoon sports. Two weeks later Al Davidson came back from a holiday, and he says, 'I hire the sports guys around here. This guy's off the air.' Davidson never talked to me.

"Barrie walks me down the hall to Warren Barker's office. I was given a part-time job, ended up doing full-time hours. But then in December of '84 Warren gave me a full-time shift. He had me filling in everywhere.

"A tough day for me is one where nothing's happening. I file 1,500 stories a year; it's not unusual for me to file six stories in three hours, and a week ago I filed five in 30 minutes."

In September of 1985 Chris was put in charge of the newsroom's beat reporters, succeeding Steve McNally. The beaters at the moment include Chris himself, Doug Strachan, Reg Hampton, Moira MacLean, Carrie Stefanson, Mike Clarke and Ted Field. Ted covers the suburban beat, and Reg and Moira add newsroom time to their beat duties. George Garrett is a beater, but he's essentially self-assigning.

"The job's mostly assigning people, timing. Sometimes I'll assign a person to a certain story based on his or her strengths, but the theory is everyone should be able to do it all. And I'll coordinate when a story breaks fast. An example: we just had that collision between a B.C. ferry and the Sealink vessel. Okay, we go into what I call 'panic mode.' The collision was at 8:25 a.m. By 9 we had Kim Emerson working on angles in Victoria, Ted Field and George Garrett were out in the field, Reg Hampton was talking to B.C. Ferries and the minister responsible, Glen Clark, and Doug Strachan was talking to the Coast Guard. Bernie Simpson, an MLA, was on the Sealink. Simpson calls George Garrett from the vessel on his cellular phone. So we add that to the mix. By the 9 a.m. newscast we had all this ready. On this one, happily, the timing was good."

Here's a story illustrating why CKNW News is so often — in fact, virtually always — first with the news. B.C. Chief Justice Allan McEachern was due to hand down his decision in a land claim case involving the Gitksan Native people. Copies of the decision would be released at 9 a.m. This was an important case, seen as setting the standard for similar future claims.

Chris is on hand at the courthouse, and he wants to get the gist of that decision onto NW's 9 a.m. news. He arrives early, obtains the receipt he needs to get a copy of McEachern's judgement from the court clerk, and stands with his nose up against the court doors. Other reporters jostle behind and around him. The doors open, and everyone surges forward. Chris takes aside the court clerk who hands him the thick document in exchange for the receipt, tells her who he is, and asks 'What page is the decision on?' '295,' she says. Chris is already heading for the street as he flips the document open, looking for Page 295. Good, he thinks, hurrying down the steps of the building to get outside where his cellular phone will work, there are good quotes there. Out onto the street, he's panting, it's 9:03 and the newscast is half over. He calls in, the desker alerts news reader Pat Markley

The first night he worked on commercial radio, someone took a shot at Chris Olsen. A real one. With a bullet.

Today, Chris is NW's assistant news director, and "beat captain." After starting at CITR on the UBC campus in late 1974 as 'The Big O on the Radio'("I was the crazy deejay; I read news, did play-by-play on campus football, hockey and basketball"), Chris started sending tapes out, and got a job offer from CKAY, Duncan. "I was to do afternoon sports, and the 7 to midnight deejay slot. My first night on the air I got shot at. I'm playing a Perry Como record and BANG, the window cracks. Then I notice the window is made of quite thick glass, and that there are several other bullet holes in it. I mentioned it to management the next day, and they said, 'Not again?'" ■

1980's Prinsendam story is a prime example of CKNW's pursuit of news. The Prinsendam was a Dutch luxury cruise liner en route to the Orient, via Alaska. The ship had recently sailed from Vancouver, carrying 524 passengers and crew. Arnold Epp and Dave Biro were in the newsroom, and heard a Mayday call on their scanner. "It was a pure fluke, a freak radio skip," Epp says, "because the vessel was well off the Alaskan coast.

"We called Search and Rescue and learned the call came from a cruise vessel in distress: there was a fire in the engine room. A U.S. supertanker, the Williamsburg, had responded to the Mayday and was coming to the rescue. To talk to the Williamsburg we have to book satellite time through an offshore marine operator in Atlanta. We call the Williamsburg, and get her radio operator. He looks out his porthole for us, and describes the Prinsendam in flames, people jumping into the water and being rescued — and we went with the story. Then we called NBC with it. They didn't believe us, even though we had

that Chris is ready, she finishes the current item and throws it to him. Standing on the street, speaking into his cellular, checking his watch to see he doesn't run long because this newscast is on the WIN network and cannot run over, Chris calmly reads the essential excerpts from McEachern's judgement and throws it back to Pat in time for her to sign off the news.

Now he'll take time to read the document in more detail for later newscasts. But not too much time. Because there's an awful lot of news out there!

"Did you hear what he said this morning?"

Everybody who ever knew the man has a story about Al Davidson. "Al," said his good friend Erm Fiorillo, "did more to attract attention and listeners to a radio station than any sports figure or personality in western Canada — in spite of any failings attributed to him." There are a lot of stories about Big Al, and they're so illustrative of this scrappy bundle of contradictions that we bring a sampling to you unadorned.

But, first, this word: likely the best tribute that could be paid to Al is to tell you that, at his funeral August 13, 1991 the 650-seat All Saints Parish Church in Coquitlam was jammed to overflowing with his friends and colleagues. There was a fine remembrance of Big Al from Father Desmond McGoldrick, and more than a few tears were shed.

- Pat Davidson remembers when Al was working in Winnipeg, and he and Pat and Al's mother were driving somewhere when a fire truck went by at full tilt. Al made a screeching U-turn and followed the fire truck even when it turned the wrong way down a one-way street. "I was petrified," Pat says. "When we finally stopped at the fire, I turned to Al's mother and asked her if she was all right, and she said, 'Wasn't that exciting?'"

- Hal Davis, on Al's first hiring as a newsman: "I thought we'd made a great deal. I picked him up at the airport. Years later Al told me he still had my first memo to him. It read: 'I'm basically a cheap person, so I'm just going to pay you $350.'"

- Hal Davis: "Al got mad at something one day and kicked a hole in the newsroom wall at 227 Columbia. Well, right behind that wall were some electrical relays . . . and Al put us off the air! Engineer Leo Haydamack rigged up a tin bakepan to cover the hole. We called it the Davidson Kick Panel."

- Hal Davis: "He was a good, aggressive newsman with a dramatic delivery, and he took that into sport. Al didn't have too many people skills, or organizational skills, so I brought in John McKeachie for balance. I remember McKeachie marvelling at Al's style; John said he read the same wire copy Al did, but Al made it *his*. He understood it was showbiz. But he couldn't help getting personally involved."

- Hal Davis on Al's rehiring, this time as sports director: "I did the actual hiring, but it was Bill Hughes' idea to have Al as sports director. Did we have any qualms? Well, we figured: sports. What could possibly go wrong?"

- Erm Fiorillo: "Al Davidson never knew what he made. He was always asking me what he made. He only cared about that mike."

- Ted Smith: "People would tell me, 'I never listen to your station because of Al Davidson. Can't stand him. Did you hear what he said this morning?'"

- Terry Spence: "Al Davidson told Bill Hughes' secretary to go f*** herself. Bill Hughes insisted that Al apologize, and said he would stand there and listen

Big Al Davidson couldn't help getting personally involved.

while the apology was made. Al stood contritely in front of the lady, and said, 'I'm sorry I told you to go f*** yourself. I shouldn't have told you to go f*** yourself. It was wrong of me to tell you to go f*** yourself."

- Ted Smith: "I used to say I got two vacations a year. One was my own, and one was Al Davidson's."
- Pat Davidson: "The whole family was going to go to Disneyland one year, but Bill Hughes protested. Bill says, 'You can't go to Disneyland, because I've just apologized about you to the Lions.' Al says, 'I am going, because it's a family thing.' Bill Hughes said, 'If you go, you won't have a job when you get back.' We went to midnight mass, and Al said to the parish priest, 'Father Swinkels, how'd you like to go to Disneyland?' So my seven children and I went to Disneyland with the parish priest."
- Paul Preston: "Al had a jeep, and he bet everyone he could drive up and over a huge pile of snow in the parking lot. The jeep high-centred and stalled. It took eight of us to get Al and the jeep off the snowpile."
- Ted Smith: "I had a cottage at Pender Harbor not far from Al's place. He came over for breakfast one morning, and in the middle of his eggs he got up to phone the station for another Seawatch Report . . . 'We've dropped the hook off Epson Point . . . it's a beautiful morning, the water's calm, and we've got spring on board . . . there are a dozen other boats here!' What a psychic Al was!"
- Dave McCormick: "Al did an item about Bobby Ackles back in November of '83, and said if it wasn't true, he'd eat crow. Well, it wasn't true, and he ate crow. Literally. Baked and served under glass by Bobby Ackles."
- John Plul: "Al and Pat Davidson were driving home from somewhere, and a cop stopped them. Al wasn't drinking then; the cop just wanted to know if he was wearing his seat belt. He wasn't. He explained to the cop he had a letter from his doctor, explaining a hernia made it impossible for him to comfortably wear his seatbelt. Where's the letter? asks the officer. It's at home, Al said. Then he said,

tape, and wouldn't take the story. So we called CBS, and they gladly used it. The *next day* NBC called us to ask if we knew anything about it.

"We followed it all, tracked all the rescued passengers as they were being taken into Alaska, interviewed some of them. We even talked to the ship's comedian! Everyone got off safely. One week later, we called a tug that was towing the Prinsendam back into port, and the fellow says, 'Funny you should call. We had to cut the line. She was taking on water. She just sank.'

"It turned out to be the largest single-ship maritime rescue in modern times, and it got us a world scoop." ∎

George Garrett's thirst to know what's happening has made him the most effective beat reporter in B.C.

"Look," and he lay down on the seat and pulled up his shirt and he showed the cop his hernia. Everything had to be drama with Al! Don't just have a letter. Show your hernia!"

- Cameron Bell: "Al was at a party once, and Bob Pickell was at the same party. Pickell was a big guy, former basketball player, well over six feet tall. Al has some kind of a mad on about him, and he's heard going around muttering he's going to punch Pickell out. Word of this gets to Pickell, on the other side of this crowded room, and he says, 'If that little son-of-a-bitch hits me, *and I hear about it . . .*'"

- Ted Smith: "Al had a car from a sponsor, took it on a fishing trip up to Pender Harbor. It was June, and he caught some spring salmon. He threw 'em in the trunk of the car, and forgot about 'em. A month later he goes back to the car dealer. This car's no good, he tells them, it stinks to high heaven. He threw them the keys and left. Then they opened the trunk."

- Hal Davis: "Al drank, and it caused problems. He missed a major sportscast one morning, during Grey Cup festivities. I went down to the Georgia Hotel to see Al. I put my arm around his shoulder. 'Al, I've always done what I've promised for you, right?' 'Right.' 'Well, I'm going to make this promise. If you screw up one more time, I'll fire you.' He went to AA, and never took a drink again. Not long after that conversation, I was at a roast for Al and I noticed a brown paper bag by his chair. I checked. It was a big bottle of Pepsi. And it was really Pepsi."

- Pat Davidson: "Al's cousin Jean was visiting from Aberdeen, and she was looking forward to a Canadian Christmas dinner with us and the family. The turkey was in the oven. Late in the afternoon the phone rang. It was Al. 'How long will it be before the turkey's ready?' I told him it was almost ready. 'Can you make some gravy fast?' 'I guess so.' 'Okay, and make about ten pounds of potatoes.' It turns out he had heard about an East End family in trouble: their power had been cut off, and they were sitting at home, cold and in the dark. Al came home, and he and I drove over to their place with the Christmas turkey and all the trimmings. When we got back home, Jean looked at us. 'What's for dinner?' she says. 'Well,' I said, 'there's some sausages in the fridge.' And that was Christmas dinner that year."

"I was bleeding everywhere . . ."

Joan Garrett on her husband George: "He hears a siren and he's out the door."

George Garrett's fabled list of contacts has gone electronic. He has a small handheld Casio organizer, in it the names of more than 600 people. And he *uses* the thing. "I add 10 or so names a week, take out people who move away, or leave their jobs, or die. Sometimes I'll scroll through, and see a name I should call just to see what's happening."

Garrett's thirst to know what's happening has made him the most effective beat reporter in B.C., a man who collects scoops like others collect stamps. As he puts it, "We don't follow newspaper stories, we break stories."

The 1982 "Clearwater murders," in which six members of the related Johnson and Bentley families were slain, was a scoop for Garrett. He got a tip from a good contact (he won't name his contacts on stories of this kind) who told him the two families had been found, all of them dead, in the Clearwater area. "I called the RCMP, but they wouldn't say anything. My source was so good I went with the story. A couple of stations on the WIN network phoned the newsroom: 'The RCMP won't confirm that Garrett story.' The newsroom said, 'Who do you want to believe? The RCMP or George Garrett?' They went with it."

Normally, newsmen don't become news items themselves. The Davie Fulton story was a rarity. So was George's May 1, 1992 run-in with some L.A. toughs. He'd gone down there to cover the Rodney King riots (some blacks had rioted when, in their first trial, the police officers who beat King were cleared). Just as Garrett was about to call in with a live report on Bill Good's show, four young black men jumped him. George told Province reporter Clare Ogilvie they grabbed the phone out of his hand and hung up. "Then one grabbed my mike and it fell to the ground. Well, if you are a reporter you can't lose your tape machine and mike, so I bent to pick it up and he put his foot on the cord and pulled it away. Then he tried to grab my machine and my notes.

"They took me into a doorway and I looked around in desperation for someone to help me but I realized I was on my own. I thought I could talk my way out of it, and I said 'Surely you wouldn't assault an old man like me? I'm just going on the air to tell Canadians about your problems.' But one of them said, 'It doesn't matter, you're white,' and with that he hit me.

"I fell to my knees and was bleeding everywhere. I'm just lucky it wasn't a knife or a gun they hit me with instead of a fist."

recorder in full view of him, and it was running. He says to the officers, 'Do you know who I am?' They ask him to get into a police car. 'Very well,' he says, 'I will not be a judge any more.' The police repeat, 'Would you get into the car, sir?' And Fulton said, 'Go to hell!' I got it all on tape.

"I confided to news director Warren Barker I had the tape. It was only a roadside suspension, not an arrest. But then it came to light that there had been an earlier accident that same night caused by Fulton. Harry Philips had done a story on that. We decided to combine the stories, and we ran the tape. The Sun and The Province were on strike, so it was The Vancouver Express that headlined the story next day: Judge Tells Cops: Go To Hell!" ∎

George Garrett once interviewed Premier W.A.C. Bennett on tape at the ungodly hour of 4 a.m. during a tense period when woodworkers were out on strike, bringing the province's major industry to a grinding halt. When George got back to NW with the interview, he discovered to his horror there was a pronounced wobble on the tape, and it made Bennett's voice quaver. Bob Giles, night news editor, said "Don't worry about it," and began the newscast: "Premier Bennett, his voice shaking with emotion, told CKNW's George Garrett ..." ∎

Two black people from the neighborhood came to George's aid, drove him to hospital in his rental car. He had a broken upper jaw and a tooth was knocked out. Ogilvie ended her story: "Garrett says his brush with death won't stop him accepting dangerous assignments. But he says he will think twice about taking unnecessary risks. At that, his wife Joan lowered her head and gave Garrett an over-my-dead-body look, which Garrett carefully ignored."

The L.A. beating was doubly annoying: in the 36 years preceding it, Garrett had missed precisely one-half day of work.

"I liked the no-rules style . . ."

Bill Good, in CKNW terms, is almost a rookie. With just six years at the station, he's the second newest of the major names. Only Philip Till is "newer." But, as you'd expect, Bill's no newcomer to the business: in 1995 he'll mark 30 years in broadcasting.

Bill was born in Winnipeg in December of 1945, came to Vancouver with the family in 1948. "At three or four years old I was walking around with a 'mike' — using a spoon or something — and I'd do things like, 'Will Brian do the dishes tonight, or will it be Shaela or Derek . . .'

"There was never any question what I wanted to do. I never ever talked about it with my dad until I actually started doing it." Bill wasn't alone in high school in ambition to be a broadcaster: fellow students included Fred Latremouille, Vicki Gabereau and Michael McIvor.

He finished Grade 12 and got a job at CFPR in Prince Rupert. There followed jobs in Terrace and Victoria, then to Vancouver's CBU to do the morning show. In 1969, when the Canucks got into the NHL, Bill was seconded into sports. "I did color on the first-ever Canucks game on CBC-TV's Hockey Night in Canada. And, of course, I was also doing sportscasts on CBC. Over time I was covering 23 annual live sports events: lacrosse, LPGA, swimming . . . In 1978 I became the first anchor of the CBC-TV Evening News. I did that for 10 years. Then I got a phone call."

The call was from CKNW manager Ron Bremner. He'd seen Good hosting a panel show, and was impressed. "I *loved* doing live stuff," Bill says, "thinking on your feet, ad libbing, getting away from the script. I thrived on it. I'd done the '78 election for CBC and got plaudits. So, yeah, I liked the no-rules style. Ron Bremner and I went for a coffee, he wanted to explore the possibility of my someday coming to NW. Gary Bannerman was having health problems . . . Well, I'd grown up with CKNW, knew it well. When I worked at CBC, *they* listened to NW. Eight months later, Ron called again. Would I come? Norm McKinnon handled the negotiations, as he does for Frosty Forst. They offered me a three-year contract, with an option.

"There are still people," Bill says, "who think I got fired from CBC. They couldn't conceive anyone leaving

Bill Good felt comfortable right from the beginning.

TV news to go to a locally-based radio station! I started on CKNW September 12, 1988. My first guest was Grace McCarthy. I felt comfortable right from the beginning. But my initial instinct was to treat these interviews as news *alone*, rather than to take a stand, voice an opinion.

"That changed."

Incidentally, both Bill Good, Sr. and Bill Good, Jr. have won Nellies, the ACTRA Awards. "I think we're the only father-and-son team to win Nellies," Bill says, "and I believe I'm the only NW personality to win a Nellie." Bill, Jr. won his as best radio interviewer.

"Get the facts together . . ."

Since his return to CKNW as sales manager in early 1987, John Iacobucci (yakko-bootchy) has seen the station reach annual billings of more than $20 million. He owes his arrival at NW to his knowledge of hockey. John worked for years for Max McNab in the Canucks' front office, and Al Davidson used to come into the office all the time and talk with him.

"Al recommended me to NW, so I went for an interview with Mel Cooper, a guy who taught me a lot about radio. Mel gave me a job in the promotion department. It was 1967. I was 25. A year-and-a-half after I started at NW, I was offered a sales position at a cosmetics company and I took it. I didn't relate to the cosmetics industry at all, but in six months I did well. So I thought, 'If I can do *that*, how would I do in a job that I liked? I went into sales at CKLG in 1969. I sold successfully, won the top sales award for the last four of my six years there."

Next up was CJJC in Langley, from there to All-Canada's Vancouver office, and then nine years as sales manager at CKWX.

In January of 1987 John returned to the station, nearly 20 years after he had left it. But this time he was director of sales. "I never made the move until I felt they really needed me — which, in hindsight, was the smartest thing I could've done."

John's experience with other stations gave him insight into how they viewed the Top Dog. "Everybody would sit back and *admire* CKNW, would respect and even fear CKNW. *But they wouldn't do it themselves.*"

"To sell," says John, "just get the *facts* together, and present them well. Jack Webster learned after leaving NW he didn't have a team behind him. It took him three years to get his ratings up to where they should be.

"I'm not a super-salesman. There's no secret to my success at NW: it's the *team*. Put me on a line with Mario Lemieux, and I'll do well."

The dream came true . . ."

John Plul's proudest moment for a promotional idea came with the world-famed journey of Rick Hansen. A driving mishap had turned Rick into a paraplegic . . . which led him in turn to a single-minded determination to raise money, millions of dollars worth of money, for research into spinal cord injuries. Rick got the world's attention by announcing he would make a journey around the world in his wheelchair, the famous Man In Motion World Tour. For months newscasts in Canada and around the world featured this courageous young man, laboriously wheeling himself through country after country.

His return to Canada, especially to British Columbia, was eagerly anticipated.

Suddenly Plul had a vision: Rick Hansen wheeling along the Trans-Canada

Bill Good's a rarity among Vancouver broadcasters: he's the son of a broadcaster who was every bit as well-known in his day. Only the Billy Browne father-and-son duo come to mind. Bill Good, Sr. was a familiar face and voice in Canadian broadcasting for decades, and was virtually synonymous with curling broadcasts in Canada. Young Bill inherited something else from his father: height. He's six foot five; his dad's six foot six. Mom Doris was average height. (He also inherited his dad's robust good humor: on a recent show, Bill Jr. said he was in the same business as his father had been: "Shooting off our mouths.") ■

Highway through Alberta, and approaching the British Columbia border. Standing at the border to greet him: the Premier of British Columbia and a huge crowd of supporters. And there, at Rogers Pass in the majestic Canadian Rockies, would be a bright yellow ribbon stretched across the highway. Rick would wheel himself with a huge smile through that ribbon to the cheers of the crowd, of British Columbia, of Canada, of the world.

The dream came true.

What's important to realize here is that vision came to Plul *months* before Hansen was anywhere near the B.C.-Alberta border.

Events like these have to be planned well in advance, like a military campaign, and at this kind of work John Plul is a master. "The yellow ribbon is a universal symbol of home-coming," he says, "so it was a natural progression. We wanted to help Rick raise money, so we planned to provide thousands and thousands of pieces of yellow ribbon to sell, with proceeds going to Rick's campaign. The lengths of ribbon would be for sale, by the foot, at Safeway stores. We approached various suppliers asking about ribbon prices. We called the RCMP, and they told us who they bought ribbon from: 3M. We called . . . and 3M donated the ribbon. Rick was famous by now, so there was no problem. The printing on the ribbons was donated, *everything* was donated."

The scene at the border in the spring of 1987 played itself out in real life, just as John had visualized it months before. There was Premier Bennett, there was the vast crowd of cheering supporters, there was the bright yellow ribbon. And there was Rick Hansen, a huge smile creasing his features, as he wheeled through the ribbon to mark his return to British Columbia.

CKNW's John Ashbridge drove the Yellow Ribbon Caravan that accompanied Rick on the last stretch of his journey. Every station on the WIN network carried live reports. People started handing their pieces of ribbon to Rick to autograph. CKNW had a lock on the Hansen journey as an event. In May, as a huge crowd of supporters cheered, Rick rolled through the same ribbon at Oakridge Shopping Centre, which he had left at the start of his journey in 1985.

This time the ribbon said, "Welcome Home, Rick!"

"He always does his homework . . ."

When CKNW was fighting CKWX for the rights to broadcast games of the brand-new still-to-play-their-first-game Vancouver Canucks, the station was presented with a problem: Medicor, the firm that owned the team, wanted Jim Robson to do the play-by-play. Jim Robson worked for CKWX.

Manager Mel Cooper invited Robson for coffee at the Sylvia Hotel. "Jim didn't even want to talk with me; he was loyal to CKWX. But I asked him, 'What do you want most of all?' And he said, 'To be the broadcaster of the Vancouver Canucks.' I pulled out a letter on CKNW letterhead with a contract on it for Jim to sign. He immediately said, 'Oh, I have a deal with WX.' And I said, 'Jim, if WX gets the rights, this contract will never see the light of day.' He signed on that basis.

"CKWX offered $75,000, and we ended up at $85,000 *and* put the team on a network. So we got the Canucks and Jim Robson to call the games."

Jim Robson's love for sports got him into Dewdney League baseball as a kid. "I was a bad right-handed pitcher." He pitched in the first junior game at Haney's Telosky Stadium . . . which he had helped build! And he pitched in the first game at Hammond Stadium, too. CKNW's Norm Grohmann, a fellow student, also played in both those first-day games. And one of the Hammond players was Larry Walker, Sr., whose son Larry is currently wielding a big bat for the Montreal Expos.

"I left school in 1952 to go work on the radio. It was odd: I'd been selected as valedictorian at MRHS, and I wasn't going to pass.

"Even as a kid I'd said in my school yearbook I wanted to be a broadcaster. I loved sports and music on the radio." ∎

When Jim arrived, CKNW's sports director was the formidable Al Davidson. Davidson quit the day Robson was hired, because he wanted to do the hockey, but they talked him out of it. "When I'd been on WX, Al used to refer to me as the Bushleaguer on Burrard. After I came to NW he became my biggest booster." For the first year Jim did play-by-play on Canucks games, and Davidson did color. Big Al didn't go on the road, so Jim did play-by-play alone when out of town.

"Robson," Clancy Loranger, a famed Vancouver sports reporter, once wrote, "has the respect of his fellow media men because he always does his homework. He's so conscientious he's usually on the scene three hours before a game, and there's not the slightest danger he'll ever miss a bus or plane."

"The difficult part for me," says Jim, "is the travel. After 31 years of travel, I'm tired. And the season's so long now: it starts Labor Day, and the Stanley Cup finals are in mid-June."

He relaxes in the summer in his big garden on Galiano Island, playing on the local nine-hole golf course, and wandering through 120 acres of woodlot.

"Call CKNW — they love your stuff . . ."

You were never quite sure where Philip Till was going to be. As chief foreign correspondent for NBC News, Till had reported from 110 countries. In January of 1989 CKNW solved the problem. They took him from NBC, and brought him to Vancouver to stay.

The legions of NW listeners who remember Jack Kyle also remember his famous hats. He wore one at the opening of the Dell Hotel. Someone stole it. "That hat had cost me $8 at the Bay. I talked about it on the air. And the station took out full-page ads in both dailies with me wearing the hat. I went back to the Bay, hoping they'd give me a replacement. But, no," he laughs, "I had to buy it again — after all that free publicity for them." ■

John Plul's proudest moment for a promotional idea came with the world-famed journey of Rick Hansen .

No matter where Philip Till went in the world, CKNW was going to find him. As the chief roving reporter for NBC Radio, Till had filed from an eye-popping range of places: Beirut, Geneva, Paraguay, Brazil, Mexico, Russia, Libya . . . He once covered an Elizabeth Taylor birthday party in Budapest ("I gate-crashed Miss Taylor's party, saw the diamond Richard Burton had given her, got hit by a bouncer, and filed my story on the Telex after bribing the operator with chocolate and a Zippo lighter.").

There's more: Gary Bannerman chased him down in London for an eye-witness account of a royal wedding; Rafe Mair tracked Philip to the shores of Scotland's Loch Ness, where he told Rafe of yet another search for the fabled Nessie; Shirley Stocker talked to him in Tripoli during the U.S. bombing of that city . . .

Till has reported from 110 countries. ∎

Jim Robson, (left) here with color man Tom Larscheid, wanted to be broadcaster of the Canucks.

"CKNW was one of 350 NBC affiliates in Canada and the U.S.," Philip says, "and we all had our favorite affiliates. For a colleague and close personal friend of mine, Fred Kennedy, it was Vancouver. Fred had gone to UBC, and he knew the area well. And CKNW had a good reputation. In a week, we'd get at least 50 phone calls from the affiliates looking for more on a certain story. I can only recall two Canadian affiliates that ever called, and one of them was NW, and they called regularly. We never turned them down."

Philip has contacts in a lot of the countries he reported from, and it brings an added depth to his show, already solid with co-host Jon McComb, and two producers. One of the two is Ian Koenigsfest, once a radio news director in South Africa. "Ian's my Rock of Gibraltar."

"I listen to BBC as much as I can, to Deutsche Welle, to Radio France Internationale. I used to have the English-language broadcasts of Radio Moscow permanently tuned in. I watch local French TV a lot. Anyone who doesn't learn at least one other language is going to miss out."

How did this spectacularly frequent flyer end up in Vancouver? "Ah! Well, once you're on the market, everyone knows. I'd been travelling eight months a year for 15 years. I got a call from a Canadian radio station, I don't remember which, and at the end of the item they said, 'Is there anything we can do for you?' I said, 'Yeah, give me a job.' And they said, 'You should call CKNW. They love your stuff.'

"I phoned Shirley Stocker. She was on vacation. I didn't even leave a message. But someone here recognized my voice, and it wasn't long before Shirley called me in London. Then Doug Rutherford called me. 'Would you like,' he says, 'to host the evening talk show on CKNW?'

"I believe I said yes."

"I didn't need the extra time . . ."

Jim Cox went into sales in 1963, continued to do sports play-by-play. "I responded to the challenge of sales. I was initially reluctant, and Bill Hughes knew that, but he said it had been the same for him at the start. Lloyd Bray was the sales manager; he taught me a lot, taught me how to organize. Hughes told me, 'I'll guarantee you'll make what you're making now in your first year. Give it a shot.' Well, I didn't need the extra time: I exceeded the target. I had Fogg Motors, Sterling Furniture, Bowell Maclean . . . My biggest achievement was getting Army & Navy on the air. I sold a year's contract to Sam Cohen, $15,000.

"In '68 I got into national sales; we had an office in the Hotel Georgia. It wasn't quite as satisfying as local retail sales. There you had the personal contact with the client, and he decides right now. In national, the accounts were bigger, you had the potential to make money. But your contact was Suzy Timebuyer, and she was just out of high school. In retail, you saw immediate results, you saw people in the store."

In 1985 Jim retired from sales, and — he thought — from broadcasting, but in 1988 NW got football back and they asked Jim to come back "and do some stuff." So he 'did some stuff' for three more years, then really retired. ∎

Jim Cox: "Ross McIntyre was a popular NW engineer in the '40s — who also did some announcing. Ross did enjoy a drink. They had these punch cards for prizes in a bar he went to, and one day he won a turkey. It was a *live* turkey; he brought it back to the station on a string. He takes the turkey and his script for the news into the studio, and ties the turkey to the leg of the table. Then he's on the air. And it's obvious he's sozzled. The turkey starts going 'gobble-gobble-gobble.' Ross puts the cough-switch on and raps on the glass, motioning me to come in. I hurry in, and he's pointing to a place on the script. 'I can't go on,' he says, 'You pick up from here.' He unties the turkey, which is now gobbling like mad, and has crapped on the floor, and he and the turkey leave. I finished reading the rest of the news." ∎

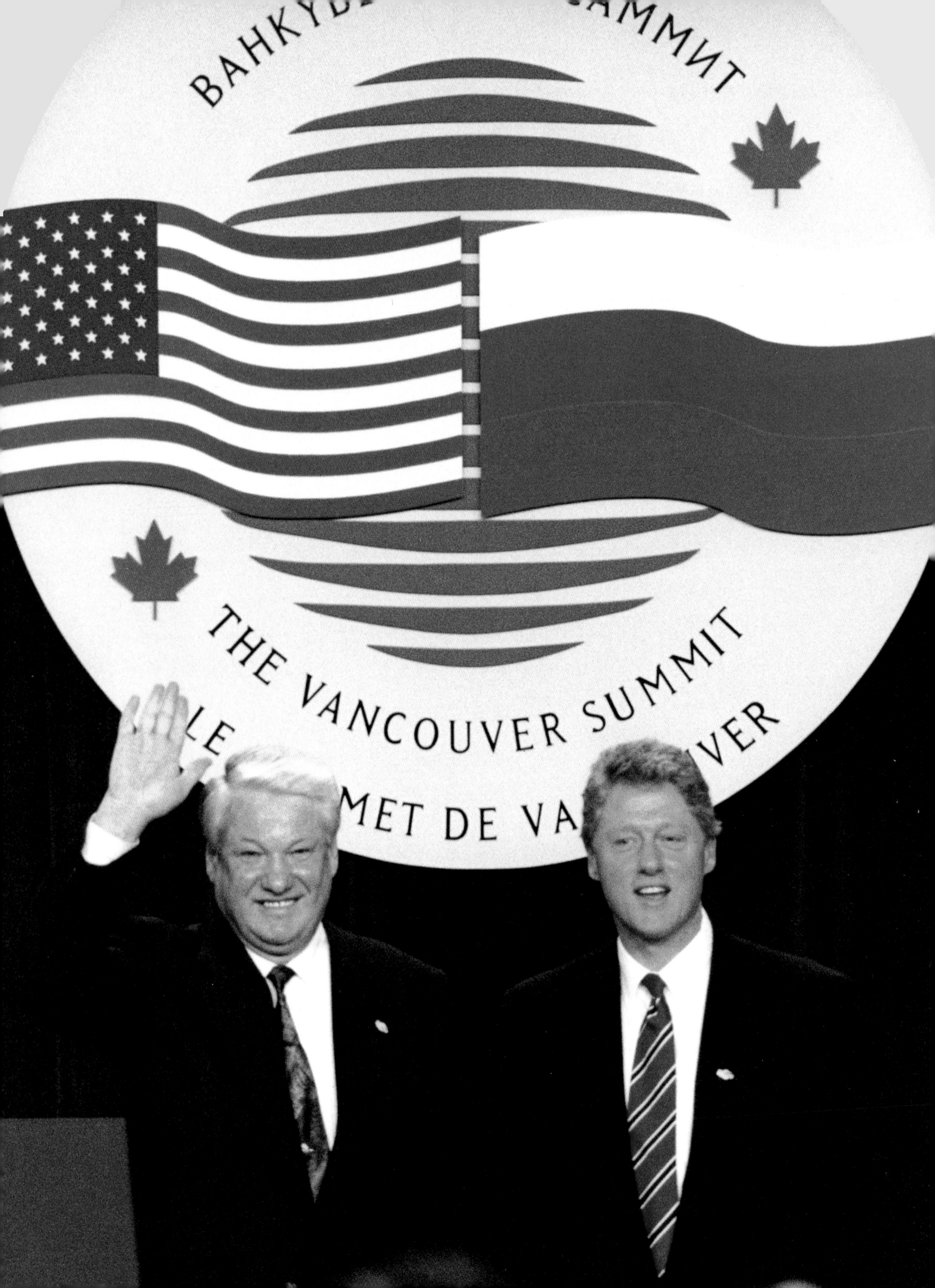
THE VANCOUVER SUMMIT

"We're More Of It Than Anyone . . ."

THE 1990S DIDN'T TAKE LONG TO GET GOING BEFORE NEW NAMES popped up to command our attention: Clyde Wells, Elijah Harper, Meech Lake, Twin Peaks, The Simpsons, Major-General Lewis MacKenzie, Roberta Bondar, Silken Laumann, and Mike Harcourt with the word Premier in front . . . We lost Barbara Frum, and turned thumbs down on tinkering with the Constitution. CKNW's Rafe Mair became de facto leader of the 'No' forces in B.C., and attracted continent-wide attention.

The Toronto Blue Jays won the World Series, Queen Elizabeth agonized over the royal family's "annus horribilis," and the U.S. rejected George Bush in favor of Bill Clinton. Up here, we would have rejected Brian Mulroney if he had let us, but he stepped aside to let others vie for the job. The famous photo of Kim Campbell's bare shoulders likely helped, rather than hurt, her successful leadership campaign.

Sinead O'Connor ripped apart a picture of Pope John II on Saturday Night Live, and Joe Pesci put it back together again a week later on the same show. Woodward's closed forever, ending a century of service to western Canada.

NW began the decade with an award from the B.C. Association of Broadcasters for Excellence in Journalism, and the Western International Network installed its very own up-link. Now programs could be fed directly from Western International Network's headquarters in the CKNW building to subscribing stations throughout western Canada. Ron Bremner left to run BCTV, and Rod Gunn succeeded him as president and general manager. Warren Barker retired and Gord Macdonald became news director, and J. Paul McConnell took the helm at sports. After more than 45 years as on-air personality at CKNW, Hal Davis laid down his 8 a.m. news microphone and concentrated on administering the Orphans' Fund. (But Hal's Sunday evening music show continued.)

Astonishingly, Hal's name pops up in every decade of CKNW's existence: he has played an important role at Top Dog for a rapidly approaching FIFTIETH year. There are few Canadian broadcasters with such a record of longevity.

In November, 1993, one month after this book hits the stands, Warren Barker will become the 1993 recipient of the Bruce Hutchison Lifetime Achievement Award, for his outstanding contributions to journalism in British Columbia. The award will be presented at the annual Jack Webster Awards ceremony for B.C. journalists.

And, in a series of changes so close to the printing deadline for this book that they're mentioned only here, and are not reflected elsewhere in the book:

CKNW's parent company is WIC, Western International Communications Ltd., in Vancouver. WIC is Canada's largest private broadcasting company. And, says chairman Frank A. Griffiths, "it all grew out of Bill Rea's little station."

Griffiths bought CJOB and CJKR-FM in Winnipeg in 1961. Those were the first outside purchases in what became the WIC empire.

In 1963 Griffiths purchased an interest in Victoria's CHEK-TV and CHAN-TV (now BCTV), more radio stations in the '60s and '70s, and, in the early '80s became a founding shareholder in Canadian Satellite Communications Inc. (CANCOM).

The past five years have seen rapid growth at WIC with emphasis on acquiring television stations and rights to pay TV and pay-per-view services. ■

Phillip Till (right), pictured here with Tony Parsons of BCTV, covers current world events for CKNW.

Fin Anthony has a deadpan — and deadly — sense of humor, and you may find yourself being gently ribbed as he gazes earnestly at you. He once told his wife's very credulous sister, when she raved about CKNW's new afternoon announcer, that the new guy couldn't speak a word of English. Bill Rea had gone out, Fin solemnly explained, and got this very expensive piece of equipment that instantly translated the announcer's German into flawless English. The device cost $60,000.

- Doug Rutherford was promoted to general manager of Edmonton's CHED, a sister station . . .
- and was succeeded as NW's program director by 27-year-old Tom Plasteras . . .
- who immediately hired David Berner to do a five hour talk show to begin after the midnight news. Already Edmonton's CHED, Calgary's CHQR and the WIN network signed on . . .
- cashed in on the popularity of Lee Powell's Prime Time sports by scheduling two hours of jock-talk from six to eight Sunday night, to be called, naturally, Prime Time Sunday.

The midnight talk show is not a totally new departure for CKNW. Rafe Mair started his NW career with just such a show — and Dave Berner's ready wit and all-around knowledgeabililty promised similar success. What is new is the expansion to a western Canadian network — with a possibilty of further growth.

NW is dominant in the market now, but it's used to being that. The Top Dog stays that way because it never rests on its laurels. It's always challenging itself. "We're not *nervous,* " Tom laughs, "but whatever it is we are, we're more of it than anyone."

The old Safeway store at 8th and McBride is bursting at the seams. "We have simply outgrown the present location," says general manager Rod Gunn. They would like to bring CKNW, CFMI, the Western Information Network and the talk shows all together in one building. There are no plans afoot at this time, but they are thinking about it and when they start to think about something at NW . . .

"Where are the orphans?"

John Plul: "Jack Wasserman once asked in his Sun column: 'Where are the orphans?' Year after year we're asked: why not call it the CKNW Children's Fund? But there's a magic to that word 'orphans.' We have 18,000 kids in the program. They're single-family kids, low income, they're in institutions. Their parents may be alive, but the family is not together."

Hal Davis: "Erm Fiorillo was active in the Orphans' Fund from its creation. Erm's likely more responsible for its success than anyone; he was particularly effective in fund-raising at Catholic events. He knew everyone!"

Erm: "When Hal took over, he began to expand the scope. It's not restricted to kids now; there are programs for retarded adults, bursaries for single mothers." In 1991 more than 60 social agencies received grants. Amounts have gone as high as the $100,000 grant made to Children's Hospital to treat children suffering from cancer. The Fund buys necessary items for children at risk; they can vary from a crib for a burned-out family, to a wheelchair for a paraplegic, to a computer for a severely handicapped child.

In 1983 $400,000 was placed in a trust to fund a chair of research into child immunology, and subsequent contributions have been made to keep research funded through the CKNW Orphans' Fund Professor at UBC.

College bursaries are awarded, and a fund has been established at Simon Fraser University, which provides a 100 per cent scholarship to a student from a welfare background. The scholarship can continue up to four years.

Erm Fiorillo: "We had hotels for special nights, at rock bottom prices, proceeds to the Orphans' Fund; we had tag days. The Women's Bowling League we started became the world's largest, and it has raised more than a million dollars alone for the Fund. The community gets involved. We get bequests: one was for $220,000, and we've had others in the range of $100,000."

The Fund's Directors meet four times a year. President for many years has been Judge Tom Fisher. (The president has always been a judge. That tradition started with Judge Sullivan, then it was Justice Monroe, now Tom Fisher. In 1993 the Directors were: Nick Carr, Marilyn Cassady, Hal Davis, Erm Fiorillo, Frank A. Griffiths, Frank W. Griffiths, Rod Gunn, Dr. Art Hister, Bill Hughes, Pauline Hughes, Gerry Mignault, John Plul, Art Reitmayer, Ted Smith and Louis Valente.) NW has never dictated to the Fund. The station picks up all expenses, but it never tries to influence the directors.

A January, 1993 meeting of the Fund's Board of Directors gives an indication of the kinds of groups that receive grants: The Boys & Girls Clubs of Greater Vancouver; B.C. Paraplegic Association; Camp Artaban Society; Children's Foundation; Family Services of Greater Vancouver; Latona Catholic Camp; Maple Ridge Family Education Centre; North Shore Disability Resource Centre Association; Rainbow Youth Excellence Society; Sunny Hill Hospital for Children Foundation; Vancouver-Richmond Association for Mentally Handicapped Persons; Disabled Sailing Association of B.C. and many more.

The Fund's Gina Steeves Award, named for an affectionately recalled NW employee, was given to Rita Ferris, an Eaton's employee. She, for many years, has done the selecting and wrapping of individual gifts for the Fund.

And the CKNW Orphans' Fund Award went to the management and staff of Playland "who do an outstanding job each year at the Orphans' Fund Picnic."

But sometimes they'd get back at Fin, too. Bill Rea had bought a huge old time clock. He intended to convert it into a decorative element for a bar. Hal Davis and someone else at NW lifted the huge thing up and put it outside the sales office door. Then they told Fin he was required to punch in when he arrived at work and when he left. "Fin," said a bystander, "went ballistic." ∎

Shirley Stocker laughs when she recalls the time she went down and collected four steaming mad women standing outside an exercise spa that had been closed by the bailiff. "I drove them to the studio to interview them. These women had spent thousands of dollars on their classes, and now they couldn't get at the equipment. They were still dressed in their exercise gear during the interview. Then there were the Gypsies. They'd been advertising their service as readers of your future, but when they got with people they were persuading them to sign things. I got the Vancouver Police Department to put me in touch with the top Gypsy, and I called him. He not only returned the people's money, he sent me roses." ∎

Mel Cooper, former CKNW promotions man, now owns CFAX in Victoria.

In 1993 then Minister of Defence Kim Campbell, B.C. Premier Mike Harcourt, and former Olympian Nancy Greene Raine were among the prominent British Columbians who joined CKNW staff at the Westin Bayshore to take part in the station's annual Pledge Day. A stunning new record was reached when the all-day event, hosted by Bill Good, raised more than $535,000. What's more, the actual amount of money sent in exceeded that figure by 10 per cent! And every penny went to the Orphans' Fund.

Station Owners

No fewer than eight former staffers at CKNW would go on to own or co-own their own stations. They include:

- Ken Hutcheson CJAV Port Alberni
- Dave Armstrong CKDA Victoria
- Joe Chesney CJJC Langley
- Mel Cooper CFAX Victoria
- Roy Chapman CKOK Penticton
- Bob Giles/Jack Kyle CHUB Nanaimo
- Les White (Henri Michaud) CJDC Dawson Creek. (This one was the family business.)

"Larscheid does all the work . . ."

CKNW has western Canada's biggest radio sports department. Sports director J. Paul McConnell heads a crew that includes Jim Robson, Tom Larscheid, Neil Macrae, Ron Barnet, Lee Powell, Abe Hefter (weekend sports) and Gary Monahan.

J. Paul was born in Ladner in November, 1945, grew up there. His first radio job was in Nelson. He followed his girlfriend to Calgary, and by 1967 was in Winnipeg at CJOB. "In '69 I went to a shopping centre holdup. A guy, a cop I'd had had coffee with a couple of hours before, had had his head blown off. CKWX heard the tape of my report and offered me a job. I went there, started working with Jim Robson. I was a newsman at WX, but if I did sports I got an extra $5.

"WX stole the Lions' rights from NW in 1971, and I started hosting the game shows and doing play-by-play in the third quarter. I did that for three years." One night in 1979 McConnell finished the 8 o'clock news at WX and walked back to his desk to find the CBC's Gordon Craig sitting there! "He said, 'I want you to come work for me.'

"I was at CBC-TV until February 1, 1989. I came back from holidays, went to use my electronic key on the back door to the CBC . . . and it didn't work. I'd been fired. Three weeks later Doug Rutherford phoned me, 'picked me up on waivers,' and here I am. I'd always wanted to work here, anyway."

J. Paul says he finds play-by-play on hockey very, very difficult. "Robson says football's more difficult. It's our different approaches. I'm not comfortable doing hockey. But I'm Robson's backup, did 10 games a couple of years ago, and I did the game the night he was inducted into the Hockey Hall of Fame."

J. Paul's comfort level rises at Lions' games. "The ball's in play about 13 minutes in a game — Tom Larscheid does all the work. When Tom gets into the game, he *really* gets into it. He used to play, he knows the game, that brings everybody up, makes it easier for everyone."

J. Paul's radio career included a short pause at CFUN. "Larscheid was my boss at CFUN, now I'm his here. I used to lie to him about my expense account at CFUN, now he lies to me about his."

"We owe Warren a debt of gratitude . . ."

In April, 1959 Warren Barker, 30, was made NW's news director, succeeding Jim Cox. He held the job for 32 astonishing years, turned CKNW news into a juggernaut. "I may not be as smart, or know as much, as the other people in the newsroom, but if I show I can work as hard and as long as anyone, they'll do the job for me. It's 'seat of the pants,' and illustration by example. I don't give philosophical talks on the nature of news."

"In an era before computers," says ex-NW newsman Cameron Bell, "in a newsroom the size of a sedan, Barker would carefully construct ongoing files for ongoing stories. They'd be put away in a filing system that owed more to squirrels than Dewey, but were available for instant recall. Barker could often retrieve information faster than most computerized databases today."

Barker set the standard for the work ethic here. In the smallest of the morning's hours he would review assignments for the coming day; contact police and fire halls across the province, select winners of the $25 news tip prize . . . and chew his way through the plastic tips of several cigarillos.

A major component of the Barker system is the call sheets: CKNW's news staff makes hundreds of phone calls every day, to police stations, firehalls, hospitals, union offices, service clubs, executive offices, courts, professional association . . . on and on.

More than a year after his "retirement," Warren still comes to the NW newsroom regularly. He does a business commentary heard just before the 8:30 a.m. news, and an afternoon editorial on whatever interests him that day.

He reflects on his early days in the newsroom: "I was never a beater; I was sent out for the occasional story, but I wasn't on the regular beat. Deskers followed up

One day members of the New Westminster Fire Department, dropping off some Fiesta entries, happened to look into the studio just in time to see the show's host opening envelopes . . . off the air. If one were cynical, one could say the host was looking for incorrect answers to string the game out longer and increase the jackpot. And one would be right.

To correct this, um, anomaly Bill Rea came up with an idea to have huge bins built to hold the entries. Then prominent business people were invited on the show to pick entries. (But another staffer has confessed that the bins were so constructed that entries had to be pulled from the bottom. They were the older entries, and not as likely to have the correct answer.) ∎

Block programming is so widespread today, virtually universal, that we don't even notice it. But it was unknown in B.C. before CKNW introduced it.

"On other stations," says Jim Cox, "if you tuned in Tuesday at 2 o'clock you'd hear a show different from the one on Monday at 2. On CKNW Bill Rea had it: when you turned on the radio at 2 o'clock you heard the same show Monday through Friday — and sometimes Saturday."

Hal Davis: "It was an American innovation. Bill Rea picked it up from people in the States. They discovered listeners would become familiar with programs and personalities that came on at the same time every day. People would actually time themselves by the program and the personality." ∎

most of the stories by phone; we made regular calls to the cop shops, checked the wire copy. I read the half-hourly newscasts; the more senior types read on the hour. We did lots of phoning, pursued *local* news. There tended to be an emphasis on New Westminster items, partly because of the weakness of our signal in Vancouver at the time. Our first beater was Marke Raines; he had a radio-telephone put into his own car. I recall Marke testing the Port Mann freeway for CKNW the day before it opened. He got up to 90 miles an hour (about 145 k/ph).

"We didn't have any women in the newsroom in the mid-50s; Susan Soskin was the first. BCTV's Pamela Martin was an early woman reporter for us."

With his promotion to news director, Warren carried on with his regular schedule of newscast reading. (That's still the rule: Gord Macdonald, Warren's successor, regularly reads a morning news shift.)

"Whatever success we had in beat reporting, two people stand out: George Garrett and Carl Waiz. George gets calls from contacts, day and night. Carl was more dogged, did more solid research. He died young of a brain tumor. My luckiest break was when George Garrett got fired as manager of CJAT in Trail, and came back to us. He found he really enjoyed the investigative work, and that's what he does now: he's a full-time investigative reporter."

On the announcement July 26, 1991 of Warren's retirement CKNW's program director Doug Rutherford sent a memo to all staff: "To try to accurately describe the outstanding contribution to broadcast journalism by CKNW vice president of information programming and news director Warren Barker in memo form would be faint praise indeed. Warren Barker has set the standard for Canadian radio journalism in a radio career spanning 44 years. He took over as News Director of CKNW in 1959. Since then, CKNW has been not only the market leader, but the Canadian leader in the radio news profession.

"We owe this success to Warren's hard work, outstanding dedication and vision, and to the professional team of journalists he has assembled . . . We owe Warren a debt of gratitude for developing a newsroom that has been, and will continue to be, the centrepiece of CKNW's long-standing success."

"Don't break the machine . . ."

It's safe to say radio was in CKNW's news director Gord Macdonald's blood. "My parents met in a radio station in Medicine Hat; my father was the program director, my mother was in copy. My dad worked at CKRD in Red Deer when Warren Barker was there in 1949. We moved around a lot: I've lived in seven of the 10 provinces. I was born in Quebec City in September, 1956. My dad was manager of a station in Regina when I was in kindergarten, and my sister Elizabeth was the first female reporter on CFRB in Toronto. She's now a United Church minister."

The Macdonalds were in Victoria in 1973, where George Macdonald became manager of CKDA. Gord took a year of political science and economics at U Vic, worked for a time as a news/operator on DA. He got an undergraduate degree from the University of Windsor, worked at CJOY in Guelph while attending. "After I graduated, I sent out about 120 applications to the west, and got a job in news and sports at CKLQ in Brandon."

Gord next spent five years as news and sports director at Trail's CJAT. Former NW newsman Peter Munoz was now at CKIQ in Kelowna, KBS's flagship station, and had introduced the Warren Barker newsroom system there. After Gord arrived

Warren Barker was NW's news director for 32 astonishing years.

at CJAT, he was sent to CKIQ to see how their newsroom operated. Macdonald returned to Trail and set up a system that, unbeknownst to him, had largely been CKNW influenced. Peter Munoz, by the way, had left CKIQ some time before to found the broadcast journalism program at BCIT. (Munoz set the NW system up at BCIT as the model for broadcast students!)

Gord himself then went to BCIT. As a teacher.

"I taught broadcast journalism from '86 to '89, and worked for John Ashbridge on weekends on WIN. And in the summer I did summer relief full time for Warren and WIN. In my third year of teaching I came to Warren and said I'd like a job. By then, he'd heard me on the air a lot and knew my work. In February of '89 Warren hired me, and I started full-time in the summer."

Warren Barker worked you hard, Gord says, but you respected him. "He never got mad at you, but on those rare occasions he told you about a mistake you had made, you felt *awful*. It was a newsroom where you hanged yourself."

In September of 1989 veteran NW newsman John McKitrick took early retirement, and Gord's life changed. "Warren gave me the coveted daytime 'pilot' shift that John McKitrick had had. The way he showed you how you were doing was where he put you on the shift. That's how Warren 'talked' to you. In the late spring of '91 we started hearing reports Warren might be retiring.

"Three of us in the newsroom were candidates to succeed him. I didn't envy the guy who would replace Warren Barker. My approach was: don't break the machine. The machine's working. We all liked the system, were all familiar with it. In September of 1991 I became news director. There was some adjustment. With Warren's departure, and John McKitrick's, we had lost 65 years of editorial judgement in 12 months. You can't make that up overnight."

1994 marks 45 years for the CKNW Orphans' Fund Picnic. More than 2,000 children and supervisors now attend. The tradition began when children from the Loyal Protestant Home were entertained for the day at a picnic on Bowen Island. Transportation was by fishboat, the captain of which was a friend of Bill Rea's. The picnic's been held at Playland at the PNE since 1957.

"The picnic," says Tanya Boguski of CKNW's promotion department, "serves as a way for less fortunate children, and in some cases adults, to spend a day at Playland enjoying all of the rides and entertainment.

"We have several sponsors who've helped us throughout the years by generously supplying treats for the kids. Dairy Queen has made sundaes; Nalley's has supplied us with bags of chips; and KFC and Coca-Cola have been very generous by giving us reasonable prices for the lunches and soft drinks. And, of course, we have to give special thanks to Playland and B.C. Transit staff: they make the day special for so many kids."

In 1956 Erm Fiorillo (left) and Hal Davis joined in the fun at the annual Orphans' Fund picnic.

Reflecting on the long and influential backgrounds of NW newsroom veterans like Jim Cox, Warren Barker and John McKitrick, Gord says: "I won't say it's humbling, but I do feel a very small and proud part of a very long heritage."

"Al invited me to come work for him . . ."
Radio is one field in which working for many different companies over the years is not a handicap. CKNW sports reporter Ron Barnet is a good example: his 36 years of broadcasting have taken him to 10 different stations. Born in April, 1940 in Manyberries, Alberta, Ron was in radio at 17, going to Grade 12 and hosting a weekly high-school show on CJOC, Lethbridge. They had him do sports, too, and he still remembers the date of his first sportscast: November 11, 1957.

Ron spent 18 years at Regina's CKCK, during which time he became the station's sports director. "I'd been a frequent guest on Al Davidson's interview shows on CKNW, and Al invited me to come work for him. I'd been negotiating to do play-by-play for the Winnipeg Blue Bombers, but decided to accept Al's offer. That was in October, 1983."

Ron didn't know Big Al was "such a loose cannon," and looked on in amazement as his flamboyant and aggressive boss went through several career crises, including the burning of his boats, his clash with Neil Macrae and, finally, his removal from the air.

"At the end of the '87 season I negotiated for and won the play-by-play for the Vancouver Canadians. Baseball's my favorite game, so I enjoyed that. I report on sports, work the sidelines at Lions games, I've done post-game shows, locker-room interviews. What do I like best? No question: play-by-play."

"That microphone meant everything . . ."
At 2:30 a.m., October 22, 1987, CKNW general manager Ron Bremner struggled out of sleep to answer an insistent phone call. The station's sports director, Dave Hodge,

was on the phone. As soon as Bremner heard who was calling, he said "What'd Al do?" Hodge replied, "How'd you know?"

Hodge was calling Bremner to say Neil Macrae said he had been threatened by Davidson at a Canucks-Bruins game the night before. Bremner climbed into his clothes and went to meet Hodge at an all-night Denny's to talk about it.

At the beginning of the third period of the game, said Macrae, Davidson had said to him, "Just so you know, my son is going to beat the shit out of you. When he finds you, he is going to shoot your ass off. He will bend you in half." Said Macrae, "Give me a reason." "He's got fifty," Davidson replied. "Just give me one," Macrae responded, and when Davidson didn't respond, asked, "Is that a threat?" Said Davidson, "No, just a promise." Macrae reported the conversation to Hodge after the game, and also to the police.

There was bad blood between Davidson and Macrae. Al, who had been sports director of NW for more than 20 years had agreed to step down in exchange for an extension of his contract. His new title: senior sports editor. Ron Bremner hired Hodge as sports director. Hodge gave Macrae, who had been with CKNW two years, some of the work on Canucks broadcasts once done by Davidson. Big Al resented that.

Ron Bremner: "We phoned Al's lawyer, Bill Berardino, first thing in the morning. 'Here's the latest problem with Al,' I said. Berardino called Al, met with him after his sportscast. Then Berardino met with me, Hodge and two of NW's lawyers. We agreed on terms that called for Al to take medical leave. Al was *furious* with us. He went over to OR and started working there, starts rippin' the #^&% out of CKNW on the air."

Pat Davidson, Al's widow: "I remember when Al called me from NW in the morning, after the Neil Macrae incident, and told me they wouldn't let him on the air. Al had been telling me for weeks that something was going on. I was used to seeing him coming home tired, but he started coming home tired and *downhearted*. 'I don't look forward to going in.'"

Al launched a wrongful dismissal suit against NW. The station said it had cause because of Al's threat to Macrae, said the threat was the culmination of a series of similar incidents, said it could tolerate Davidson's conduct no longer. (The list of controversies, arguments, and physical confrontations Al was involved in both inside and outside CKNW was, admittedly, astonishingly long.) Davidson, in turn, denied the remarks were a threat, said the incident was blown out of proportion, and had been deliberately distorted to get rid of him.

Davidson, said Judge Ian Donald, when he handed down his decision May 25, 1990, was "by all accounts a difficult man. He is short tempered, irascible, hypercritical and abrasive. But he is also witty, engaging and extraordinarily hard working. He possesses a roguish charm . . . The broadcasting style he employed was unique to the man. It was aggressively controversial. The station wanted listeners and did not care whether they loved or hated Davidson, so long as they tuned into CKNW — and they did in satisfying numbers." The judge described Al's threat as "childish and silly; the kind of thing one little boy says to another in a school yard," and said Macrae's behavior afterward indicated he, Macrae, didn't really take the threat seriously.

He found that NW's reference during the trial to earlier, similar incidents involving Al were irrelevant, since they had gone unpunished at the time. "The defendant

The picnic lasts just one day, but takes weeks of planning. Invitations are sent out to more than 50 schools and institutions. B.C. Transit takes the resulting data and sets up an intricate schedule to pick up the kids and their supervisors at various locations throughout the Lower Mainland. When they arrive, they're treated to rides, balloons and entertainment.

Weeks before the event, calls are made to arrange the services of St. John's Ambulance, the band, face painters, local athletes and mascots.

"The kids aren't the only ones who enjoy the day at Playland," Tanya says, "The 'grown-up' kids at CKNW enjoy it, as well!" ∎

Rafe Mair, whose dexterity at operating the "kill" switch leaves something to be desired, recalls one particular night early in his NW career (he was doing a midnight to 2 a.m. talk show) when the theme was sexual activity. One caller, carried away by his enthusiasm for the subject, used an obscene word. There is a seven-second delay on talk shows, so Rafe had seven seconds to act. (Appropriately, it was a seven-letter word.) He fumbled for the button that would beep out the offending word before it got out on the air . . . and managed to cut off everything the caller said BUT that word. It blared out loud and clear, after a seven-second beep guaranteed to attract every listener's attention. ∎

(CKNW) put up with Davidson's quarrels with other employees because it was in its economic interests to keep a difficult, but highly entertaining, character . . ." Davidson, said Judge Donald, was "hardly an ideal employee. But he was not hired to work as a clerk in an insurance office; he was an entertainer whose special talent was bound up in an abrasive personality."

The judge essentially agreed with most of what Al and his lawyer claimed. He said the firing, under the unique circumstances of Al's role at the station, was not justified and awarded Al $326,000 in lost income. From that, he deducted income Davidson had earned at CJOR and elsewhere in the year he spent after NW dropped him, for a net of just over $262,000.

The OR job was the last Al had on the air. "He was there about a year," Pat Davidson says, "and then in 1988 they went rock and roll. He took the staff members who could go down to the Granville Island Hotel. He didn't drink any more, but he got them all drinks."

More painful to him than the loss of income, says Pat, was the loss of a mike. "That microphone meant everything to him. When it was taken away . . .

"In the summer of 1991 Al started having difficulty in walking. We thought it might be some shrapnel he still had in his body from World War II. And he was diabetic. He fell badly, twice. He was due for a checkup, anyway, and our family doctor suspected a cranial problem. Al was scheduled for a scan at VGH. He had an appointment to go for a test on August 8th, but when I called them to describe his condition they said to come in right away.

"He'd been sedated, but then he went into a coma. All the family were there except Marcia, who was in Australia."

Big Al died of a brain tumor August 9, 1991. He died before seeing the money awarded him by Judge Donald, because of an appeal against the decision by CKNW. The station lost the appeal and Pat got a cheque. "But if people think I'm sitting on a pile of gold after we won that settlement award," she says, "they're crazy."

Lee Powell and Prime Time Sports

Lee Powell's Prime Time Sports on CKNW is an example of a new phenomenon in commercial AM radio: a talk show devoted entirely to sports. CKNW didn't waste any time reading the public mood on this one. In September, 1991 they launched Lee's show . . . and it's a hit. (Lee's CFMI counterpart, Dan Russell, has had a similar FM success with Sports Talk for many years.)

In July of 1992 The Province's Howard Tsumura asked Lee what the fascination was in sports talk radio. "People like to trade opinions," Lee said, "and today sports is tougher than ever to follow. It's our job to sift through it all, and find the nuggets." NW's Doug Rutherford told Tsumura Lee's show was a natural extension for a station whose high sports exposure was already established. "Lee . . . is so knowledgeable, and it just shows through."

Lee was born in Vancouver in October, 1958, graduated from the Broadcast Communications program at BCIT in 1978, worked in Castlegar, Vernon, Kamloops, Brandon and at AM 1040, which became Coast Radio.

"I spent a year as sports director at AM 1040, but left when they changed their format to rock. Al Davidson was leaving NW, and people were being shifted around there; Dave Hodge hired me in the spring of 1987. I did weekend sports, some reporting . . . then began to fill in for Dan Russell on Sports Talk, and became his regular guest host for a couple of years. I eventually did 'drive sports' during Rick Honey's show.

"Is there a difference in the calls between hockey and football? Yes! Football doesn't always draw the *passion* hockey does. Hockey can get really heated."

We're talking at Champs Sports Pub Extraordinaire where Prime Time Sports is live. Producer Chad Varhaug's gesturing now for Lee to get to the mike, the show's about to begin. The first half-hour, featuring Trevor Linden, goes quickly. There's a big cheer from the crowd for rookie Dixon Ward (he had just assisted on Pavel Bure's 50th goal, the first time a Canuck had reached that level), and a big laugh when he responds to a question from Lee about Ronnie Stern. "I'm not gonna say anything bad about Ronnie Stern," Ward drawls, "because he's a friend of Trevor's, and Trevor's sitting right beside me!"

A mike's been set up for pub patrons to ask questions, and that attracts a few of the bolder types. Later, when the inevitable question about the Canucks' ineffective

Macrae's abrasive style often leads to abrasive comments from listeners.

power play comes up, Dixon Ward says "everybody knows the Vancouver media is very negative," and that gets another cheer from the crowd. A few minutes with goalie Whitmore and the show is done for another night.

It hasn't escaped the attention of CKNW management that sports brings a younger audience to AM radio. Sports talk radio — and Lee Powell's Prime Time Sports — is here to stay!

"You gotta do a show . . ."

Neil Macrae: "Frosty likes my style . . . abrasive, witty, fast. I'm willing to set myself up for his stuff; I don't care if people poke fun at me. Frosty needs someone who can fire back. It's not rehearsed; I have no idea what he's going to say. His mike's open when I'm talking, and he'll say things. He's the only deejay I know who's right on top of current events, including sports.

"I've always been abrasive. There's not a lot of difference between me and the average sports fan talking. I have a microphone. When you get people going to the office and saying, 'I missed Macrae, what'd he say?' you know you're doing it. You gotta do a *show*."

His abrasive style often leads to abrasive comment on Macrae from listeners . . . and competing media types. (The Province's Kent Gilchrist, dubbing him Kneel McKnock, once described him as "a big-mouthed, air-headed, evil Ronald McDonald clone . . . the mouse that roared on Frosty's morning show," and accused Macrae of stealing ideas from the paper's sports columnists.) "It shows

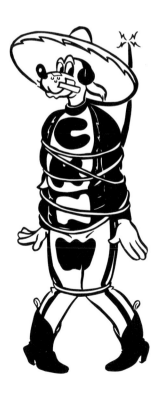

they're listening when they devote a whole column to you. If *I* take a shot at someone, I don't expect them to get upset. So vice versa, no problem."

"People seemed to like it . . ."

For a fellow born in Ephrata, Washington (May 20, 1953), who grew up in Tucson, Arizona, CKNW newsman and World Tonight co-host Jon McComb sure sounds Canadian. Jon has been, in his words, "hanging around" radio stations since he was 12. He came north of the border in 1972, started at Vancouver's CKVN. It was back to the States (Portland) in 1975, and then on to CFCF in Montreal in 1977. Less than a year later he was doing afternoon news at CJAD, at 25 the youngest they'd ever had in that time period. He had that job until May of 1980.

"I wanted to go back to school, *and* freelance. So I went to Simon Fraser University, and in 1980 started part-time at NW. By the end of '80, beginning of '81, I was working virtually full-time for NW, but then a buddy of mine had an idea that turned into a company called Sunshine Cabs. All the cabs would be Cadillacs! In the fall of '81 I left CKNW and started driving, dispatching, and administering Sunshine Cabs. In '83 I came back to NW part-time as a beat reporter, was on Western Information Network, worked every shift imaginable. John Ashbridge came off the desk in 1985 to run NW's Expo operation and I replaced him. That's what I was doing until Philip Till showed up, and NW launched The World Tonight.

"I was really interested in international stories and current events, and Philip and I hit it off personally from the beginning. We'd do a colloquy on the international stories, and that seemed to go well. That turned into what we do now from 6:30 to 6:40.

"I'd first heard Philip when he was with NBC, and his reports were carried on CKNW. His coverage of the bombing of Tripoli was particularly memorable. When we started working together, I was thrilled. This is *Philip Till*. Phil and I began to develop an on-air relationship, a very positive one. People seemed to like it.

"He asked me one day if I'd ever considered talk. I said no. 'Why not,' he asked, 'When I'm away you can do the show.' So we broached it with Shirley Stocker and Doug Rutherford, and I started to fill in more: first for a couple of days, then a week, then three weeks when he's away on holiday.

"In '91 the show moved up to 5:30 and I moved up to a full-fledged co-host. There's a lot of variety: last night we had Mike Harcourt on about a cabinet shuffle, an environmental group on mining in B.C., international segments, and a singing psychic. The off-the-wall stuff is fun."

Jon McComb has been around radio stations since he was 12.

Jim Robson's been the Canucks broadcaster since the franchise began more than 20 years ago, and has called more than 1,500 games. He leaves nothing to chance. He reads the Game Notes prepared for the media by the Canucks front office, jots notes on individual players, and checks statistics.

But things can still go awry: "I used to do away games by myself," Jim says, "hang a mike over the box to get crowd noise, have a pencil mike on a loop around my neck so I could take it off and interview someone. I remember an AHL game in Providence, there was no phone for

Joy Metcalfe isn't really everywhere at the same time, it just seems that way. She started on air at CKNW in November, 1987.

"My main job? Get it first."

Joy Metcalfe isn't really everywhere, it just seems that way. Her "items column" of the air, Joy's Journal, is one of CKNW's most familiar soundmarks, heard twice daily. (Her 8:35 a.m. report has well over 100,000 listeners.) Into the few minutes she's on, Joy crams in a whole day's events: openings, premieres, interviews, news conferences, celebrity sightings . . . it's fast-paced, energetic, and effusive, like the lady herself.

Winnipeg-born Joy's natural promotional abilities got her a publicity job at the Vancouver Playhouse, and she became the first in-house public relations person at Palmer Jarvis Advertising.

In 1976 Joy started doing an items column at The Courier, "just about the same time Earle Bradford started doing his items show on CKNW." Joy recalls that Earle, anxious in his new role, would call and ask what her lead item was. "I wouldn't want to say, and he'd get mad. And every morning after his broadcast, he'd phone me and ask 'How was that?'"

With her Courier column, and daily NW shows, you'd be hard pressed to think of a public event at which this irrepressibly curious woman isn't present with her note pad. "My main job in life? Get it *first*."

That ferocious pursuit of scoops brought Joy to the attention of the city's radio fraternity. Both CKNW's John Plul and CJOR's George Madden began pursuing her. There was a special urgency at NW: Earle Bradford had become seriously ill, and was in hospital. Joy had no intention of stepping into Earle's shoes while he was ailing,

the broadcast, so I'm using the concession phone. There's a tremendous rush down the ice by Vancouver, and I'm roaring into the mike, and suddenly the listeners hear someone say, 'We need five dozen more buns.'" ∎

Tom Plasteras is prepared: 'If we lose, play this cart.' 'If we win, play this cart.'

and so accepted the OR offer. It would prove to be a short stay, but a valuable learning experience. "I remember John Plul from NW was calling me virtually every day: 'You're sounding okay now, come on over.' I told him, give me six months. But I was still not going to go there over Earle's sick body. Then Earle himself called from the hospital. 'Get your ass out of CJOR,' he says, 'and get over to CKNW. Otherwise that job won't be there when *I* get back.' So nine weeks after I started at OR I went over to CKNW. I went to a Jack Cullen bash at Expo, and Jack told his listeners I was coming to NW. That's where my boss at OR, George Madden, heard the news. I started on-air at CKNW November 2, 1987; Earle Bradford died November 5."

Joy was nervous at first about being on Frosty Forst's morning show. Forst, a razor-sharp ad-libber, can be intimidat-

On April Fool's Day, 1990 George Garrett pulled off a great gag. He announced he'd come across "confidential drawings" showing B.C. government plans for a rapid-transit line to whisk British Columbians quickly, safely and conveniently down to Bellis Fair, a big shopping mall . . . in Bellingham, Washington. Bob Robertson portrayed Premier Bill Vander Zalm on the phony item, commenting favorably on the plan. Meanwhile, out in the real world, Rita Johnston, transportation minister at the time, heard the item, immediately realized it was an

ing. And initial reaction to Joy's bits was not uniformly favorable. But Frosty calmed her down. "You'll do okay," he said. "It's my show, I'll decide. Just relax." She did, and she's still there, still getting it *first*.

"Hold back your modesty!"

"I get a charge out of being *prepared*. Last year, during the CFL playoffs, there was a game every two days. I prepared carts for Frosty's morning show, and they're labeled: 'If we lose, play this cart.' 'If we win, play this cart.' Jim Conrad voiced them, we had music and effects. Rahib 'Rocket' Ismail of the Argos was getting a lot of hype at the time, but as it happens we beat the Argos. Next morning there's the 'win' cart, already prepared, Frosty hits it, and it starts: 'SO MUCH FOR RAHIB!!!!'

That's NW's assistant program director Tom Plasteras (plas-TEER-ess) talking. When he took his practicum in his second year at BCIT they sent him to CKNW, where he started as an operator.

"Around July of '89 Paul Preston, the production manager, asked if I wanted to work full time. I started in commercial production September 1, 1989. They started adding CFMI work to my production chores, and I thought I should be making more money. In the spring of '90 I got fed up, and asked for more. I wrote a pleasant, but firm letter, and the result was they gave me Studio 2. That's considered a step up. And Doug Rutherford told me later the letter was a factor in his appointing me assistant program director."

Another factor occurred in October 1990: "I'm in Studio 5 gabbing with the guys and Doug Rutherford walks through. 'Plasteras, your studio.' We go in, the door shuts, Doug says, 'You interested in programming?' I say, 'I think I'd be good at it.' Doug says, 'Hold back your modesty!' Well, Doug has to think about this stuff for a long time. Finally, he came back. 'OK,' he says, 'you wanna be assistant program director?' I said, 'Sure!'"

Originally, the job encompassed shift scheduling on the programming side, supervising the operators, and doing some work in production. It's expanded since. One of the more enjoyable facets is talking about music: Tom had always loved music, played guitars and drums, and now he regularly sits in with Doug Rutherford and Frosty Forst and the three talk about the songs played on CKNW. "We discuss every song we play. Our music policy is: 'familiar, familiar, familiar.' We do so many *kinds* of programming that our music has to appeal to everybody. The single most important song of the day is the one Frosty plays at 5 minutes to 8."

Tom fills in for Doug Rutherford now when the latter's away on holidays or business. And he deals with the public a lot. He'll talk on the phone with NW listeners who are pleased — or not pleased — about the station's shows or personalities. "I get a lot of calls about Neil Macrae."

"Rafe shows me the buttons . . ."

Shell Busey has 280,000 listeners tuning in to his Home Improvement Show, originating on CKNW. When this Owen Sound native came to B.C. in 1974, he'd been the youngest manager in the 100-store Beaver Lumber chain. After he left Beaver he bought a Windsor Plywood outlet in Delta.

Shell's contact with Windsor Plywood put him in contact with Windsor's Al Wightman. Wightman used to work at CKNW. He was familiar with radio, and thought Shell would make an excellent guest on Rafe Mair's show, then on CJOR. "I'm on for half an hour with Rafe," Shell says, "and it must be going well, because he asks if I can stay for another half hour. So I did. And after, Rafe says he's going to have to have me back. Renovation Week was coming up in a few weeks, so I went back. The lines went wild. After the show, OR's manager Harvey Gold asks if he can talk with me. 'Would you be interested in hosting a regular show?' Sure! So I was slated to do 90 minutes on Saturday mornings.

"Now I'm going to be doing a show myself, I have never been so scared in my life. Rafe shows me the buttons, and I'm on my own. But I can call on him, he says, if I need help. He goes for coffee. The show's going along well, and then there's a newscast and I go out for a stretch. 'Where's Rafe?' 'Oh,' the switchboard lady says, 'he said you were doing so well, you didn't need him. He went home!' "

During 1988 B.C. Hydro came to see Shell. "They were just about to launch their Power Smart (power conservation) program, and they wanted to do a radio show. David Brown of Hydro and Ray Dagg of WIN arranged everything, and the Home Idea Show started May 13, 1990. Well, going from CJOR to CKNW was like going from a Volkswagen Beetle to the fastest race track. And WIN made it faster. We started with 32 stations, now there are 62, making it the largest network show in B.C.

"By the way, know who broke me in on the board at NW, showed me how the buttons worked? Rafe Mair!"

"I thought I'd gone to heaven . . ."

Dr. Art Hister pops up all over CKNW's schedule — he does the Medical Minutes, he's a regular guest on Bill Good's show, and he conducts his own phone-in show, House Call, on Sunday mornings. He graduated in 1970, at 24, and interned at Montreal's Jewish General Hospital.

"I also got married in 1970. My wife Phyllis wanted to go to Library School. She got accepted at UBC. 'I'm going to Vancouver,' she tells me, 'Wanna come?'

April Fool gag, and phoned to ask George if she could join the fun. The next newscast featured George's original story, then Rita coming on and elaborating on it, making it an even more ambitious project!

The result was every April Fool prankster's dream: someone bit, and bit big. A delegation of executives from Surrey Place, a big mall on the King George Highway, actually drove down to Bellingham to protest! ∎

Bill Good in the studio with Vancouver Alderman Gordon Price.

Jim Cox remembers emceeing a 1940s appearance at the Town Hall by Bob Crosby's band. Crosby hadn't been told 30 minutes of the band's performance would be broadcast — and was startled when teenager Jim strode from the wings, set up a CKNW mike stand and began to introduce him. It wasn't legal, but Crosby shrugged and carried on.

The room had an unusual cooling system: a ceiling arrangement of vanes, hanging down about four feet, would periodically

Well, I knew nothing about Vancouver, except it had a new NHL team. So, what the heck, sure. Our timing was very good: the city was looking for assistant medical health officers. The chief MHO at the time was Gerry Bonham; he tells me the guy running the Pine Street Free Clinic is leaving. Do I want to take it over? The patients were old hippies, and drug freaks. I fell in love with the place; I thought I'd gone to heaven. The Clinic started off small, but it grew very fast. In fact, I thought it got too big, so I left after about seven years. I went into private practice as a GP, and I did that right up until 1991.

"The media stuff started in '85 with Phil Reimer. The B.C. Medical Association was launching a series on CBC-TV, and they were advertising for a doctor/host. The producer was a woman named Nijole Kuzmickas and Phil Reimer was executive producer. They chose me as host. The show was called Doctor Doctor, and ran three years.

"Then I approached CKNW's program director, Doug Rutherford, and suggested a feature called Medical Minutes. He says, 'Let me get back to you.' Later I bumped into Doug at an awards event, and I forgot who he was! But he remembered *me* and told me he wanted to do the Medical Minutes idea."

Art's 1000th Medical Minute was broadcast just before this interview. And now the feature is heard on the Western Information Network, comprising dozens of stations in B.C. and Alberta. By the time you read this, Toronto, Ottawa and Montreal will have been added.

Next, Bill Good wanted to do a regular feature on medical matters on his show. "And then," Art says, "Doug came up with a concept: my own show. I was scared to death. I came home after the first show, and said to Phyllis, 'I don't know . . .' But it's worked out."

House Call debuted September 17, 1989.

"I kept thinking, "What if I'm wrong?""

"The show is a blank easel every day," Patti Mair says. "Rafe trusts me to fill it. I book stuff, and he goes with it, even things he's not personally interested in. Part of what guides us are the moods of the day: there are two. There's a daily mood; that's created by concern over a current event. And there's a 'wave' mood, a continuing feeling about something like, say, the deficit. And that wave mood doesn't break down demographically: *everybody* has the same concern.The audience now is very sophisticated, very knowledgable."

Rafe weighs in. "The whole of talk radio has changed dramatically in the last 10 years. The public is a hell of a lot smarter than they're given credit for by some radio programmers. They want to learn, they want to delve into serious issues." Serious certainly describes the Meech Lake constitutional debate. Rafe took an immediate stance against that agreement, and argued long and fiercely against it on his show. "NW kept asking me, 'Why do you keep going on about this? People don't care.' I said they will. And they did."

Response to Mair's shows on the constitutional question was explosive. Rather than tuning out, listeners — many of whom vehemently disagreed with his stance — began to tune in regularly. The cogency and force of Mair's arguments against a 'Yes' vote on the Charlottetown referendum began to articulate for many British Columbians the things they had difficulty expressing. He found himself at the centre of a storm of controversy, and other media began to take notice. The Vancouver Sun dubbed him 'Dr. No,' and soon, to his utter and unfeigned amazement, Rafe Mair found himself being cited in magazines and newspapers all across Canada and beyond: The Globe and Mail, The Georgia Straight, The Sunday Times (London), The Toronto Star (which reported that Prime Minister Brian Mulroney was "livid" about Mair's marshalling of the No forces), The New York Times, The Times-Colonist, The Montreal Gazette, US News and World Report, British Columbia Report, TIME, The Financial Post Magazine . . . and countless other newspapers.

"There was real incredulity from the eastern media when they actually listened to my shows. There were no rednecks! Callers were informed and intelligent. But I have to tell you, I kept thinking, 'What if I'm wrong?'"

When the results of the referendum came in, the strongest No vote (68.1 per cent) was in British Columbia, and it's no exaggeration to say Rafe Mair played a huge part in that result.

An occasional bone of contention between Mair and NW is what he calls "blood wars" over the Vancouver Canucks. Rafe won't hold back on attacking the Canucks if he thinks it's war-ranted, and that has led to "hot arguments." "I've told them to take back my contract if they don't like it," he says. Patti con-curs: "We don't have anyone we won't bite."

begin swinging slowly back and forth to circulate the air. It was noisy, and looked bizarre, but the dancers were used to it. No one told Crosby about the vanes, and when they began their slow sweep to and fro, he stopped conducting and gaped up at them. "Boy," Crosby said into the mike, "*everything* swings at the Town Hall!" ∎

The show is a blank easel every day for Rafe Mair.

Hal Davis doesn't make the claim himself, but an argument could be made he began the talk-show phenomenon that makes Vancouver radio unique. (Unique because of its muscular ratings, unequalled elsewhere in Canada!) When CKNW and other stations had to kill contests like Fiesta, Hal started driving around North America with his ears peeled for new ideas. From San Francisco he heard the famed talker Ira Blue, and in Winnipeg heard a phone-in show on household hints. Hal put the two ideas together, and had Wally Garrett begin a phone-in show, still titled Fiesta, partly on household hints, partly on a question of the day. "Wally could feel the thing happening," says Hal, "and started going longer than the five minutes of talk per half-hour we'd started with." The ratings were excellent. CJOR countered with Pat Burns . . . to whom CKNW responded with Jack Webster . . . and the rest is talk-show history. ∎

And there are the real satisfactions, like being nominated for the Michener Award for a series on child custody services, a series that led to B.C.'s ombudsman recommending changes in legislation.

At his contract re-signing in 1992, Rafe turned to program director Doug Rutherford before a roomful of prominent invited guests, and said, "Doug, over the last eight years I've said and done a lot of things that have really upset you. I just want you to know that during the next three years there won't be a damn thing changed."

In 1993 Rafe Mair was named Broadcaster of the Year by the B.C. Association of Broadcasters.

"Hire the best, then leave them alone . . ."

"CKNW is constantly changing," says general manager Rod Gunn, "but the changes are imperceptible. When we make a change, we plan it well in advance. As an example, Doug Rutherford and I are looking at Roving Mike right now. Bill Hughes may want to retire from that show. The ratings are still strong for it, so what do we do? George Garrett, who fills in for Bill, is good at it, so maybe we groom him to take it over if Bill decides to let it go. Is the program beginning to wear? Could something else go in in its place? Sales would be involved in that decision, so John Iacobucci would sit in. John Plul would advise on how best to phase the show out, *if* it's phased out. Or maybe we should make it weekly?

"We're thinking right now about the possibility of an all-night talk show. Maybe it would go on WIN, even go national . . . We're reflecting Vancouver's ethnic mix more in our existing talk shows, wondering if we should have a reporter to cover the Chinese community, the 'Chinatown beat.' Bill Good did a recent show on Hong Kong arrivals, and it got tremendous response. We think about these sorts of options all the time."

There's a conscious continuity to NW's internal staff movement: "Our preference for hiring," says Gunn, "is (1) inside the station (2) inside Westcom Radio Group (3) outside." That doesn't always apply to on-air people. CKNW has a well-deserved reputation for plucking rising stars out of competitors' hands. "That's right. We hired Jack Wasserman once because we didn't want anyone else to get him. Why did we hire Gary Bannerman back? Same story. I always thought Gary was good. He was doing his show when I left to manage Calgary, so getting him back wasn't a wrench for me. And the potential that he could go against us on CHQM was there.

"In a market of this size, only one talk-station will work. And you've got to have awfully deep pockets."

Is there a management style at CKNW? "'Y' know, it's almost an honor for me to be the manager here. There's such a tradition over 50 years: Bill Rea, Bill Hughes, Mel Cooper, Hal Davis, Ted Smith, Ron Bremner . . . Some say Bill Hughes was a tyrant. Well, I worked for Bill Hughes and his style was right for the time. If there's a 'secret' to our management style, it's this: our owners believe you hire the best, then leave them alone. They do that with me, I do that with the staff."

"CKNW is going to be the showcase . . ."

Here's why CKNW stays the leader in the information field.

One day during the researching of this book, CKNW aired a bulletin that Vancouver was to be the scene of a summit meeting between U.S. President Bill Clinton and Russian President Boris Yeltsin. In minutes chief engineer Dave Glasstetter was on the phone to B.C. Tel ordering line facilities from the summit headquarters in the Vancouver Trade and Convention Centre. When he called, Dave didn't *know* if CKNW would do extensive coverage, but he knows how the station works, so he put in the order, anyway.

Around the corner in his office, news director Gord Macdonald, who's beginning to look more and more like a clone of his predecessor Warren Barker, has already pulled the shift sheet for the week before the summit dates, and is starting to move people around. Gord's making notes on who should be where to provide the best coverage. Who will be available? That's a foregone conclusion. Everybody.

Tucked into the Western International Network office between Dave and Gord, John Ashbridge has pulled notes from a CKNW broadcast of five years ago — the Commonwealth first Minister's Conference — and is looking at the logistics.

The bulletin went on just 20 minutes ago, and already this place is in high gear! While Glasstetter, Macdonald and Ashbridge are working, program director Doug Rutherford sets a summit planning meeting for Monday, March 9. Doug has already received a fax from World Tonight host Philip Till, down at NW's B.C. Place studios, with some suggestions based on his experience. Till has covered every summit meeting in the past 15 years.

Assistant program director Tom Plasteras sits in on the Monday meeting; so does talk show producer Shirley Stocker. Shirley and Gord Macdonald will coordinate Summit coverage for NW. Shirley and Philip have come in from Vancouver. General Manager Rod Gunn sits in.

Doug Rutherford, chairing, looks around the room. "CKNW," he says, "is going to be the showcase for the summit." Then he asks a question: "How do we make our coverage outstanding?" The meeting gets down to work. Till's input is invaluable. He knows about the security arrangements, the fact that President Clinton may want to jog when he's in Vancouver, what sort of people will accompany the two leaders, where they're likely to stay, how world media will behave, what CKNW can offer them, what happens to traffic, how proceedings will be announced to the media . . . etc., etc., and etc.

Newsman Ted Field has been cut loose from his regular duties, and will spend the week doing nothing but Summit background.

NW's engineers will put together a complete studio set-up inside the Convention Centre, making things right to bring CKNW's listeners wall-to-wall coverage of the Summit . . . except for two hockey games. The coverage is modified to work around them. After all, NW listeners have their priorities!

Philip Till brings solid experience to The World Tonight.

Erm Fiorillo: "When I joined the station in 1950 as credit manager I made sure advertisers paid their bills. I found it necessary at times to take some of Bill Rea's advertising friends off the air for being delinquent in their payments. The first time I did that the client phoned Bill to complain, and he put them back on the air. That prompted me to go into his office and tell him, 'Either I'm going to be your credit manager, or you are.' From Day One we had that kind of relationship; we spoke very openly to one another, and he developed respect for me. From then on, whenever I took his friends off the air, Bill had a stock answer for them: 'I might own this station, but Mr. Fiorillo runs the Credit Department. What he says goes.' There's no wonder you'd bust your ass for that kind of a boss." ∎

What was behind that famous April 18, 1991 on-the-air tirade in which Rafe Mair attacked CKNW, his employer, over its re-hiring of ex-NW talker Gary Bannerman? "That had nothing to do with Gary personally," Rafe says. "I'd seen one of CKNW's executives on BCTV talking about the hiring, and I sat in my office for nearly three hours thinking about it. I decided to go for a preemptive strike. I believed the station had behaved immorally, and maybe even illegally. I knew the *real* reason CKNW hired him had to do with wanting to preempt his going to CHQM. I knew that if the matter was raised on the open line — which it was bound to be — I would answer my callers truthfully. I thought it better to say my piece right up front rather than appear to be reacting sourly.

"Now that he's here, Gary and I get along very well." ∎

When Summit Week starts Philip Till is in Washington, D.C. with his producer, probing his sources for background news. He calls in all week with behind-the-scenes stuff (some of it more easily gathered in faraway Washington!), and reports on The World Tonight with Jon McComb anchoring at Vancouver. They do the two-man broadcast via satellite, as if they were sitting face to face. On Tuesday, just before he flies back to B.C., Till guests on Rafe Mair's show with the latest scoop from Washington.

On Saturday and Sunday regular programming goes out the window and three reporters join the Till/McComb team in the Trade and Convention Centre. Two of them work outside all day both days, and one works overnight in the event of an emergency. A security lock-down traps the reporters inside the Convention Centre.

No fewer than 25 news and production staff from CKNW work to bring the Summit coverage to life, and 15 of them live with it full time for a week. The result: everything you wanted to know about the meeting between Clinton and Yeltsin. The coverage moved back and forth from Washington to Vancouver to Moscow to the airport to UBC to the Stanley Park jogging path to meeting rooms . . . unfettered by time, print deadlines and the need for cameras.

Summit freaks got it all on CKNW. A visiting reporter from Seattle's KOMO summed it up: "I've never seen anything like it in my 30-year career. You guys were a treat to observe and listen to." And B.C.'s Premier Mike Harcourt sent a note of appreciation: "Your extended coverage was exceptional."

"We're all working for him . . ."

Frosty Forst: "I was doing what today is called the afternoon drive show. The salary was pretty good; they were keeping me around for Bob Hutton's retirement. I used to come in here in a suit and tie and carry a briefcase! I see them doing it now here, and I don't know what's in there: their medicine?

"I did Bob's show when he went on holidays, so there was a kind of phase-out. He'd read kids' jokes on the air, and 'Let's have the morning march!' Our styles were different. It was fun doing the show for Hutton when he was away; it became less fun when I started doing it myself."

Frosty's day ends at 9 p.m. when he goes to bed. It begins at 3:30 the next morning. "I set the clock for the last possible moment. When I hear it, bam, I get up. None of that 'snoozing' crap. I collect the jokes I've written the night before, bits of business I'll do with Neil Macrae, and I jump in the car with a handful of prunes or some other kind of fruit.

"I listen to talk radio on the way in, syndicated talk shows on KIRO. I'll catch the 4 a.m. news on CBS in the car. If the topic doesn't interest me, I'll flip to my classical cassettes. There's a newsman waiting for me to arrive, because I'm the best coffee maker in the building. There's grapefruit juice for me in the fridge. I sit down and write Norm Grohmann's material for the weather thing we do; it's based on stuff I learned that morning. I glance at the papers, the news wires, keep the Today in History stuff and birthdays. Then I go on at 5 a.m., and start making a fool of myself.

"I don't like someone else in the room when I'm on the air. I'm not a superstar, I find it distracting and intimidating. I'm my own operator. To be immodest, I'm a good operator."

He is that. And he thinks fast. NW was running a promo for TSN's sportsman Dave Hodge, and Frosty found it a tad too enthusiastic. While the spot was running

Frosty's day begins at 3:30: "I set the clock for the last possible moment. When I hear it, bam, I get up."

Frosty recalled a special cart he keeps aside, and slapped it on. The next time Hodge's name was heard, it was followed by a chorus of ladies all going "oooh" and "aaah." Later that day, manager Rod Gunn says, "Uhh, Frosty, was that ooh and aah stuff already on the Hodge promo?" Frosty just smiled seraphically.

"My style was always making *fun* of things. I'll make fun of this ad, or that sponsor, stick it to the boss. It's the easiest thing to do. It's marketable smartassedness." Sun columnist Jack Wasserman dubbed him the "sabre-tongued" Frosty Forst.

"You've got to be *fast*. I'm my own best audience. I play to myself. If Norm or Neil come up with a funny line, hit the commercial. Use the commercial as the rim shot.

"I pick my own music. My system? Instinct. I've always had a knack for music. I was music director here, and at several other stations. The playlist goes back a maximum of 30 years. I keep a dozen oldies on the back wall, and another half-dozen that I'll choose as I go. I may have seen the Emmys the night before, so I'll get one or two of those in. It used to be you'd play music if you had nothing to say. Now, it's think of something interesting to say, have a funny conversation.

"I don't even glimpse at newspapers when I'm doing the show. It's distracting. I'm *on*.

"I'm a real TV nut, I watch TV all day. When I get home, I'll have taped all the news shows: 20/20, Dateline, 60 Minutes, CNN . . . I keep abreast of things. I know what 'schwing' means; my mother wouldn't have at my age. I'll have taped Letterman and Leno, Saturday Night Live. I'll use lines from Cheers, Seinfeld, Shandling. I keep notes. It's 10 in the morning when you and I are talking. I'm worried right now about what Norm will say tomorrow. I think about it during the day.

Wally Garrett recalls a "professor" hired to "coordinate" the news. "He had written for Lorne Greene. He came in at 10, by 1 p.m. he'd be drunk. When he left, they found his desk full of empty mickeys."

His name was 'Professor' Ed MacDonald, and he's remembered by many others, too. "Every time I passed the Professor's office," Hal Davis laughs, "he'd slide his desk drawer shut, and you could hear the clinking of the bottles. You'd always hear the clinking. He'd arrive at the station in a taxi five minutes before his broadcast, and usually he'd already be half-sozzled. I remember Bill Rea looking down through the window one morning to see the Professor pull up in a cab, and he said, 'When they start arriving by taxi, you know the end is near.'"

Was the Professor at NW long?

"About a caseful," Hal says. ∎

Women in the newsroom Clockwise from left: Janet Larmour, Michelle Cyr and Beth Leighton.

Sometimes the clients have to be persuaded to go with an idea. When sales rep Barb Welsh wanted to have fun with the fact Morrey Nissan is run by identical twins, the Morrey twins were not enthusiastic. "We're in our fifties. We don't wear identical outfits any more."

But their own staff thought it would be fun to play with the idea — and Barb and Jan Evanski, CKNW's creative direc-

"I have a say in who I have on. It's my show. I choose my own music, the woman in the sky, I picked Norm Grohmann, Neil Macrae. If anything goes wrong with the ratings, fire me. But it has to be *my* show. I don't enjoy listening to other local deejays; they have nothing to say. We win everything by default. Where's the other morning man? There's number 1, then there's 4, 5 and 6." (In fact, a senior CKNW executive was once heard to say, "Don't tell Frosty, but we're all working for him.")

Brian has suffered from severe migraine headaches for years, takes medication now that helps, but the migraines occasionally force him to take time off. When that happens, Rick Honey usually fills in for him. A mean gag heard at the station was that when Doc Harris (a potential rival) appeared on the scene Frosty's migraines mysteriously cleared up. They haven't. He spends more than $1,000 a month on medication, carries it with him at all times. The frequency of the attacks lessens when he's on holiday.

"My family life? None. Luckily, I have a Thai wife who doesn't understand this stupid business. I first saw her dancing at the Thai Cultural Centre in Bangkok. She isn't interested in going to movies, or plays, or social events. She's happy to stay home. Darapon and I have been married 10 years, and have two kids, four and nine. I have two older kids from an earlier marriage.

"People in radio ask me if I want to work in Toronto. Why? More money? So I can come back here for a holiday?"

"Take a look at the ratings . . ."

The World Tonight brought a solid new tone to CKNW's evening broadcasting. The reason: the solid experience of host Philip Till.

Till's resume is about half as long as this book, but here are highlights: he was born in 1951 in Stoke-on-Trent, England, began his career at 16 with United Press International, London, as a copyboy. He rose in the ranks until by 1971 he was reporting on such events as Polish food riots, Romanian political changes, a Yugoslav earthquake, the Hungarian Communist Party Congress and political disruption in Bulgaria. For that last bit of reporting, he was declared 'persona non grata' in Bulgaria. Later in the '70s he reported on Germany's terrorist Baader-Meinhof Gang.

As an NBC News correspondent, Till went to every hot spot a turbulent world provided: Cyprus, Jordan, Egypt, Iran . . . and won an award for his reporting on the fall of the Shah. Over the years, Till has won many of the prestigious Overseas Press Club Awards, and he and Fred Kennedy shared a Peabody Award for a documentary on the turbulence in the world's banking system. The two men shared "a wallful of awards" for their coverage of the U.S. air strike on Libya.

As Chief Foreign Correspondent for NBC News in the 1980s, Philip Till went everywhere, saw everything, talked to everyone: summits, presidential visits, NATO meetings, OPEC meetings, Arms Control Talks . . . the amazing list goes on and on. Philip speaks English, French and German. That combination of languages serves him well in gathering global news for The World Tonight.

NW newsman Jon McComb is now a permanent ingredient of The World Tonight. "At the beginning," Philip says, "we just did the eight-minute international newscast together. But Jon was just so good, his role grew larger. I suggested he be my back-up. We're now close personal friends."

Till has other friends, all over the world, and there's a good chance you'll hear them on The World Tonight.

Continuing his globe-trotting ways for CKNW, Philip covered the German elections on the scene. He took the opportunity to drive to Croatia for a look-see. He covered the Exxon Valdez story with NW's George Garrett, went back to Alaska a year later. Out of that second visit came a two-and-a-half-hour documentary that asked the question: was B.C. prepared for a massive oil spill? And he went to San Francisco after their massive 1989 earthquake, filing a report on what B.C. was and was not doing to prepare for a similarly destructive event. For that incisive job of reporting and analysis, Philip Till won the 1991 Jack Webster Award.

"For the first time in my life I'm putting down some roots. It feels good. Some people have told me there isn't a market in British Columbia for extended international news. That is crap. Take a look at the ratings."

"I'm likely to lead with a human element . . ."

Back in 1978 when Susan Soskin (now Susan Fine) was working in news at CHNL in Kamloops she sent a letter and a tape to Warren Barker. Barker drove to Kamloops and listened to Soskin's work. He liked it, and hired her. She became the first woman to work in the NW newsroom. "I started inside in 1978," she says, "with Dave Rutherford training me. A few months after I began, Doriana Temolo started, so she was the second. I went out on the beat occasionally. I was there for three years, and would have stayed longer . . . but I got married, and my shifts were crazy, and my husband was articling. Then I had kids, and just never got back into it. But I enjoyed it a lot."

tor, developed a series of spots that stressed the twins . . . and how they agreed on taking the stress out of car-buying with their one, non-negotiable, fair price. Soon, people were coming into the Morrey Nissan showrooms and — while looking at cars — would grin and ask to see the twins.

The campaign worked: it gave Morrey Nissan a different identity, made it stand out.

And they sold cars. ∎

Dick Abbott, Jack Cullen and Hal Davis — part of the history.

Today, there are several women in Top Dog's newsroom: Yvonne Eamor, who was once full-time, now works there part-time when not at her full-time job as department head of BCIT's Broadcast Journalism program. Janet Larmour, Pat Markley, and Moira McLean are full-time writer/reporters.

Pat has been at CKNW and CFMI since September, 1981. "I started as an operator at CFMI, and did traffic ground control, working with Kathy Morse. I'd graduated from UBC with a double major in psychology and Canadian history, then I went into Broadcast Journalism at BCIT. I think both my majors helped me in the newsroom — especially," she laughs, "the psychology.

"I started doing news on CFMI, but it was 'lifestyle' news, and I wasn't that enthused about it. I started doing the NW Community Cruiser, and when a news story came up where they couldn't get a reporter, I'd rush over and cover it.

"That led to a job writing news for the WIN network, where I worked for four years. Then I got into the NW newsroom, and I've been there since. I could see a difference in coverage with the arrival of women in the newsroom. To cite just one example, when toxic shock syndrome was in the news, the guys wouldn't touch it. I guess it embarrassed them. But it was an important story for women.

"You're more likely to have a guy lead his newscast with an economic story, whereas I'm far more likely to lead with a human element ... something involving a child, say. I think the balance is a good idea, the mix is good.

"Am I going to stay in news? Yep, it's a life sentence. I'd like to go back to university and get my masters in Canadian history, but I'd stay in news. So many people don't like their jobs. I love mine."

"I don't want to be the Log Lady ..."

Fanny Kiefer, born in Billings, Montana, came to Vancouver in 1966 straight out of university. "In 1978 I started at CJOR as an assistant to Chuck Cook, salary $200 a month. Then he went into politics, and my job ended. When Terry Moore's producer quit, I got that job; then Terry leaves. But by now I'm established and my job is extended to full-time. My very first interview was with B.C. health minister Rafe Mair!

"I have a tiny claim to fame: I was the last person on the air on CJOR. Ever. The station signed off at noon, and signed back on as CHRX.

"The first thing I did at NW was fill in for Bill Good in the summer of '92. He was on holiday for three weeks. I told Doug Rutherford I was going to Toronto, he says, 'Don't go, we'll get something for you here.'"

CKNW listener Mrs. Elizabeth Ibbetson writes to say CKNW "holds a special spot in my heart. I came here as a war bride in May, 1946 from South Wales. I was so homesick and lonely. My husband went to work and returned 12 hours later. I had CKNW on all day long, and felt it really kept me going. I loved the country and western music, and what happened to Arnold Nelson? His name has always stayed with me. There was a man who used to yodel, and the trio Mike, Marc and Jack.

"I still turn on CKNW as soon as I wake up. I am alone now, and do you know, still a little

"So, if Bannerman can't do Rafe's show, I do it. And I'm the regular replacement on Bill Good's show. And I have a Saturday morning show on the environment, called Down to Earth, and it's going well. We have guests, and phone-ins. NW had wanted to do an environmental show for a long time, needed a sponsor. We have one now in the Forest Alliance.

"I like the show, but I don't want to do it forever; I don't want to go down in history as the Log Lady!"

"It all grew out of Bill Rea's station . . ."

In 1991 the Globe and Mail interviewed Frank Griffiths. "Western International Communications," said the G&M, "has 350 employees through all its affiliated companies, 250 to 275 of them in its wholly owned companies. Most of the management teams at the wholly-owned companies are still the same as at the time of Western's takeovers, a fact Mr. Griffiths credits to a 'human' approach on the part of senior management.

"'Every year since 1955, Bill Hughes, my wife Emily and I have made a point of seeing every employee of our wholly owned subsidiaries. Each December we meet with everyone — and we go to them. We talk about their successes and tweak them about their failures. This takes us away from being just names in the distance. They can see we are as human as they are, with the same problems and interests they have. I think it's part of how you make a team work, and it results in a lot of long-service people. After all, if you have people working for you, they should also be working with you.'"

In a 1992 interview with the author, Frank Griffiths said "CKNW was the key to Western International Communications. WIC is capitalized at $300 million, the largest broadcasting company in Canada. Profits today are in the multi-millions. It all grew out of Bill Rea's station."

A Closing Note

Like any history, this one encountered differing interpretations of events and variation in recollections. To cite an early example: Bill Rea's daughter Annabelle says her father didn't graduate from Illinois' Northwestern University because he refused to take accounting. Duty compels me to report that Northwestern has no record of Rea ever attending at all. Still, so many of the family cite his attendance there (even recalling the name of his fraternity) that I didn't pursue the matter.

One former staffer recalls suggesting to Bill Rea in 1949 that he begin hourly newscasts — a totally new idea then. Alas, the record shows that NW began hourly newscasts the very day it signed on, August 15, 1944. Another ex-staffer claims he gave "Frosty" Forst his nickname. Sorry, Brian was known by that on-air nickname before he came to Top Dog.

I have four different versions of how Rene Castellani came to work for NW: he was hired by Mel Cooper for a promotional gimmick as a bogus "Maharajah"; no, he was hired by Hal Davis and Bill Hughes as the Maharajah to counteract another station's promotional efforts; no, he was a friend of CKNW engineer Bill Collins and got the job through him; no, he was a friend of NW deejay Gerry Davies and Gerry told him the station's promotion department needed someone.

The Davis/Hughes version came with most supporting evidence, so that's the one I chose.

To close on a personal note: if you enjoyed reading this book as much as I enjoyed researching and writing it, then we both had a very good time. ■

homesick for Wales. But I fell in love with Vancouver, and am still here . . . I love the 9 to 11 p.m. music on a Sunday evening, and of course Jack Cullen. I started to donate to the Orphans' Fund, and still do. When I had my children they used to give me some of their pennies, and they remember it now.

"Thank you, CKNW, for the years you have given me pleasure, especially these past years which were pretty tough. You really helped . . ." ■

THE END